THE QUEST FOR SELF-EXPRESSION

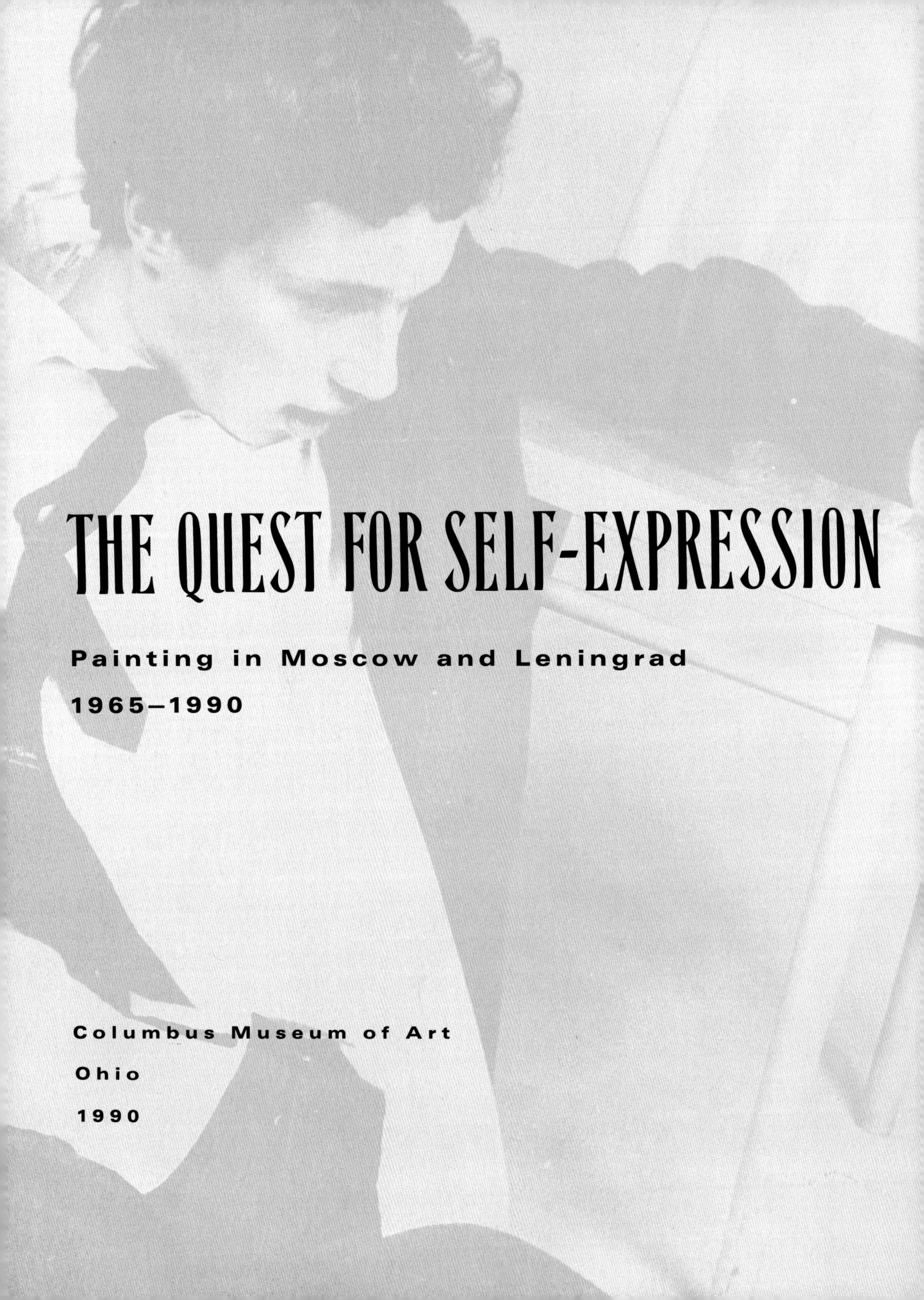

THE QUEST FOR SELF-EXPRESSION

Painting in Moscow and Leningrad

1965–1990

Columbus Museum of Art

Ohio

1990

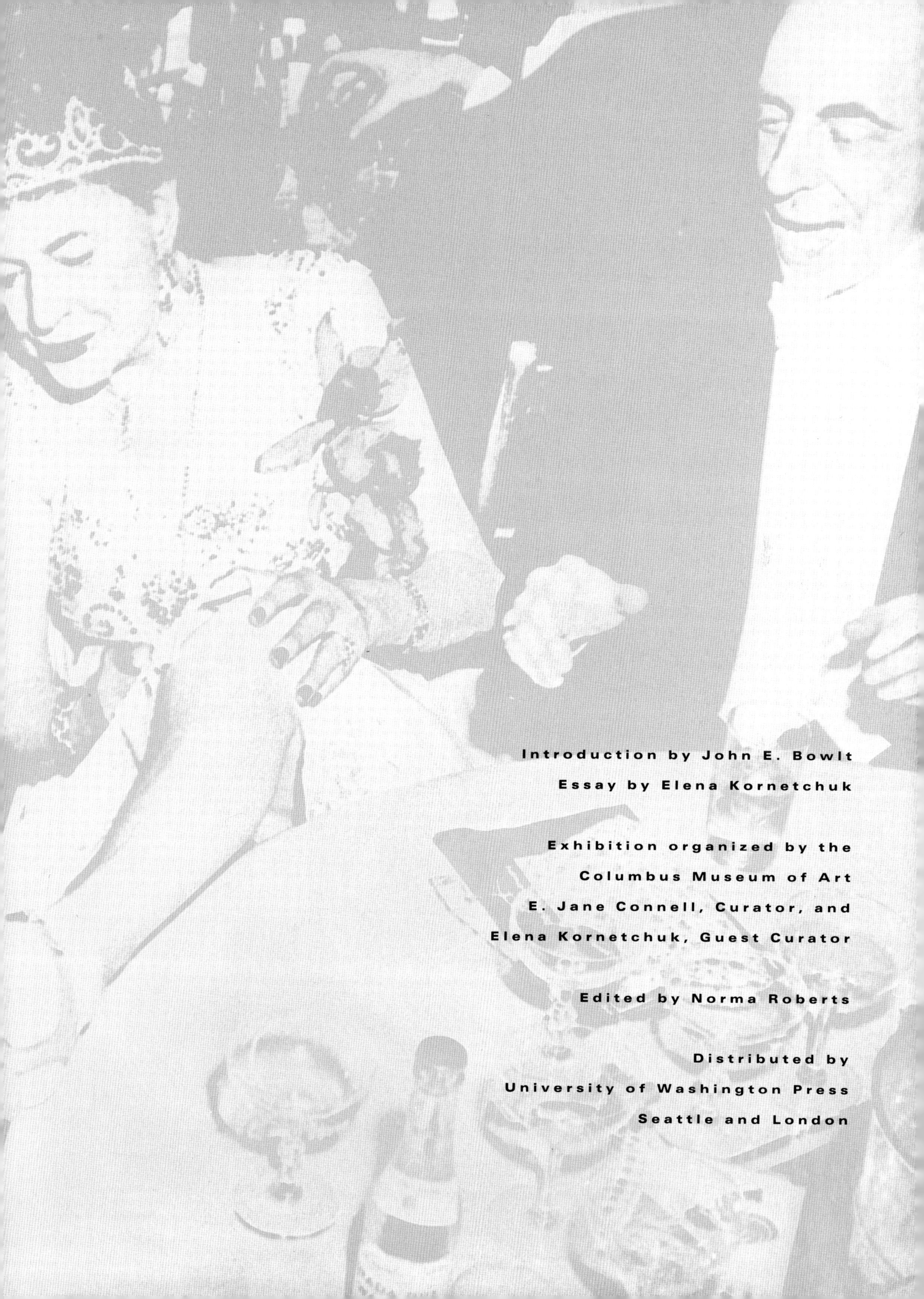

Introduction by John E. Bowlt

Essay by Elena Kornetchuk

Exhibition organized by the
Columbus Museum of Art
E. Jane Connell, Curator, and
Elena Kornetchuk, Guest Curator

Edited by Norma Roberts

Distributed by
University of Washington Press
Seattle and London

Exhibition Itinerary

Columbus Museum of Art, Columbus, Ohio
September 16–November 25, 1990

Weatherspoon Art Gallery, University of North Carolina
Greensboro, North Carolina
January 13–February 24, 1991

Arkansas Art Center, Little Rock, Arkansas
March 14–May 26, 1991

Produced by Marquand Books, Inc., Seattle
Typesetting by The Type Gallery, Inc., Seattle
Printed and bound in Japan by Toppan Printing Co.

Front cover: Olga Bulgakova, *Dream about the Red Bird*, 1989
Back cover: Evgeni Rukhin, *Untitled*, 1975

Library of Congress Cataloging-in-Publication Data is available.
ISBN 29597061-8

Grateful acknowledgment is made to the following for permission to reprint from previously published material:
Excerpt from *Rukhin*, published by Gallery 1912, Los Angeles
Excerpt from "About My Work," *Contemporary Russian Artists*, published by Museo d'Arte Contemporanea Luigi Pecci, Prato, Italy

Photography Credits
Photographs of works of art reproduced in this catalogue have been supplied by the owners or custodians of the works. Exceptions and additional credits follow.
E. Jane Connell: pp. 68, 92, 114
Courtesy Hal Bromm Gallery, New York: Pl. 51
John Kopp: Pls. 2, 5, 6, 7, 12, 18, 19, 40, 44, 45, 49, 53, 54, 68, 70, 71, 72, 73, 85, 86, 89; and figs., pp. 20 (Rabin), 25
Jennifer Kotter, courtesy Ronald Feldman Fine Arts, New York: p. 98
Robert Lodge: Pl. 23
Charles Martin: Pls. 30, 31, 32, 36, 39, 41, 42, 63, 66, 67, 87
UPI Bettmann Newsphotos: p. 35

Partial funding for the exhibition has been provided by the Wexner Arts Fund of the Columbus Foundation, Abbott-Ross Laboratories, and the James W. Overstreet Memorial Exhibition Fund.

CONTENTS

ADVISORY COMMITTEE

American Participants

John E. Bowlt
Professor of Slavic Languages and Literature and
Director of the Institute of Modern Russian Culture
University of Southern California

Myroslava Ciszkewycz
Associate Professor of Art History
The Ohio State University

Matthew Colopy
Director of International Programs
Ohio Arts Council

Norton Dodge
Director
The Cremona Foundation

Milton Esterow
Editor and Publisher
ARTnews

Irina Fiks
Art historian
Specialist in contemporary Russian art

Alison Hilton
Associate Professor of Art History
Georgetown University

Janet Kennedy
Associate Professor of Fine Arts
Indiana University

Wayne Lawson
Director
Ohio Arts Council

Merribell Parsons
Director
Columbus Museum of Art

James Scanlan
Director
Center for Slavic and East European Studies
The Ohio State University

Marilyn Scanlan
Community liaison, Columbus

Miriam Schwartz
Specialist in Russian language and literature
Community liaison, Columbus

Soviet Participants

Marina Bakuleva
Art historian
Former Director, Art and Export Salon,
Artists Fund, USSR Union of Artists, Moscow

Nina Frolova
Art historian
Director, International Department
USSR Union of Artists, Leningrad

Pavel Khoroshilov
Art historian
Art Director, Soyuz Gallery, Moscow

Vitaly Manin
Art historian
Secretary and member of the Board of Directors
USSR Union of Artists, Moscow

Alexander Sitnikov
Artist

LENDERS TO THE EXHIBITION

Guram Abramishvili

Val and Majid Arbab

Claude Bernard Gallery

Farid Bogdalov

Gleb Bogomolov

Hal Bromm

Olga Bulgakova

Nancy and Norton Dodge

Evgeni Dybsky

Jon C. and Peggy Feder

Elena Figurina

Olga Grechina

Dr. Michel and Victoria Hersen

Viktor Kalinin

Bernard and Miriam Landman

Mireille Levy

Valeri Lukka

George Mayers, Gallery 1912

The Menninger Foundation

Montreal Museum of Fine Arts

Museum of the History of Leningrad

Tatiana Nazarenko

Vladimir Nemukhin

Regina Padleckas

Alexander Petrov

Arkadi Petrov

John G. Pickard

Evgeni Rastorguev

Russian Museum

Alexander Sitnikov

Andrei Tutunov

Vatenin Family Collection

Andrei Yakhnin

Dmitri Zhilinsky

Private Collections

DIRECTOR'S STATEMENT

"Art must be free, because man is not."
—Anatoli Zverev

The Columbus Museum of Art is especially pleased to present the exhibition *The Quest for Self-Expression: Painting in Moscow and Leningrad, 1965–1990*. As the Soviet Union struggles to redefine itself after some seventy years of totalitarian rule, this exhibition provides a timely opportunity to investigate the cultural milieu of its largest republic—Soviet Russia—and its major art centers, not only during the past twenty-five years but throughout the twentieth century. In the context of this exhibition there are fascinating insights into a society long closed to the West, in which some art was acceptable and some was not, and in which definitions were imposed by the state. Since 1985, in the time this exhibition has been in preparation, freedom in the arts has been realized in Soviet Russia and distinctions between official and unofficial art have ceased to apply. Soviet art is on the threshold of a new era, the seeds of which may well have been sown in the works chosen for this exhibition.

In producing this exhibition and catalogue, the museum staff has relied on the expertise, support, and encouragement of many prominent scholars in the field of Soviet art. We are most indebted to Guest Curator Elena Kornetchuk, who has contributed the principal essay and much of the research on participating artists. Dr. Kornetchuk earned her Ph.D. in Russian Studies at Georgetown University and has continued to study contemporary Russian art for fifteen years as a lecturer and contributor to journals and exhibition catalogues. A provocative introduction has been provided by John E. Bowlt, well-known scholar and author of definitive texts on twentieth-century Soviet art. And an eminent advisory committee consisting of distinguished art and cultural historians and collectors from the United States and the Soviet Union has helped to formulate and implement the exhibition and its many components. The museum is deeply grateful to all of these.

Of crucial importance in an undertaking of this magnitude is the generosity of lenders. Nearly half the works are from artists' studios in Moscow and Leningrad. Twenty-one are from the collection of the Cremona Foundation, whose director Norton Dodge has assembled what *Art in America* has called "probably the largest and most comprehensive collection [of unofficial Soviet art] in existence." Additional loans from the Russian Museum, the USSR Union of Artists, and private collectors round out this representation of Russian art from the sixties to the present. We are deeply grateful to those who have entrusted these marvelous works to this exhibition.

Many members of the museum staff deserve recognition for their enduring devotion to this project. Curator E. Jane Connell, along with Dr. Kornetchuk, has been a part of the project since its inception and has engineered the numerous aspects of exhibition development. The educational components of the exhibition have been expertly developed by Director of Education Sharon Kokot and her staff, and the many details of catalogue editing and production have been diligently orchestrated by Editor Norma Roberts. To these and many others whose contributions are vital to the success of the exhibition, the museum community is profoundly grateful.

Most important are those who have made the exhibition possible through generous contributions for its support. Our deepest debt of gratitude is due the Wexner Arts Fund of the Columbus Foundation, Abbott-Ross Laboratories, and the James W. Overstreet Memorial Exhibition Fund. Through the foresight and generosity of individuals and institutions such as these the arts are nourished and continue to thrive.

It is our sincere hope that the exhibition will inspire further scholarship in the field of Soviet art, and that visitors to the exhibition will be rewarded with greater appreciation for this art that only recently has been made available to Western audiences.

Merribell Parsons

CURATORS' STATEMENT

Like the phoenix rising from its own ashes, artistic self-expression in the Soviet Union has taken wings after years of repression. This rebirth of creativity is the subject of the exhibition *The Quest for Self-Expression: Painting in Moscow and Leningrad, 1965–1990*. Ninety-four works have been selected to represent the rich diversity of art that has emerged and survived during the past twenty-five years in the two major art centers of the Russian republic. Forty-three artists of the sixties, seventies, and eighties are represented here. Their works mark the tortuous progress from the beginning of artistic liberation in the post-Stalin years known as the Thaw to the many significant new directions of the present time.

Planning for the exhibition began in the summer of 1985. Several concepts were considered in detail, including an exhibition of works from the Baltic republics of Latvia, Lithuania, and Estonia; a focus on the republic of Georgia, where some of the most innovative Soviet art is being created today; a concentrated look at Moscow artists; and a combination of all of these. In the end, exhibition planners decided that the most meaningful and timely contribution this museum could make to the scholarship on Soviet art would be in the current area of most intense cultural and aesthetic inquiry: the art of Moscow and Leningrad. Several decisions were made at the outset. Because we wished to gather together a major group of significant objects, we decided to focus on one medium—painting. In order to provide a solid historic foundation for the exhibition, we decided to concentrate on the twenty-five-year period beginning shortly after the landmark Manezh exhibition of 1962. To illustrate the continuum of the art of the mid-sixties through the eighties, we further decided to concentrate on the vision of artists who have remained in Moscow and Leningrad. The catalogue reflects the content of the exhibition and addresses subjects outside its parameters, including well-known emigrés such as Oskar Rabin and Lydia Masterkova and pre-1965 historic and political events.

To assist the museum in developing the exhibition and various phases of scholarship, education, publicity, and community outreach, an advisory committee consisting of prominent American and Soviet scholars, artists, Union of Artists officials, collectors, and community liaisons was established. With their full support, the selection process was accomplished over a two-year period, during which the curators made three trips to Moscow and Leningrad (in May 1989, December 1989, and May 1990). The procedure was to first compile an encyclopedic master list of major artists. Then each Soviet member of the advisory committee was asked to submit his or her ideal list. The lists were collated, and the artists common to all lists became the foundation of the exhibition. On the advice of the American advisors, the core group of artists was expanded to more fully represent and articulate the exhibition goals for an American public. Until now the breadth and depth of artistic creation that existed outside the dictates of Socialist Realism have not received extensive consideration in American, European, or Soviet exhibitions. This exhibition presents the work of both unofficial artists and their official colleagues, often nonconformist—or left-wing—union members such as Vladimir Weisberg and Anatoli Kaplan. All were at some time or another blacklisted by the government. A number of artists, such as Viktor Popkov, Evgeni Rastorguev, Zaven Arshakuni, and Valeri Vatenin, are being introduced to the American public for the first time.

Soviet artists are especially affected by political climate, history, and aesthetic traditions of the past and present. Self-expression has been influenced in particular by the Russian icon and national folk traditions, the Russian avant-garde movement of the 1920s and 1930s, and Western modernist movements such as surrealism and Pop Art. Paintings reflecting this diversity of subjects and styles were chosen directly from artists' studios and from American, Canadian, European, and Soviet public and private collections. In May 1989 the curators visited an exhibition of recent acquisitions at the Russian Museum in Leningrad, one of the finest public collections of contemporary art in the Soviet Union. We were able to study in detail a comprehensive selection of works and to make arrangements for loans of especially rare pictures. Representative works of exceptional quality were of premium importance. Sometimes surprising gems of unusual scale and complexity were discovered, such as Andrei Gennadiev's *Self-Portrait with Ladder*. Better known, published works of historic significance were also sought, including Dmitri Zhilinsky's *Man with Slain Dog*, Ilya Kabakov's *Path*, and Tatiana Nazarenko's *Pugachev*. In addition, every effort was made to represent each artist with works from the decade with which he or she is most closely associated, but this was not always possible due to lack of available works, especially from the sixties. We are fortunate, however, to have some excellent examples by Nikolai Andronov, Francisco Infante, Zaven Arshakuni, and others in the exhibition.

As the selection of works was refined, a single picture was sometimes deemed worthy to represent the spirit of the artist, such as Pyotr Belenok's *Despair in Space*. At other times more than one work was needed, such as examples of Vladimir Weisberg's still lifes, portraits, and nudes. Sometimes an artist wished to be represented by particular works, as in the case of Vladimir Nemukhin, who selected an "installation" of two still-lifes and a bronze sculpture dedicated to Weisberg; these are complemented with two earlier classic examples of Nemukhin's oeuvre. Works such as *Construction* by Igor Kopystiansky, a Ukrainian artist who now works primarily in Moscow, were chosen to challenge the limits of the definition of painting and to present new directions for the medium. More than half the works have never been seen in the United States. Others have rarely been exhibited, and most have not been included in a museum-organized presentation.

The Columbus Museum of Art hopes that this exhibition and catalogue will be significant contributions to the scholarship and understanding of contemporary Russian art. It is our further hope that the works gathered here will stimulate the appreciation of a vast audience and promote a greater sensitivity to the very complex quest for artistic self-expression in the Soviet Union.

E. Jane Connell
Elena Kornetchuk

ACKNOWLEDGMENTS

Our deepest gratitude is due the many colleagues and friends who have given of their time and expertise to bring this project to fruition—

Merribell Parsons, who, as the new director of the Columbus Museum of Art in 1987, carried the project forward with enthusiasm;

The curatorial staff of the Columbus Museum of Art, whose dedication has been unfailing: Rod Bouc, Kathy Ferguson-Nell, Lisa Greenberg, Greg Jones, Brian Maloney, John Owens, and Martha Torres;

Other members of the museum staff, whose commitment to the publication cut across departmental lines and was especially appreciated in the rush to meet production deadlines: Kathy Bonnette, Carole Genshaft, Karen Kneisley, Sharon Kokot, Kathy Meyers, Annette Oren, Beth Roach, and Jim Weidman;

Budd Harris Bishop, former director of the Columbus Museum of Art (1976–1986), who initiated the exhibition concept in 1985 and encouraged its development; and Steven White Rosen, former chief curator of the Columbus Museum of Art (1977–1989), who continues to support the museum and this exhibition;

Art historians Michele Kapur and Patricia Tanner, whose constant enthusiasm and conscientious research on all aspects of this project have been invaluable;

Dawn M. Moore, who thoroughly researched the biographical material on the artists and helped with the endless checking of details in all parts of the manuscript;

Charles M. Wiebe, who coordinated photography and helped with proofreading;

Jenifer Roulette, who worked many odd hours to prepare the manuscript for typesetting;

Elena A. Boleukh, Moscow art historian, whose contributions ranged from scheduling visits with artists to compiling biographical information and artists' statements, to securing photographs of artists and paintings;

Larisa A. Kashuk, Moscow art historian, who provided introductions to several nonconformist artists and contributed information on them;

The many artists and their families, art historians, and friends in Moscow and Leningrad who provided generous hospitality and good cheer during the curators' visits;

The staffs of the USSR Union of Artists and Soyuz Gallery, who coordinated loan arrangements and shipment of works from the Soviet Union to the Columbus Museum of Art;

Elena Duzs, Steven R. Eschner, and Bogdan Kokot, who conscientiously translated artists' statements and other materials from the Soviet Union;

Myroslava Ciszkewycz, who took time from her busy schedule to read and advise on the final manuscript draft;

All members of the Advisory Committee, whose commitment and expertise have added increments to the quality of the project.

Finally, we acknowledge with profound gratitude the support provided by the Wexner Arts Fund of the Columbus Foundation, Abbott-Ross Laboratories, and the James W. Overstreet Memorial Exhibition Fund.

E. Jane Connell
Elena Kornetchuk
Norma Roberts

THE QUEST FOR SELF-EXPRESSION

John E. Bowlt

In 1920 Evgeny Zamiatin finished his extraordinary novel *My* (We). Written in the aftermath of the October Revolution, *My* told the story of an imaginary society that lived in perfect order. Supervised by Big Brother, each inhabitant bore a number and a permanent social status, and everything down to the most humble physical need was computed and prearranged. Here was almost total harmony, the so-called Single State, that moved in unison except for two enemies—imagination and the outside world. But even these hostile elements were about to be vanquished, for imaginations were being removed surgically and the community was protected from the outside by a hermetic glass dome through which, like some monstrous *Kunstkammer*, remnants of the old world could still be seen.

My is a strong novel, for Zamiatin made an uncanny prediction of what almost happened in Soviet Russia under Stalin. In a society of forced labor that presented itself as the proletariat's kingdom come, in a society where statistics were distorted or invented, in a society that worshiped light (the electrification of Russia) and the sacred word (the behests of Marx and Lenin), a semblance of uniformity would, indeed, be implemented by the abrupt removal of artistic imagination. Many of the artists whose works appear in *The Quest for Self-Expression: Painting in Moscow and Leningrad, 1965–1990* were born during the Stalin era, learned the values of dialectical materialism, and studied with the masters of Socialist Realism. But many of them also contributed to the emergence of the first generation of dissident artists and writers of the 1960s who, in spite of a long legacy of false regimentation, still recognized the deep division between "here" and "there." While functioning (or disfunctioning) during the Khrushchev and Brezhnev eras, freedom-fighters such as Evgeny Yevtushenko, Ilya Glazunov, Ernst Neizvestny, and Andrei Voznezensky looked beyond the glass dome of their closed capsule and yearned to savor the delights of alternative styles and the luxury of irrationality and disorder.

In general terms, that first generation of underground artists (Eli Belyutin, Erik Bulatov, Ilya Glazunov, Pyotr Belenok, Ilya Kabakov, Vladimir Nemukhin, Edik Shteinberg, and Anatoli Zverev) waged a desperate war for freedom of expression, and they waged it against the severe bureaucratic control of the humanities exercised by the state mechanisms responsible for artistic affairs: the USSR Ministry of Culture, the USSR Academy of Arts, and the USSR Union of Artists. All three agencies continued to advocate the doctrine of Socialist Realism first formulated in 1934 that insisted artists depict concrete reality. Still, the aesthetic oppression of that time stemmed not so much from the philosophy of Socialist Realism as from the intractable sycophants who repeated its formulae in order to maintain their material and political power. When those first "nonconformist" artists challenged the establishment—for example, at the famous exhibition *Thirty Years of Moscow Art* at the Manezh Hall in Moscow in 1962—they were perceived more as enemies of the Party than as enemies of art, and, of course, they were.

But if, during the Stalin and Khrushchev years, the Soviet Union was still an isolated power, jealous of its political and cultural identity, how could young artists perceive alternative systems outside the glass dome? In order to answer this question, we should remember the profound effect generated by the occasional exhibitions of Western art that came to Moscow and Leningrad during the "Thaw." One of the most famous was the *Exhibition of American Painting and Sculpture*, organized in Moscow by the Archives of American Art, at which young Soviet artists such as Neizvestny and Nemukhin were able to see works by Jackson Pollock, Willem de Kooning, Georgia O'Keeffe, and others. This gradual exposure to contemporary Western art was also encouraged by the increasing interaction, often clandestine, between Western diplomats, students, and correspondents and the new Russian poets and painters. Particular reference should also be made to the indigenous traditions of experimental art—to the shades of the old avant-garde—that still lingered in Soviet cultural life in spite of Stalin's removal of imagination. In fact, artists such as Bulatov, Nemukhin, and Viktor Popkov learned to question the monopoly of Socialist Realism by heeding the sentiments of those few older artists who had been organically linked to the old avant-garde and yet, miraculously, had survived the Stalin regime. The ethical and aesthetic stance of artists such as Nikolai Akimov, Robert Falk, Anatoli Kaplan, and Alexander Tyshler was of crucial importance to the establishment of the unofficial movement in the late 1950s onward, and their loyal apprentices—Nikolai Andronov, Belyutin, Vladimir Weisberg—helped carry the torch that illuminated one of the darkest corridors of Russian culture.

Of course, without those initial protests, experiments, and conflicts (the apartment exhibitions, the smuggling of works to the West, the smear campaigns), the new avant-garde would hardly have been possible. The richness in form and content that we see today would have been unthinkable twenty years ago, and the sheer stylistic diversity of the Moscow and Leningrad art communities—from kineticism (Francisco Infante) to realism (Anatoli Nikich), from nostalgia (Dmitri Zhilinsky) to religion (Andrei Tutunov), from Photorealism (Simon Faibisovich) to Expressionism (Viktor Kalinin)—entitles them to a leading position in the international art market. The young artists of Moscow and Leningrad have achieved their mobility because the glass dome has been dismantled, because "here" and "there" are now more closely linked than ever before, and because fantasy is allowed to flourish. The picture looks bright, even if some of us experience an acute nostalgia for the severity of the Stalin era and the "period of stagnation," when to be a radical artist in the Soviet Union was to be a martyr to the cause of artistic freedom, and when to paint an abstract painting was to risk ostracism and imprisonment. As we look at the early, powerful works by Belyutin, Nemukhin, and Evgeni Rastorguev we should never forget that they and their colleagues were the first to crack the smooth surface of the glass dome and to restore an integrity of artistic imagination to modern Soviet culture.

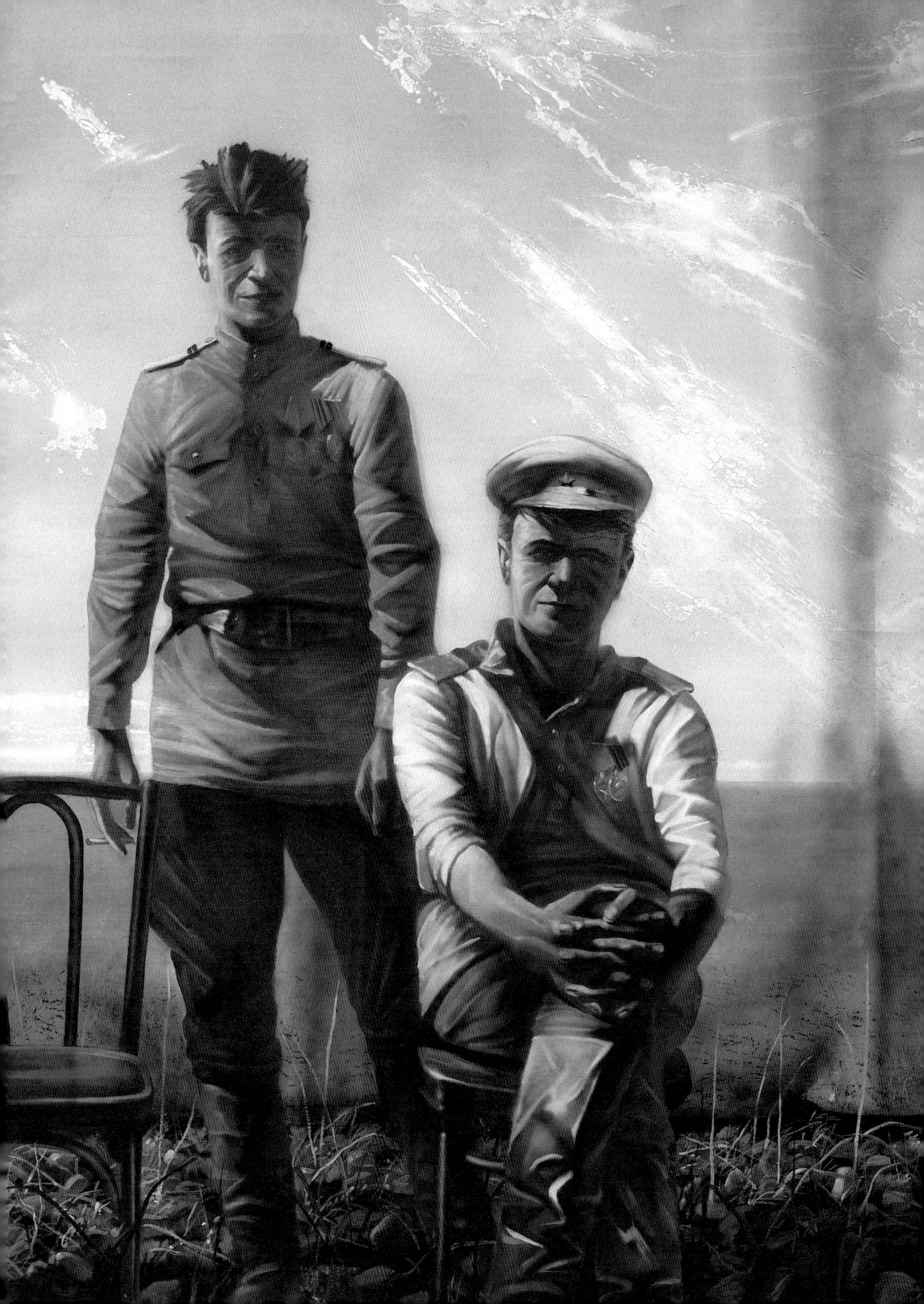

SOVIET ART AND THE STATE

Elena Kornetchuk

Although control of the arts under the authority of the Soviet State has been pervasive, enduring, and severe, the use of art for political or educational purposes was not a new historical phenomenon. For centuries Russian artists had been discouraged from exercising their creative imagination, painting instead according to the requirements of an ecclesiastical primate, a patriarch, or a czar. But in 1863 the winds of change began to stir as a group of artists who called themselves *Peredvizhniki* (Wanderers) broke away from the official academic system and became the first Russian artists to pursue their personal aesthetic beliefs. The *Peredvizhniki* believed that art is—or should be—a vehicle of social exposure and criticism. By the turn of the century, the movement they began had evolved to produce the most experimental art in the world. Known today as the Russian avant-garde, this movement encompassed a period of twenty-five to thirty years[1] and included such artistic luminaries as Wassily Kandinsky (1866–1944), Marc Chagall (1887–1985), Kasimir Malevich (1878–1935), and Vladimir Tatlin (1885–1953).

The brief era of the early avant-garde ended with the Russian Revolution and the Communist Party's rise to power after 1917. Despite the misgivings of early leaders such as G.V. Plekhanov, Russia's first Marxist theorist and critic in literature and arts, who warned that turning the muse of an artist into a "state muse" would inevitably lead to a decline in art,[2] the government set about the task of determining an official artistic language of the proletariat. In their efforts to establish guidelines for Soviet art, officials were aided by groups of artists who had organized in order to have a voice. One of these newly formed artists' organizations, *Proletkult* (the Proletarian Cultural Educational Organization), placed itself at the service of the Communist government in an attempt to dominate Soviet art.[3] Their influence was ended in 1920 by Lenin, who believed that a monopoly by one school of art was both ideologically and practically harmful.[4] *All* artists were encouraged to relate their activities to the Communist state. *Proletkult* became ineffective, but other organizations sprang up to replace it. Ultimately, one of these, AKhRR (Association of Artists of Revolutionary Russia), a very large organization that extended its influence to many cities and fully aligned itself with Communist Party ideology, became the most powerful.[5] In its desire to make art comprehensible to the common man, AKhRR adopted the slogan "Art to the Masses," rejected abstract art, and advocated "heroic realism." Much of the responsibility for curtailing artistic inquiry in the Soviet Union and for repressive state control of the arts belongs to the influence of AKhRR in the years following the Revolution.

As a result of the trend toward heroic realism, avant-garde art began to disappear from the public scene. Avant-garde artists tried to integrate their art with life and society, but many gradually abandoned the world of painting for what they felt to be more publicly oriented fields: film, utilitarian design, theater, political posters, and architecture.[6] Artists who did not become assimilated—Wassily Kandinsky, Marc Chagall, Naum Gabo (1890–1977), and Antoine Pevsner (1886–1962), for example—emigrated from the Soviet Union; some continued to paint, but without hope of exhibiting. As Stalin gained control of the Communist Party in the late 1920s, even less experimentation was tolerated in art.

In 1928 Stalin drew up his first Five-Year Plan (1928–1932), primarily to establish policies for economic restructuring but also to set an agenda for the arts. What emerged was a new doctrine known as Socialist Realism, which prescribed that artists present an optimistic view of socialist reality and of Communist doctrine in order to educate the masses. Government control of the arts became more direct in 1932, when the Central Committee of the All-Union Communist Party issued a decree, "On the Reorganization of Literary and Artistic Organizations," calling for the disbanding of all private writers' and artists' organizations and the formation of government-directed unions for practitioners of the various arts. So ended AKhRR's preeminence. At first all works inspired by Communist ideology were proclaimed to be representative of Socialist Realism, but before long the government adopted a more organized approach and began to enforce a government-approved, standardized style. For an artist to continue to work in a nonfigurative—or abstract—style was to defy the government and to be labeled a "formalist." In the great purge of 1936–1938, following the murder of one of Stalin's associates, the government sought to eliminate dissidents of all kinds, sentencing them to death or hard labor. Thus the Soviet avant-garde was forced into the underground. Socialist Realism was the only "true" art form. The state was in control.

During World War II artists were mobilized to paint national and historical subjects or war scenes, and authorities in general relaxed their vigil regarding style and content. Once World War II had ended and relations among the Allies had degenerated into a "Cold War," an ideological alert went into effect in the Soviet Union, resulting in cultural rigidity and isolationism, a strengthening of controls, and denunciation of modern Western culture. The Communist Party stressed that Soviet art had to be simple and obvious enough to be understood by everyone. The avowed mission of art was to provide propaganda to advance Communism.[7] Because the collection of the Moscow State Museum of Modern Art failed to meet these criteria, the holdings were dispersed.

In retrospect, it can be seen that for the first thirty-six years of Communist rule the Party was trying to define a role for art within a political context. Many artists participated voluntarily, offering to work for the state, perhaps unaware that they would be instrumental in curtailing aesthetic freedom. Art had become a tool for those in power. Not until the post-Stalin era would there be changes in the official doctrines of Socialist Realism as applied to the visual arts.

GOVERNING THE ARTS

Because a fundamental premise of the Soviet system of government is that art must educate the people in the spirit of Communism, an organized means of achieving this objective had to be devised. Consequently, several organizations were created to oversee the art world.

The USSR Ministry of Culture

While the Ideological Committee of the Communist Party exercises ultimate control over the arts, day-to-day management is the responsibility of the Ministry of Culture, which is composed of two special committees: one for fine arts, and one for the protection of monuments. The Ministry directly supervises some of the most important art institutions in the country—such well-known museums as the Tretyakov Art Gallery in Moscow and the Hermitage Museum in Leningrad, three art publishing houses, and the Central Scientific Research Laboratory for the Conservation and Restoration of Works of Art. In addition, the Ministry organizes major exhibitions in the Soviet Union and abroad, and—with the advice of a special commission—buys and commissions artworks. Thus the Ministry is the major employer of Soviet artists, awarding those who distinguish themselves for exceptional achievements and services with much-cherished awards, medals, and honorary titles. "People's Artist of the USSR" is the highest honorary title given to a person contributing to the fine arts, and the Lenin Prize is the highest medal awarded for the creation of exceptional works of art.

As the supervisory body of the entire organization of Soviet art, the Ministry of Culture is also responsible for the administration of the USSR Academy of Arts, and the USSR Union of Artists.

The USSR Academy of Arts

Established by the Council of Ministers in 1947, the Academy is the highest educational and scientific center for the fine arts in the USSR. The Academy's main functions are to implement the Party line in the fine arts and oversee the training of professional artists. The Surikov Art Institute in Moscow and the Repin Art Institute in Leningrad are both under the Academy's direction, as are the art studios provided for graduates of these institutions.

The Academy consists of members (academicians), honorary members (foreign artists),[8] and associate members (nominees), divided into sections according to their specialty (painting, sculpture, or graphic arts). During its periodic sessions and conferences, the Academy holds discussions on current problems in aesthetics that are of particular concern to the Soviet art community. One of the early goals of the Academy was "... to combat formalism, naturalism, and other features of contemporary bourgeois decadent art."[9] Though a rigid outlook evolved and still exists, by the end of the 1980s official enforcement of the principles of Socialist Realism became more relaxed. In the era of *glasnost* (openness), the Academy has been criticized for being overly conservative, for promoting exclusivity, and for remaining isolated from the mass of Soviet artists.[10]

The USSR Union of Artists

Of all the branches of government, the USSR Union of Artists has the greatest daily impact on Soviet professional artists, since it is their major official employer. The Union follows precedents established by *Vsekokhudozhnik* (the All-Russian Cooperative of Artists), founded in 1929 under the leadership of Yu. M. Slavinsky. A Party-controlled organization of painters, graphic and decorative artists, sculptors, and architects, *Vsekokhudozhnik* dispensed commissions, recommended purchases, lent money to artists, and contributed to setting up exhibits. Official artists' unions similar to *Vsekokhudozhnik* were founded throughout the Soviet Union as the result of the 1932 Central Committee resolution "On the Reorganization of Literary and Artistic Organizations."[11] The development of artists' unions and the formulation of a national art style precipitated the need for a national regulatory agency. In 1939, the Soviet of People's Commissars of the USSR passed a resolution "On the Formation of a Union of Artists of the USSR."[12] An organizational bureau was created, but work was delayed by World War II and postwar recovery. In 1957 the first All-Union Congress convened to form the USSR Union of Artists, a central agency that was to oversee the activities of all member unions.

The USSR Union of Artists has member unions in all fifteen Soviet republics. Union members and nonmembers alike receive monetary support in the form of commissions similar to those given by the Ministry of Culture. Members may also receive legal assistance, funds for construction of studios, and other benefits. The Union, like the Ministry, has a publishing house, which produces books, albums, catalogues, reproductions of Soviet art, and magazines such as *Iskusstvo* (Art). One of the basic concerns of the Union is the organizing of exhibitions, often with the help of the USSR Ministry of Culture. Thus all three major Soviet art organizations—the Union, the Ministry, and the Academy—offer Soviet artists opportunities to display their works.

In 1990 the USSR Union of Artists counted only about twenty-three thousand members.[13] To apply for admission artists must submit a written application, works of art or art criticism (for art historians), and three recommendations by Union members. Though most applicants are graduates of art institutes, an art diploma is not required. Elections are held by secret ballot not more than three times yearly. Upon acceptance into the Union, artists must follow its regulations. Even minor infractions, such as failure to pay a membership fee for two consecutive years, can result in dismissal.

In the past the Union has been held in high esteem by government officials. In 1969, the Presidium of the Supreme Soviet of the USSR awarded the organization the Order of Lenin. In the Gorbachev era, however, this highly complex bureaucracy with a relatively small membership has been openly criticized. Member artists have come to question the Union's ability to encourage and stimulate artistic work. Observers seem to agree that the Union has displayed a lack of vigor and a disinclination to promote change and innovation. As the decade of the 1990s begins, a new openness permeates the Soviet system, and the Union as well as the Academy must answer to a much broader constituency. History has shown that to remain rigid in such a climate would almost certainly be disastrous.

Other Artists

A number of artists are not members of artists' unions. Some of these, known as "nonprofessional" artists because they have not been academically trained, support government criteria for art and work independently at home or in studios at local clubs. In some republics and regions, the Soviet Union has set up special museums of "national and nonprofessional art" so that these artists too will have opportunities to exhibit. Some nonprofessional artists eventually pursue formal studies in art and graduate from art institutes.[14]

Among others who do not belong to artists' unions are those who work for publishing houses or are members of organizations such as the United Committee of Graphic Artists of the Workers' Union of Culture (also known as the Gorkom Grafikov, or Graphics Union) in Moscow, and the Fellowship of Experimental Visual

Arts in Leningrad, loose associations of official and unofficial avant-garde artists. Generally, these organizations are less rigid than the unions, permitting more experimentation in the work of their members. Indeed, the Graphics Union in Moscow was a prime force in supporting innovation and self-expression during the Brezhnev era, known today as "the period of stagnation."

In addition, there is a comparatively small number of artists who in the 1970s came to be known under a variety of names such as unofficial, nonconformist, dissident, avant-garde, underground, or left-wing. These artists began to emerge from seclusion during the cultural relaxation which took place under Khrushchev, but until the advent of *perestroika* (restructuring) in 1985, artists who did not subscribe to the doctrines of Socialist Realism were perceived by the Soviet government to constitute a challenge to the official system.[15] As a result, they incurred the hostility of the government bureaucracy. In their efforts to remain independent, some artists refused to join official organizations, although in most cases they were simply not welcome to do so. Many were forced to support themselves by holding jobs unrelated to their art work. Others were able to sell their works privately to members of the scientific elite, the intelligentsia, or the Moscow diplomatic community. Not until the late 1980s did it become possible for these artists to sell their art through official organizations and to openly mount their own commercial exhibitions. Though free now to create as they wish, unofficial artists believe they are not given due recognition in their own country. On the other hand, Soviet art historians apparently believe that unofficial art has received too much attention in the West, especially in the late 1980s and into the 1990s, when works by unofficial artists have become especially popular.

THE KHRUSHCHEV YEARS

Before the Thaw

Several months before Stalin's death in 1953, there was a turning point in contemporary Soviet art. Mikhail Suslov, the Communist Party's chief ideologist and an arch-conservative, said that Soviet art had become both "sweet and empty."[16] Because artists were afraid to attempt anything that contradicted official dogma, Suslov argued, they were shying away from subjects that dealt with issues and their art had become stagnant. Thus, after thirty-five years of Communist Party insistence on depicting the positive aspects of Soviet life, artists were invited to introduce an element of controversy in their artworks. According to an official dictum, they were to show the Soviet people overcoming obstacles as they sought to establish a Communist society.[17] The new climate in art favored abandoning old themes. To paint such famous defenders of old Russia as Pugachev and Kutuzov, certainly "safe" topics in the past, was no longer considered socially helpful. Because the USSR had successfully survived World War II, emerging even as a conqueror, the Party apparently concluded that reinforcing the idea of Soviet Russia's might was no longer the primary concern in art. Depicting the people and their positive role in developing society—even through struggle—was now deemed important. Ironically, nearly thirty years later, when artists were much freer to choose their subject matter, one, Tatiana Nazarenko, would reintroduce the theme of heroic leaders in *Pugachev* (Colorplate 43), in which the rebel leader is transformed into a Christlike figure, himself suffering under authoritarian rule.

This new direction in Soviet art after 1953 was by no means an invitation to broad experimentation. Nevertheless, artists were tempted to go beyond the bounds as they tried to overcome the strictures of Socialist Realism. Anatoli Zverev, a painter of brightly colored abstracts (see Colorplates 92–94), was dismissed from the 1905 Art Institute for openly teaching formalism. In Leningrad, the first known group of underground artists was formed. This small group—ten artists in all—was dedicated to the art of Pavel Filonov (1883–1941), an artist of the Russian avant-garde and a member of the Russian Futurist movement.[18] Later, in the 1960s, some members of this group would become leaders in the Leningrad dissident art movement.

Stalin's death seemed to open the way for discussions of problems in art policy and practice and even debates on the thematic and formal dimensions of Socialist Realism. As it became more common to criticize the status of Soviet art in the post-Stalin period, artists' unions as well as the style and content of Soviet painting came into question. Artists and art historians felt that the "theory of nonconflict" (*beskonfliktnost'*), which was manifested in the theme of happy workers, had distorted art and had led to a romantic view of reality. However, when subjects depicting any type of struggle were introduced, officials said the works were pessimistic and withheld them from exhibition.[19] Other officials supported the artists: one, Boris Ioganson, Chairman of the Organizational Committee of the USSR Union of Artists, shifted the blame from the artists to the system, criticizing arts organizations and their leaders for suffocating creativity.[20]

An important breakthrough occurred in 1954, precipitated by the publication of Ilya Ehrenburg's novel, *The Thaw*. The protagonists of this landmark work were artists: Pukhov, a successful Party-line painter, and Saburov, who produced original works. To the public, an artist who produced original works opposed the Party line and was thought to be "abnormal" or "schizophrenic," terms applied to some artists in the USSR into the 1980s. But beginning in 1954, quite possibly as a result of the novel, Saburov types began to surface more frequently in Soviet art. Eli Belyutin was one. A young professor of painting at the Polygraphic Institute in Moscow, Belyutin founded the Studio of Experimental Painting and Graphic Arts and encouraged his students to experiment in free-form techniques. Belyutin believed that art should promote spiritual emancipation, should lead to knowledge of the self and to understanding of the creative process. His own works (see Colorplates 5–7) are vivid, emotional, vibrant expressions. He developed a considerable following in Moscow, and his students came to be known as the Belyutintsy.[21]

The general, thematic classifications for the subject matter of official Soviet art of the post-Stalin period were little changed from those of preceding years: collective farms (*kolkhoz*), industry, history, sports, everyday life, the struggle for peace, and wars of liberation. Missing from this inventory is the theme of "the leader and his companions-in-arms." Apparently hero worship in the USSR had been superseded by other values—those of collective leadership and the preeminence of the nation over the individual. The most visible new trend, no matter what the subject, was toward simplicity. The constant use of forced pathos in artworks disappeared. Instead, artists began to describe genuine gloom and mute incomprehension in the face of suffering and death. Eventually this new approach developed into what is now called the Severe Style, in which dark colors and the pain of life became the principal focus. Among the chief proponents of the Severe Style were Pavel Nikonov and Nikolai Andronov, whose *Monday in Ferapontov* (Colorplate 2) exemplifies the change from the bright, optimistic hues of Socialist Realism.

By 1955 the definition of Socialist Realism began to change again, for the first time embracing the concepts of Impressionism. The revision of the official interpretation of art was marked by the exhibition *Fourteenth- to Twentieth-Century French Art*, held at the Pushkin Museum in Moscow in 1955. All the works in the exhibit came from the collections of Soviet museums, which until this time had not exhibited French Impressionist paintings.[22]

Some young Soviet artists were quick to respond to this perceived thaw in official policy, laying the groundwork for the unofficial art movement of the 1960s. In Moscow in the mid-1950s, sculptors Vadim Sidur, Vladimir Lempert, and Nikolai Silis organized a group of artists interested in modernist trends; and another group of unofficial artists, calling itself The Icon, was founded at the Orlov Art Institute in Yeletz. About the same time, painters Anatoli Zverev and Vladimir Weisberg—the former an unofficial artist, the latter a left-wing union member who produced paintings based on his own theories of color perception (see Colorplates 84–87)—began to sell their works to the Moscow intelligentsia and Western collectors.[23] While liberalizing policies continued, so also did occasional and possibly perfunctory warnings from some leaders.[24]

For the first time, Stalin's reputation as well as his policies were attacked from the highest podium in the nation, when in 1956 Khrushchev gave his so-called Secret Speech at the Twentieth Communist Party Congress, intoning Stalin's crimes against the Party and the people of the USSR. Shortly after the Secret Speech, large paintings and busts of Stalin were removed from the Tretyakov Art Gallery in Moscow, and Stalin's artistic dictums came under fire. Art historian A. Ginevski, for example, claimed that deviations in Soviet art were the result of the Stalinist "cult of personality," a form of hero- or leader-worship in which first Lenin and then

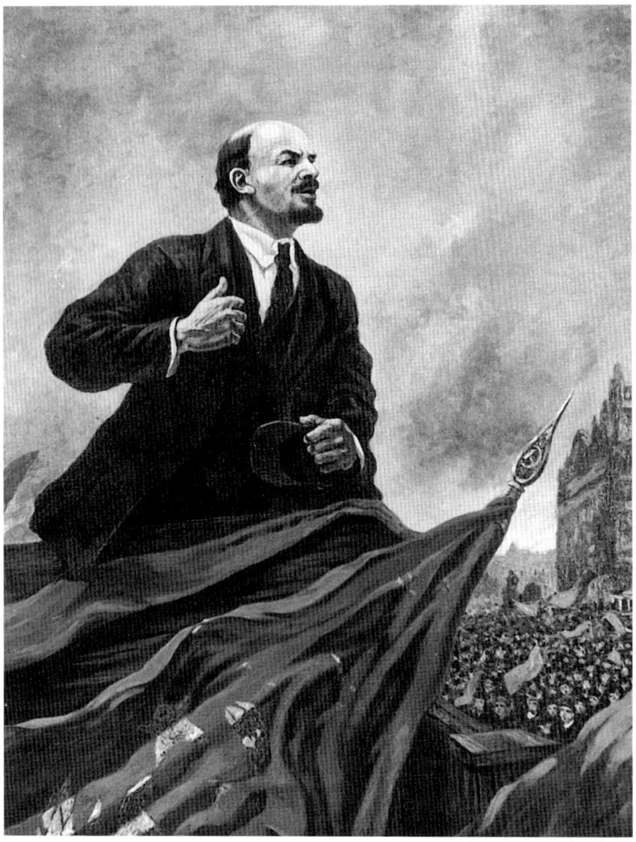

ALEXANDER GERASIMOV
Lenin on the Tribune, 1930
Oil on canvas
Central Lenin Museum, Moscow

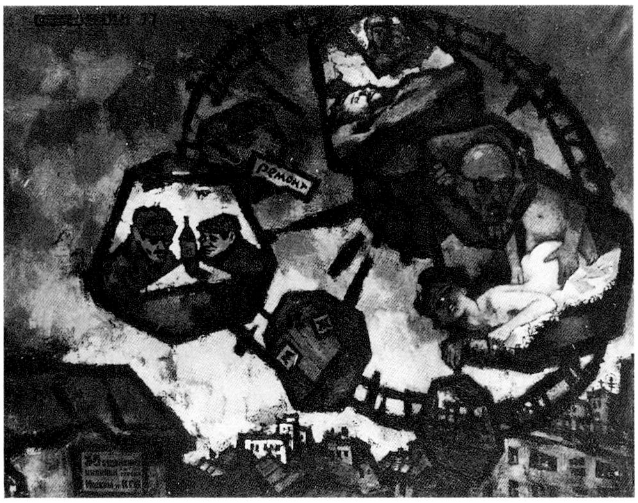

OSKAR RABIN
Ferris Wheel—Evening, 1977
Oil on canvas
Collection of Nancy and Norton Dodge

Stalin were venerated as the embodiment of the spirit of Communism and as such the prime subject matter for artists. Ginevski described the turning point in art, often referred to as the *perelom* (or *perelom v iskusstve*), as the "... aspiration of artists toward subjects depicting the life and interests of simple folk ... and by the striving of artists to depict life more poetically, more artistically, more figuratively."[25] Ginevski criticized A. Gerasimov (1881–1963) for ignoring Impressionism and suppressing art critics, who Ginevski felt were important to stimulating artistic productivity. So antagonistic to experimentation was Gerasimov, according to Ginevski, that during his reign, "... the entire large collective of MOSSKH [the Moscow Union of Artists] was listed in the camp of the formalists."[26]

After years of suppression, the necessity for innovation was finally being accepted. Artists would no longer be judged by their conformity or nonconformity to government dictates, but their works would be judged individually and criticized objectively. Even Gerasimov, who had been dubbed "Stalin's court painter," had a change of heart. He finally admitted that "... the cult of personality had done considerable harm ... [had caused the creation of] pompous pictures bearing the imprint of machine production."[27] Reversing his stance of previous years, he began to favor greater freedom of style and subject matter and, despite his earlier opposition to Impressionism, came to recognize its contributions to the history of painting. In all this, he became an embarrassment to official policymakers, and by the end of 1956 he was forced to resign from the presidency of the USSR Academy of Arts.

With the broadening of the Party line in art, officials allowed a much wider range of foreign art to be exhibited in the USSR. *Seventeenth to Twentieth Century English Art* opened at the Pushkin Museum in Moscow in 1956. Works by Pablo Picasso (1881–1973) and Henri Matisse (1869–1954), formerly labeled formalist and bourgeois, were exhibited at the Hermitage in Leningrad the same year. To celebrate Picasso's seventy-fifth birthday in 1956, an exhibition organized in his honor by Ilya Ehrenburg, author of *The Thaw*, was held in the Pushkin Museum. Picasso contributed a large number of his own works to this show, which Ehrenburg wrote about in his memoirs as follows: "Too many people came to the opening.... The crowd broke through the barrier.... I spoke into the microphone: 'Comrades, you have waited twenty-five years for this exhibit, now wait patiently twenty-five minutes....' "[28]

Many young artists of that time claimed that the Picasso exhibition had an important influence on their work.[29] They became emboldened, exhibiting their own nonconformist art more frequently. Oskar Rabin, a dissident artist from Riga, Latvia, moved to Moscow, where he began his rise to prominence as a leader of the Moscow unofficial artists movement.[30] Apartment exhibitions organized by members of the intelligentsia and scientific elite became popular in the capital, providing a semi-public forum for artists whose works were normally not shown in official state exhibitions.

Meanwhile, several changes were occurring at the highest levels of officialdom. To improve the economic status of artists and to encourage them to create more new artworks, the USSR Ministry of Culture developed a system of awarding commissions and established specialized stores—quasi-art galleries—for the sale of paintings, prints, and sculpture. For the first time since the Stalin era began, art had become a consumer item, not merely a form of propaganda. To further encourage artists, spacious studios were constructed in Moscow, Leningrad, and Kiev.[31] Every effort was made to improve the well-being of the Soviet artist. At the same time, Khrushchev's policies opened the way for momentous changes in the arts. His affirmation of "peaceful coexistence" with the West, for example, permitted thinking of Western technology as separate from its ideology and made technical tools such as airbrushes acceptable for use in Soviet art. But artists who were hoping that the same consideration would be given to content were disappointed when uprisings in Poland and Hungary temporarily jeopardized any liberalizing tendencies.[32] Nevertheless, the momentum of the Secret Speech and its effects in all areas of art were irreversible. Artists knew they had to tread the Party line, but they were eager to preserve their newly gained freedom.

An attempt to define a new Party line in art marked the first four post-Stalin years, when the art establishment and its officials were clearly reevaluating Socialist Realism and in general attempting to expand its interpretation. All seemed to realize, along with Hungarian Marxist philosopher and literary critic Gyorgy Lukacs, that "... Socialist Realism has turned into something [called] 'government issue naturalism.' "[33] By the late 1950s such prominent Soviet artists as Arkadii Plastov (1893–1972), Martiros Saryan (1880–1972), Alexander Deineka (1899–1969), and Pavel Korin (1892–1962), who had been criticized for their views in the 1940s, could no longer be dismissed as formalists and their works withheld from exhibitions. Officials agreed that experimentation in art could originate from new, though officially dictated, content, and that innovation in form could be permitted when it augmented the approved content. Artists were to remain the Party's helpers in educating society, and despite the *perelom* they were to continue integrating Marxist-Leninist theory in their work, but they could now do so creatively.

The Thaw

A new liberalism swept Soviet art as Khrushchev gained increasing control of the Communist Party in the second half of the 1950s. The first All-Union Congress of Soviet Artists met in March 1957 and unanimously condemned the effect of the Stalin era on Soviet art. The Congress agreed that Soviet art had become uniform and that labeling any departures from uniformity as formalist was unreasonable. In a momentous decision, the Congress announced that no art movement was to be rejected without study.[34] As a result, Soviet artists were encouraged to become knowledgeable about formerly forbidden schools and movements of art. Officials reasoned that because studies of the philosophers Kant, Berkeley, and Hegel had been permitted, modern Western art movements could also be explored. Furthermore, the Congress recommended that formalist works by Soviet artists should be exhibited in Soviet museums, because, they said, the artistic ideas of Kandinsky, Malevich, and Filonov were more interesting than those of contemporary Western modernists.[35] Thus, in 1957, it appeared that if Soviet artists and art officials were to have their way all Soviet citizens would be exposed to the works of the Russian avant-garde more than thirty years after they had been banned.[36]

Although many artists developed an "inner censorship"[37] and perhaps out of fear or mistrust stifled their artistic initiative and research, others became more courageous. The young Leningrad artist Ilya Glazunov opened a controversial show at the Moscow Central House of Workers of Art in February 1957. In particular, authorities objected to a pastel titled *Morning* (1956; collection of the artist), which depicted a nude woman (modeled by the artist's wife Nina Benois) reclining in bed while her lover gazes through a window overlooking Leningrad. Though nudes had periodically appeared in Soviet art,[38] there seemed to be an unwritten rule against depicting such subjects. Glazunov, the *enfant terrible* of Russian art, was testing the new expansion of Socialist Realism. Not only was his painting executed in an Impressionist style—as yet unpopular in the Soviet Union—but it also failed to deal with social themes and reflected what the Soviets considered to be modern bourgeois ideals. Moscow's leading literary newspaper, *Literaturnaya gazeta*, defended Glazunov and applauded his courage.[39]

Whereas the 1957 All-Union Congress of Soviet Artists initiated only hesitant questioning of the relationship between Socialist Realism and formalism, the VI International Youth Festival held in Moscow in the same year demonstrated an astonishing level of free and open discussion on the subject. Forty-nine countries, including the United States and representatives of Eastern and Western Europe and the Third World, participated in the May Festival organized by the USSR Ministry of Culture.[40] For the first time since the Stalin era, works of every school and art movement were on exhibit in Moscow. For some Soviet artists this was the first visual confrontation with abstract art forms.

The festival, its exhibits and discussions, made a permanent impact on Soviet art, sparking debates about the merits of abstract art that would continue into the 1980s. The Soviet press printed many of the arguments given by proponents of modern art. The public could openly view the artworks—abstract or realist—by artists who defended one or another viewpoint. Arguments ranged from that of American abstract painter Harry Coleman, who claimed that the main source of art is the personal psychological world of the artist,[41] to that of Russian sculptor Ernst Neizvestny, who renounced abstract art, saying, "Why doesn't my generation in our country accept abstract art?... It would seem mockery to us to leave our comrades, who are not artists, without an art comprehensible to all. I personally consider it a crime to make the incomprehensibility of art a slogan."[42] Coleman's response to Neizvestny was simply that the enemies of abstract art were innocent victims of cultural isolation.[43] Ironically, Neizvestny and Oskar Rabin, two Moscow artists who received recognition for their work at the festival,[44] would assume leading roles in the Russian nonconformist art movement of the 1960s. Both left the USSR in the 1970s for greater artistic freedom.

In the wake of such discussions, conservatives retrenched. The arch-conservative painter Vladimir Serov, known for his paintings of Lenin, feared losing control over the direction of Soviet art. He warned that Socialist Realism was not a "rubber sack" which had no bottom or sides; in other words, Socialist Realism was not flexible enough to incorporate all art forms. Serov felt that artists should return to their "Party paintings," creating works that would be comprehensible to the masses.[45] Similar warnings to the art community came from Khrushchev, who feared that artists might commit excesses in their searchings.[46] Official artists who had made hesitant steps toward liberalization once again elected to defend realism. Reverting to a conservative stance in comparison to his earlier pronouncements, Boris Ioganson, now president of the USSR Academy of Arts, said: "And, of course, the realistic form, tested by centuries of the development of art, appears as the only form capable of expressing deep content. This position is an axiom for us, Soviet artists. It is not debatable."[47] But although artists who experimented were harshly criticized, the new wave of reluctant tolerance for disagreement and debate prevailed.

The years 1957 and 1958 were revolutionary times for Soviet artists who had become accustomed to living and painting by strict official guidelines. By 1957, they no longer had to be members of artists' unions to participate in exhibitions; instead, shows were juried.[48] Some Soviet artists began to experiment with Impressionist techniques, and Impressionist paintings were commonly reproduced in Soviet art magazines.[49] Works from the early Russian avant-garde period were more frequently exhibited. Avant-garde artists such as Nicholas Roerich (1874–1947) and Robert Falk (1886–1953) had one-artist shows in Moscow in 1958.[50] In addition,

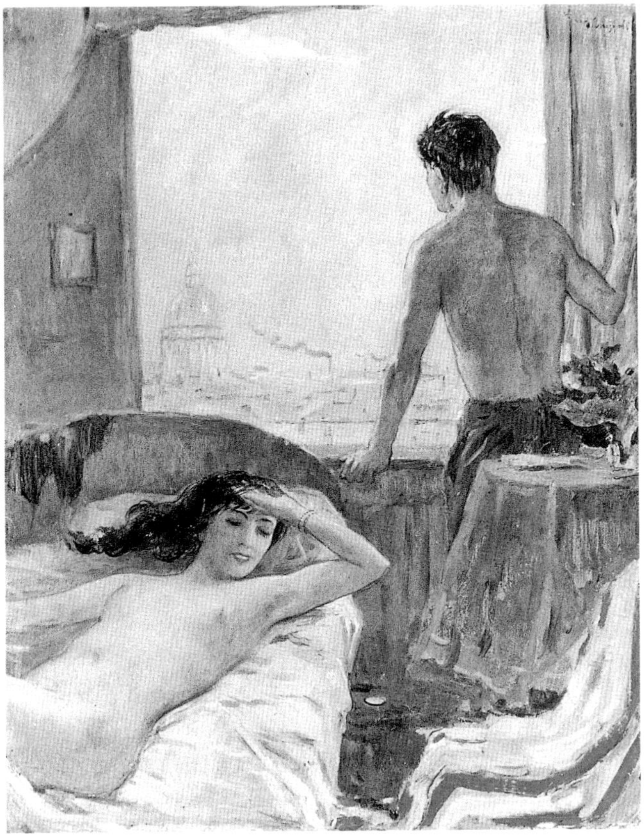

ILYA GLAZUNOV
Morning, 1956
Collection of the Artist

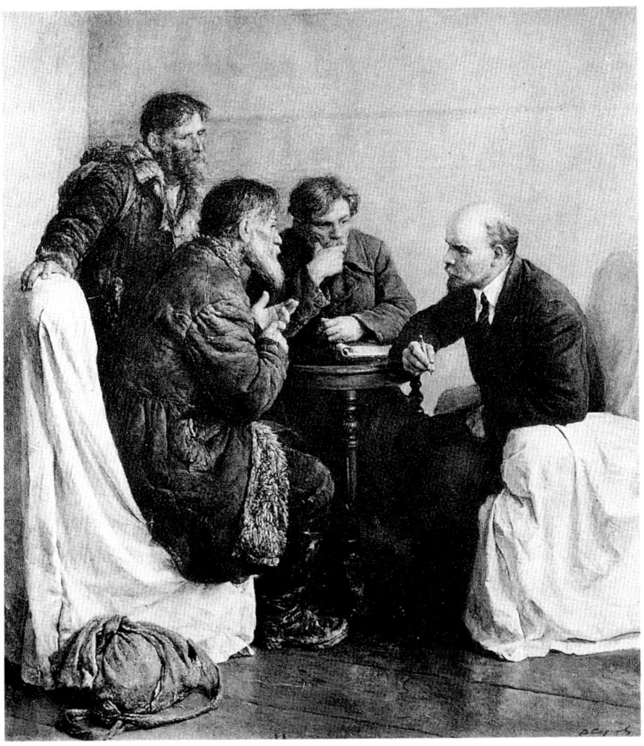

VLADIMIR SEROV
Peasant Delegates Talking to Lenin, 1950
Oil on canvas
Tretyakov Art Gallery, Moscow

books were published about modernist art: Eli Belyutin and N. Molevoi co-authored *The School of Anton Aschbe*, which discussed Aschbe's pedagogical principles and their influence on the Russian avant-garde; Andrei Sinyavskii (who was to be tried in Moscow in 1966 for printing satirical works in the West) and Moscow art historian Igor Golomshtok (who immigrated to Paris in the 1970s) wrote *Picasso and Matisse in Moscow*.[51]

As Soviet artists became more conscious of Western art movements, they responded in various ways. Some founded groups within their own communities to study modernism. The Group of Eight, seeking peaceful methods to broaden Socialist Realism, launched a movement within the Moscow Union of Artists.[52] A number of independent artists gathered around Rabin in Lianozovo, a suburb of Moscow, to further their explorations in modernism. Nonconformist groups in Moscow organized several small shows of works by young experimental artists Mikhail Grobman, Dmitri Plavinsky, and Vladimir Yakovlev.[53] Similar activities began in Leningrad, but no unified group was founded there in the early days.[54]

While the Soviet government worked on "thawing out the cold war," officials exhorted artists to chronicle the changes occurring in Soviet society. N. A. Mikhailov, the Minister of Culture, reiterated the need for contemporary themes, pointing out the absence of space subjects in Soviet art despite the successful launching of the first Sputnik in 1956. Years after this theme began to appear in Soviet art, it continues in the works of Olga Grechina, Sergei Sherstiuk, and Pyotr Belenok, but in works such as Belenok's *Despair in Space* (Colorplate 4), painted in 1978, the subject is viewed as an environmental cataclysm. The Soviet government would not have condoned such an avant-garde approach in the late fifties, when Minister of Culture Mikhailov was proclaiming that "Soviet art, along with the art of a number of other countries of the socialist camp, is conducting a struggle against diverse modernist movements."[55]

Despite Mikhailov's denunciation of Western modernism, the debate over abstract art reached the general public through articles and lectures. When Alfred H. Barr, Director of Collections of the Museum of Modern Art, gave a well-received slide lecture about contemporary American art in Moscow in 1959,[56] artists and art historians were prompted to suggest a role for abstract art within the Soviet context. Soviet critics rejected the concept of using abstract forms purely for the sake of form, but they agreed that "before conducting a struggle with abstractionism, as though it were a senseless and harmful movement of easel painting, one should discuss its possible utilization in decorative and applied arts."[57] These critics argued that abstract motifs were acceptable in the case of three-dimensional objects if they were subordinated to the dictates of "higher aesthetics." In other words, a vase had to remain functional and could not be abstract but could integrate abstract forms as design motifs. In its pure form, abstract three-dimensional art was only acceptable if it represented the national character of its creator; thus modern African sculpture was approved, since it was based on African tradition.[58] Despite this reluctant acceptance on one front, abstractionism in easel painting remained "senseless and harmful" in the eyes of officials.

Once limits on the use of abstract art forms were officially defined in 1959 and 1960, experimentation became less acceptable. Expressionism and surrealism were entirely rejected, and their existence in the West attributed to "Mister Business."[59] By 1961, the Moscow Union of Artists, which had been denounced for its favorable attitudes toward formalism during the Stalin years, came under renewed attacks for supporting the rebellious Neizvestny and for allowing too much experimentation. Khrushchev reinforced an official anti-modernist stance on the occasion of a September 1961 exhibition of French modern art in Moscow, when he proposed a toast to "... the real French art, not the kind we saw here. I mean the kind of art where you don't have to ask whether it is a cow or a horse."[60]

The desire for a unified national image in art received additional impetus in 1960 when the first Congress of the Russian Artists' Union met and overwhelmingly reaffirmed the tenets of Socialist Realism.[61] But something else happened on this occasion; for the first time there were open discussions of underground artists. Sergei Gerasimov, a conservative artist and an official of the new union, warned young underground artists such as Anatoli Zverev that they were being utilized by the West to discredit Soviet ideology. He exhorted all artists "... to fight even for those few who like flies are attracted to the treacle of bourgeois fashion."[62] As if to ward off further Western criticism and to demonstrate government control of the arts, immediately following the meeting of the Congress, Khrushchev held a meeting with the leaders of the Soviet intelligentsia[63] in which he emphasized the importance of Party guidance in the arts.

In spite of government efforts to combat it, the Soviet underground art movement was gaining momentum. Rabin's house in Lianozovo attracted visitors to weekly Sunday exhibitions of works by unofficial artists;[64] avant-garde art exhibits were held in apartments around Moscow; and George Costakis, a leading collector of the early Russian avant-garde, had a permanent exhibition of works by artists such as Zverev, Alexander Tyshler and Vladimir Weisberg.[65] In addition to apartment exhibitions, in 1960 there were also exhibits in clubs, scientific institutes, and elsewhere.[66] Most nonconformist exhibitions were unofficial, but some were held with official sanction.[67] The works may have been dubbed "formalistic vagaries [and] a chaotic conglomeration of colored spots,"[68] but they were not banned from exhibition. Despite official displeasure with "useless experimentation" and continuing criticism of abstract art, "the left artists" seemed to be carving their own niche in Soviet society.

Thirty Years of Moscow Art—The Exhibition

Prelude

On the occasion of the Twenty-Second Congress of the Communist Party in 1961, fifty exhibitions opened in Moscow.[69] Not all paintings at these exhibitions were thematic, nor did they contain political overtones. Some artists strayed so far from acceptable norms of Socialist Realism that they were chastised by union officials. Nevertheless, encouraged by the official tolerance of such exhibits, the "new left" pushed for additional gains. Small public and private showings of their work were held for the Moscow intelligentsia, and Moscow University held an exhibit of sculptures by Neizvestny and esoteric abstract paintings by Vladimir Yankilevsky. Mikhail Chemiakin had his first one-artist exhibition at the club of the *Zvezda* journal in Leningrad. The *Dvizhenie* (Movement) group, founded by Lev Nusberg in Moscow and including artists such as Francisco Infante, began to experiment with kinetic designs and constructions (see, for example, Infante's *Spirals* series [Colorplates 30–32]).[70] Pianist Svyatoslav Richter sponsored several exhibits of new-left modern art in his Gorky Street apartment. And a show by Yevgenii Kropivnitskii, the mentor of the Lianozovo group, was scheduled for an official opening at the Exhibition Hall on Yermolayevsky Street.[71] Apparently the condemnation of the cult of personality had released enormous creative powers.[72]

With all this activity, the modernists seemed to be on the verge of a breakthrough by 1962, when several exhibitions of early avant-garde works were held in the Mayakovsky Museum in Moscow: in February, paintings by the Expressionist Pavel Filonov were shown; in May there was an exhibit of works by Malevich and Tatlin. Such exhibits seemed to demonstrate tacit official recognition of the Russian avant-garde of the 1920s. Moscow art historian Nikolai Khardzhev, who was responsible for the exhibits, indicated that more would be held: "If we are to write the history of Soviet art, it must include the facts.... Malevich played an important role in the Soviet art of the early days, and nobody can deny that."[73] Georgy Nissky, a proponent of "artistic truth," called for the opening of a museum of new Western art and Soviet art of the 1920s; such a museum, he explained, would save young artists the problem of discovering what had already been discovered, and it would help them to avoid many mistakes. Nissky postulated that only those artists who experimented would play a role in society; those who lived in the past would soon be forgotten. Art critic Vladimir Turbin, in his book about aesthetics entitled *Comrade Time and Comrade Art*,[74] paralleled Nissky's views. Turbin compared abstractions in modern science to abstractions in modern art, implying that both were necessary.

The new left became increasingly bold in vocalizing theories and creating avant-garde artworks. Neizvestny, who was in the forefront of leftist activities, said: "... I have decided the following: an artist has the right to be incomprehensible...."[75] Though he himself opposed straightforward formalism, Neizvestny published his liberal views in defense of artistic innovation in the leading Russian art magazine *Iskusstvo*,[76] pleading for everyone to accept experimentation so that the Soviet Union

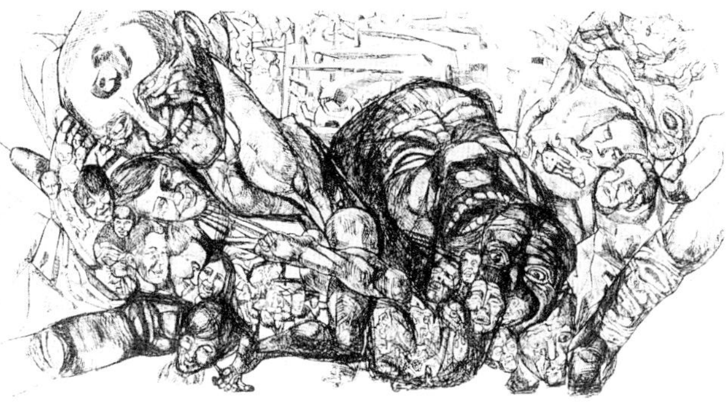

ERNST NEIZVESTNY
Untitled, n.d.
Etching
Collection of Nancy and Norton Dodge

could catch up with the West not only on the industrial front but also in the fine arts.

Liberal success in Moscow in the early 1960s is perhaps best measured by the undisturbed activities of Eli Belyutin and his followers. Belyutin had taught at the Polygraphic Institute in Moscow until 1959, when he was denounced for his modernist ideals by the painter Goncharev and subsequently released from the institute faculty. After leaving the institute, Belyutin authored several books about art theory and taught part-time in official institutions and in his own Studio of Experimental Painting and Graphic Arts. In the summer of 1962, Belyutin, who had become known for his innovative teaching,[77] led a group of students on a study trip by boat down the Volga River from Moscow to Astrakhan. In the fall, he and his students held a one-evening exhibition at the Moscow Cafe Molodyezhnoye and a longer exhibition at the Moscow Literary Institute. On November 26, thirty Belyutin students exhibited about seventy-five abstract paintings in a public showing held in Belyutin's studio. Other well-known members of Moscow's official and unofficial art world also participated—artists such as Neizvestny, Ulo Sooster, Yankilevsky, and Yury Sobolev.[78] It was the first public exhibition of Soviet abstract art since Stalin had achieved full power in the Soviet Union. Foreign correspondents were invited to the exhibit, a possible indication that some members of Soviet officialdom were ready to publicly acknowledge their approval of abstract art.

Abstract Art at the Manezh

Following the successful exhibit in Belyutin's studio, an unexpected invitation was issued by Dmitri Polikarpov, head of the Cultural Section of the Central Committee. According to Belyutin, Polikarpov telephoned him with a request that he exhibit the work of the Belyutintsy at the Manezh, Moscow's Central Exhibition Hall. Reportedly Polikarpov told Belyutin that his group had a chance to gain complete official acceptance by showing their art to leaders of the Party and the government. Belyutin, accepting the invitation, said that he expected either "provocation or recognition."[79]

The jubilee exhibition, called *Thirty Years of Moscow Art*, opened on November 4, 1962. Two thousand paintings, prints, and sculptures were on view.[80] Within one month of its opening, the Manezh exhibit had been visited by more than one hundred thousand people. The exhibit aroused many arguments and discussions about artists such as David Shterenberg (1881–1948) and Robert Falk who had abandoned the traditions of Socialist Realism. Falk's *The Nude* (Tretyakov Art Gallery) was found especially objectionable. Members of the younger generation adversely critiqued were Pavel Nikonov, Andrei Vasnetsov (who in 1988 became Chairman of the USSR Union of Artists), and A. Pologovaya,[81] all members of the Moscow Union of Artists. The official statement proclaimed that the exhibition had stimulated honest discussions about urgent matters in art, but artists and art critics had failed "to clean house" after "combating" the difficult period of the "personality cult."[82]

There was little journalistic coverage until members of the Party and the government came to view the exhibit on December 1. The viewing took several hours. Explanations of the art were given by, among others, the First Secretary of the Board of the USSR Union of Artists, Sergei Gerasimov; the President of the USSR Academy of Arts, Boris Ioganson; and the First Secretary of the Board of the Russian Artists' Union, Vladimir Serov.[83] Khrushchev's severe pronouncements on the works of the Belyutintsy were ignored by the Soviet press, which published only his much milder commentary on the main exhibit. Months later, the British magazine *Encounter* printed what it described as "a hitherto unpublished stenographic account of some of [Khrushchev's] remarks."[84]

In criticizing some of the paintings, Khrushchev reminded artists that the "lofty mission" of Soviet art was to "truthfully depict the life of the people, to inspire people to build Communism, to educate man to the very best, noblest feelings, to a deep understanding of the wondrous."[85] He stated that the better works depicted Soviet creative goals. Pausing before Nikonov's painting *The Geologists* (Russian Museum, Leningrad), which particularly irritated him, he said: "A picture should elevate, ennoble man, inspire and lead him to a noble deed. But can such pictures really fulfill such high social aims?"[86] The painting, now a classic of the Severe Style, shows a group of men at work in an icy snowstorm. Their faces are gray and disfigured from frostbite. One of the men is sitting in the snow, removing his shoes, because his feet are frozen. Measured by the standards of Socialist Realism, this painting had failed. It did not depict robust, optimistic workers, nor was it cheerful, nor did it inspire confidence. Khrushchev was further infuriated when in discussions with the artists he discovered that some were indifferent to public opinion. He responded that a painting which is understandable only to the painter could not be taken for real art.[87]

After his review of the main exhibition halls, Khrushchev and the leaders of the Party, the government, and arts organizations continued to the upper halls of the Manezh to view the works of the Belyutintsy. When he entered the private rooms, Khrushchev is said to have exploded in anger. The magazine *Iskusstvo* explained that the "so-called abstract works" aroused feelings of bewilderment and indignation in Khrushchev and that to him these works were devoid of sense, content, and form.[88] According to the Soviet press, when Khrushchev asked the artists what they were depicting and what thoughts they were trying to communicate to viewers, the response was "inarticulate conversation testifying to the spiritual squalor of the authors of those works."[89] In one of the exchanges, Khrushchev asked Belyutin to explain his semi-abstract painting, *The Spassky Gate* (collection of the artist), which depicts one of the entrances to the Kremlin. After Belyutin explained, Khrushchev responded, "What are you talking about, what sort of Kremlin is this? This is mockery!... And see here, Belyutin, I am telling you, as the Chairman of the Council of Ministers, all this is unnecessary to the Soviet people."[90] To the conservative artist Serov, who had been guiding the leaders through the exhibit, Khrushchev said: "But you, Serov, also don't know how to paint well. I remember we visited the Dresden Gallery. They showed us a picture in which the hands were painted in such a way that you couldn't see the brush strokes even through a magnifying glass. Now you can't do that either."[91] In the midst of his scathing remarks Khrushchev asserted:

> ... such "creativity" is alien to our people, they reject it. This must be pondered by these people who call themselves artists, yet create such "pictures" that you cannot tell—were they drawn by the hand of a person, or daubed by the tail of a donkey. They must understand their errors and work for the people.[92]

In addition to his remarks to the artists present, Khrushchev criticized some of his leading colleagues in the Party: "... if pictures like these appear, it means that we are not doing our work properly. This includes the Ministry of Culture and the Central Committee's Commission on Ideology."[93]

In spite of such high-level condemnation, the general public seemed supportive of the Manezh exhibit; the criticized paintings, especially, attracted large crowds. An official tour guide was even heard defending the merits of one painting that had been censured.[94] One young man, admiring Nikonov's *The Geologists*, which Khrushchev had singled out for his harshest criticism, announced to a group of about a hundred people crowding before the painting, "I like this picture. It has captured a mood."[95] An older man added:

> Listen, comrades, I myself am a geologist. I know what the work of a geologist is like. The artist has hit the nail on the head. I have seen other pictures with this theme. All have made our work showy and prettified it! But this picture is real. It shows the truth. It is not always rosy. Life is not made up of happiness.[96]

Though Belyutin was optimistic about the outcome of Khrushchev's visit to the Manezh, and later felt that Neizvestny had provoked the Party leader, he laid the ultimate blame for the condemnation of the event on Suslov, the Party chief of ideology. According to Belyutin, Suslov had maneuvered Khrushchev into the Manezh with a warning concerning the role of the intelligentsia in the Hungarian uprising of 1956. Certain officials attempted to protect Belyutin and his followers, but for the time being they had lost the battle. The mistake committed by the Belyutintsy and other liberals was that they attempted to push the Party too far, too fast, in order to rescind the entire cultural policy of Stalin. For now, Serov, representing the conservatives, could joyfully exclaim, "The most incredible, understand me, incredible thing has happened. We have won!" The works of the Belyutintsy were locked away in the upper rooms of the Manezh for the duration of the exhibit and not released for public viewing.[97]

Aftermath

Following the Manezh exhibition there was a new wave of conservative posturing which continued for months. The USSR Union of Artists confessed its failure to form a united front against formalistic aesthetics[98] and elected conservative A. Gerasimov to its membership. Another conservative, Alexander Laktionov, was elected to the directorship of the Surikov Art Institute, Moscow's leading educational art institution.[99] Ioganson, the liberal president of the USSR Academy of Arts, was replaced by the conservative Serov, who had escorted Khrushchev around the Manezh exhibition.

Other official arts organizations attempted to justify their actions so that they would not be implicated by the Manezh debacle. The magazine *Iskusstvo* defended its posture by quoting from a series of conservative articles it had printed over the years and by refuting a recently published article on Neizvestny. The revised opinion of Neizvestny's sculptures described them as "devoid of humanistic content, alien to realism, imitating the works of Western abstractionists."[100] The article also criticized Moscow artist Nikolai Andronov for his position that artists of the Russian avant-garde should be fully rehabilitated. *Iskusstvo* now took a position advocating the resurrection of Stalinist art of the 1930s and 1940s, which the magazine claimed had been debunked by critics who had correlated all works of the period to the personality cult.[101]

Amid the verbal warfare, liberals steadfastly pursued their goals. Perhaps to appease them, the Ministry of

Culture, on January 17, 1963, opened an exhibition of three hundred paintings and ceramics by the French Cubist Fernand Léger. The exhibition continued for three months at the Pushkin Museum in Moscow.[102] The Ministry also approved an exhibition at the Tretyakov Art Gallery of paintings by Mikhail Nesterov (1862–1942), a Russian nationalist who had not been exhibited since the Revolution. Other exhibits followed. The abstract works of Edik Shteinberg and Mikhail Grobman were included in a one-day exhibition at the Dostoevsky Museum.[103] And Neizvestny was given a show at Dubna, the Soviet atomic research center (scientists being among the most enthusiastic supporters of the new art in Russia).[104]

Abstract art once again came under fire in 1963 when in a speech Khrushchev severely lashed out against the artists he had assailed at the Manezh. He referred to Neizvestny's sculptures as "nauseating concoctions," and he went on to say that Neizvestny was not the only Soviet artist creating "ugly abstractions." In comparing the self-portraits of the orthodox painter Alexander Laktionov with those of Boris Zhutovsky, a member of the Belyutin group, Khrushchev said: "It is clear to any sensible person with unspoiled taste that the painting by Laktionov holds one's attention through its humanity.... But whom has Zhutovsky portrayed? A freak."[105]

Orthodox artists were encouraged by Khrushchev's speech. Some members of the intelligentsia recanted. Of the artists who had exhibited at the Manezh, Neizvestny was among the few to retreat, promising "to work more and better"[106] but in no way apologizing for his criticized works. The sculptor Tomsky, who had become increasingly experimental in his work during the post-Stalin thaw years, in a turn-about recommended that young Soviet artists be sent to work in industry and agriculture as part of their art education to help them learn the true meaning of life, and, as a result, to paint according to official precepts.[107] Many remained silent: Belyutin, for example, did not engage in self-criticism.

The Second Congress of the USSR Union of Artists met in 1963 and upheld "the re-establishment of Leninist principles in art after the liquidation of the personality cult,"[108] but the proceedings were milder in tone than the Khrushchev speeches. Abstract art and naturalism were criticized, as were some of the artists who had exhibited at the Manezh, but there was little name-calling. Young Leningraders were upbraided for their formalism, Georgian artists for adhering to French Pointillism, and Latvian artists for "cosmopolitan modernism" in their watercolors.

Despite the tides against modernism, the deposed liberal head of the Academy, Boris Ioganson, took a strong stand, saying that "modern" artists should not be cast out by society. In a somewhat prophetic statement he warned that accusing artists of "foreign ideologies" might in fact turn them toward these ideologies. He recommended that the government help these artists by providing them with the proper conditions for their work.[109] Moscow sculptor Lev Kerbel did not share Ioganson's views and complained about artists who refused to accept the Party's criticisms, but he was pleased that official policy toward "rule-breakers" had changed: "When serious critical remarks were made about some works of literature and art, I was pleased that the struggle was not against people who made mistakes. The struggle was for [the benefit of] those people...."[110] Orthodox as well as liberal members of the art community were breathing a sigh of relief that one could be criticized one day and still be working in one's studio the next.

The Yoke Loosens

As 1963 progressed, events began to favor new liberal gains. Katharine Kuh, a noted American curator and critic, visited the USSR and in a *Saturday Review* article reported a free exchange of thoughts among artists. She observed that Khrushchev was not the only reason for the negative attitude toward new forms of art, but that some of the more reactionary painters and sculptors exerted pressure to stifle innovation among younger artists because they perceived them to be artistic and professional threats.[111] Similarly, John Canaday, art critic and Moscow correspondent for *The New York Times*, observed a "freeing up" of the situation in Soviet arts. Canaday pointed out that as many as four hundred Moscow artists were working in the modern style and artists of the stature of Neizvestny were exhibiting "just about as they please," since their international reputation would make persecution undesirable. Abstract artists, Canaday claimed, were not making political statements but were "searching for 'a lasting perception of life'... a universalization connectable with the Socialist Realists' desire to depict life in hope-inspiring terms."[112]

The renewed sense of freedom in the arts could be measured in terms of commercial activities as well. In the fall of 1963, Eric Estorick, a London art dealer, signed a landmark contract with V/O Mezhdunarodnaya Kniga, a Soviet foreign trade organization, for the exportation of Soviet paintings and graphics to the West.[113] The works of Anatoli Kaplan, Nikonov, and Neizvestny were included in the trade agreement, as were the works of Rabin, leader of the unofficial Lianozovo artists.[114] Possibly, the sale of such works to the West served propaganda purposes, showing that artists were creating openly and freely in the Soviet Union. Certainly, the large-scale exhibition of Soviet prints, including the lithographs of Jewish artist Kaplan, that opened in the Time-Life Building in New York in November 1963, served this purpose.[115]

Unfortunately, it was becoming more and more apparent to Soviet leaders that many artists were leading a double life. A. Kozlov, for example, who was criticized for his "expressionistic tendencies," was said to be producing works at home that were even more formalistic.[116] During the day, it was said, Odessa artist Sokolov advocated realism, but at night he created abstract paintings with such titles as *The Atomic Power Station Run on Sexual Energy* (whereabouts unknown).[117] Officials who noted that the most daring works were being produced surreptitiously alluded also to the patrons—scientists, scholars, writers, composers, and actors—who purchased artworks directly from artists. Such sales were frowned upon, but they were not illegal.

Other members of the new left openly experimented and even thrived. Belyutin founded another workshop for his students in Abramtsevo, an artists' colony outside Moscow. Nusberg and his group of Moscow kineticists, which included Francisco Infante, held exhibits at the Youth Club on Prospekt Mir (Peace Avenue) and at the Historical Museum. Ulo Sooster had "Tuesday Salons" at his apartment, where he exhibited his avant-garde works. Muscovite Mikhail Shvartsman created a new system of painting he called "Synthesis and Metaphysics." With Grobman and V. Galatski from Moscow and Chemiakin, M. Ivanov, and O. Lyagachev from Leningrad, he wrote the "Manifesto of Synthesis in Painting." Though Leningrad members of the new left experienced more opposition than their comrades in Moscow, they too continued to experiment. Chemiakin, Lyagachev, Valeri Kravchenko, Vladimir Ovchinnikov, and Vladimir Ufliand organized a March 1964 exhibit of *Working Artists from the Hermitage Staff*, which opened at the Hermitage but was closed three days later by authorities.[118] Nevertheless, one of the future leaders of the Leningrad unofficial artists' movement, Evgeni Rukhin, was able to go about educating himself in modernist art, a pursuit that eventually led him to Moscow and a close association with the Lianozovo group. In Moscow, Rukhin met George Costakis, a Greek-Russian collector, whose collection of the early Russian avant-garde was to have a profound influence on his work.[119]

One Soviet artist who successfully and legally maneuvered himself into a position of prominence in the years after the Manezh exhibition was Ilya Glazunov. Glazunov's painting style was based on that of the icon painters of the fourteenth and fifteenth centuries, in particular, Theophanos the Greek and his pupil Andrei Rublev (ca.1370–ca.1430), and his themes ranged from biblical and old Russian to contemporary life. A Russophile by conviction, Glazunov had a stylized approach to art, which was a departure from strict Socialist Realism. As a result, the artist was repeatedly refused membership in the Moscow Union of Artists. Because he was not supported by the union, Glazunov worked as a book and magazine illustrator and, through a variety of friendships in the Western diplomatic community, received portrait commissions. He achieved a certain amount of notoriety, which attracted the attention of the Russian intelligentsia and brought additional commissions for artworks. So much favorable attention protected him. Because of his popularity, the Ministry of Culture granted him a license to give private art lessons and allotted him a studio. He was even permitted to visit Italy on a painting assignment. Finally, Glazunov succeeded in opening his first one-artist show at the Manezh in Moscow on June 15, 1964, the first showing of his works since the 1957 exhibit in which he showed the controversial pastel of a nude woman.

The decision to display Glazunov's works was made by the Ministry of Culture, which said that "despite opposition from conservative elements of the Union, Glazunov should be judged by 'public opinion' " and after the end of the show a public debate should take place.[120] In spite of this show of official approval, there were last-minute problems. At 4:00 p.m., when the exhibit was scheduled to open, the militia posted a handwritten notice postponing the exhibit indefinitely. Apparently, the Ministry of Culture was reacting to a protest from the artists' union. Some two hundred people who had gathered for the exhibit remained and protested. Alexander N. Kuznetzov, the first Deputy Minister of Culture, arrived to review the show, had two paintings removed, and ordered the exhibit to be opened. According to a bystander, the minister said, "I don't like the looks of this. I don't want any trouble."[121] With the opening of the exhibit Glazunov gained a victory over the entrenched power of the artists' union and demonstrated that the Ministry of Culture had become more flexible in its policies of dealing with artists. To a lesser degree, the exhibit also demonstrated the effect of public pressure.

Four months later, on October 16, 1964, the surprising official announcement came that Khrushchev had been released from the Presidium and the Secretariat and as Chairman of the Council of Ministers. The Khrushchev era, which had shown that the Party could maintain control over artists by alternating the use of the carrot and the stick, as Stalin had done more vigorously, was ended. The pendulum of liberalization had swung to and fro several times since Stalin's death in 1953, and each time the net result was a gain for those who aimed at broadening the area of creative freedom. As the new regime attempted to bring artists into line, it would be confronted with a more sophisticated and powerful intelligentsia than ever before. When he dictated his memoirs, Khrushchev himself finally realized that "any kind of limitation is like a yoke on the creative process."[122] Yokes by any definition cannot be tolerated indefinitely.

BREZHNEV AND THE ARTS

The new leadership that came to power after Khrushchev's fall intended to retain control of the arts,[123] but among art officials there was a more relaxed attitude. On January 16, 1965, Boris Ioganson was elected chairman of the board of the USSR Union of Artists, replacing the deceased conservative chairman Sergei Gerasimov.[124] But while liberals gained more support in the Union of Artists, the Academy of Arts remained the stronghold of conservatives. Serov was reelected to the presidency of the Academy in 1966, despite official displeasure over his failure to help young artists organize exhibitions.[125]

Since young artists could not enter artists' unions immediately after graduating from art institutes without first exhibiting their works for approval, they were left to their own resources. Many had no access to studios or money to purchase art supplies and, according to government assessment of the situation, were forced to take odd jobs. It was believed that this situation resulted in unprofessional works and attempts at "fashion" or "modernism."[126] More and more young artists were associating with groups of unofficial artists. Thus in 1966 the Union of Artists resumed the young artists' exhibits that had been abolished at the Second Congress of the USSR Union of Artists in 1963, enabling artists thirty-five years of age or younger to participate in annual exhibits. Moreover, Tair Salakhov, secretary of the Union of Artists, invited young artists to contribute new, interpretive paintings to a major national art exhibition commemorating the fiftieth anniversary of the Soviet Union.[127]

In 1967 the Fifth Plenum of the USSR Union of Artists met jointly with the Collegium of the USSR Ministry of Culture, and once again modernism was deemed objectionable. Innovation, however, was declared acceptable. Artists found it difficult to separate the two. But all hopes for innovation were smashed with the Soviet decision to reimpose orthodox Communism in Czechoslovakia and to replace the liberal reforms undertaken by Czech Party leader Alexander Dubček. When Soviet and Warsaw Pact forces invaded Czechoslovakia in August 1968, there was no turning back from the reimposition of conservatism in art. At official meetings and conferences artists reaffirmed their dedication to the Party and their intent to combat ideological inconsistencies.[128] Renewed pressure for conformity was on.

In this atmosphere the Third Congress of the USSR Union of Artists opened in Moscow on November 23, 1968. Present were Leonid Brezhnev and Aleksei Kosygin.[129] Amidst the usual rhetoric, came the usual admonitions: "... we must strengthen the ideological stability of the Soviet peoples and their ability to oppose any form of bourgeois influence."[130] There followed a period of ideological watchfulness, during which the Party decided to shake up the complacency of the official artistic elite, starting with the Art Fund, the commercial organization of the USSR Union of Artists.

Under Khrushchev, there had been two drives against fund officials, one in 1954 and another in 1964. In 1965, under Brezhnev, officials of the Moscow Union Art Fund were accused of using the fund for personal gains.[131] By 1969 the flagrancies were so great that *Pravda* published an exposé, listing the people involved in the misappropriation of funds. According to the article, "a cartel consisting of N. Andronov, A. Vasnetsov, and Elkonin... designed a wall panel for the Moscow Theater. For five months of creative endeavor, each of those three designers designed a sum of fourteen thousand rubles in his own pocket."[132] *Pravda* also said that from 1967 to 1968, I. A. Titov, the former chairman of the Moscow Union of Artists, had paid himself an average salary in excess of two thousand five hundred rubles monthly. Some administrators engaged in extortion or bribery, while others illegally amassed collections of old masterpieces. As a result of official investigations of the fund, the union was forced to change its payment policies and establish a new administrative structure.[133]

After the invasion of Czechoslovakia, artists were warned against "deliberately or inadvertently softening the reactionary essence of modernism."[134] The terms "reality" (*realistichnost'*)[135] and "realistic innovation" (*realisticheskoe novatorstvo*)[136] were more frequently used than "realism," but no clear definitions were given. Though the young artists exhibitions were resumed, the artworks were severely criticized for their depressing and overly philosophical content and because they reflected a renunciation of contemporary life.[137]

The Twenty-fourth Congress of the Communist Party of the Soviet Union met in the spring of 1971, and stressed a "middle-of-the-road" position on all issues, which differed little in substance from that of the Congress of 1966. Brezhnev criticized both liberals and hardliners in the arts and claimed that the personality cult of the Stalin era and the subjectivism of the Khrushchev era had been overcome. He reaffirmed his commitment to Socialist Realism. Artists who belonged to unions were encouraged to strengthen their ties with those who did not belong. Plenary meetings of unions were to be held to uphold the wishes of the Congress.

Officials continued their efforts to influence and improve the work of young artists, but they remained dissatisfied with the results. The 1972 *All-Union Exhibit of Young Artists* was regarded as "overly intellectual." Some works, it was said, showed a preoccupation with the personal thoughts of the artist, while current social issues were ignored. Old Russia was idolized, and a style reminiscent of early icon paintings was gaining popularity.[138] Yuri Nekhoroshev, chief editor of *Tvorchestvo*, reviewed the exhibit for *Literaturnaya Rossiya*:

> The masterly ability to reproduce the exterior of a subject has turned into an end in itself. The content of the works has developed into a formal skill of creating an illusion of three-dimensionality. And imperceptibly, the distinction between realism and naturalism has been obliterated.[139]

The problem of dealing with young artists became a focal point of the Fourth Congress of the USSR Union of Artists during its May 1973 meeting in Moscow. The Congress decided to safeguard young artists from the influence of modernism by directing their attention to an "in-depth study of life's processes and their truthful and realistic depiction."[140] Furthermore, it was decided that the period between graduating from an art institute and entering a union was too long for artists to be left to their own devices. As a result, the Congress created commissions to work with young artists[141] in order to advance their ideological education and presumably to keep them under control.

In addition, the Fourth Congress launched a crackdown on modernist practices. "The ideological struggle against bourgeois aesthetics needs to be intensified.... We must show intolerance to every form of ideological influence on Soviet art.... We must resolutely uphold our ideological and aesthetic positions," proclaimed Nikolai Ponomarev, chairman of the Union's board.[142] Soviet artists were to "express the principal ideas of the time... that is, to follow the ways of Soviet realist arts."[143] The disfavored alternative would be to "use one's ability and energy... to the doubtful amusement of those whose world outlook... is narrowed by elitist views... and for whom art is fun or sometimes simply commerce."[144] As a warning to those who were failing to comply with the government's directives, artists were told that "everyone has the right to make a choice, but this will be his principal choice in life."[145] The seriousness of the conservative campaign was dramatized on February 13, 1974, with the expulsion of Alexander Solzhenitsyn from the Soviet Union, an event that overshadowed all others in Soviet cultural life at the time.[146]

But as official Soviet art evolved during the first decade of Brezhnev's reign there were several encouraging developments: the rise of national art schools, the official acceptance of the Russian avant-garde of the 1920s, and the firm entrenchment of unofficial art. A crucial spark in this new wave of liberalism was Ilya Glazunov. Ironically, Glazunov was the leading representative of a group of Russian poets, writers, painters, and composers who organized to create a national art free from Western influences. By 1965, the organization had become known as SMOG, an acronym for the Russian words *smelost'*, *mysl'*, *obraz*, and *glubina* (courage, idea, image, and profundity). Aiming to become the leading school of Russian art by the end of the sixties, SMOG drew up a "Manifesto of Creativity," declaring: "Modern Russian art has entered a blind alley from which it cannot extricate itself. It has become so saturated with foreign literature and art that it has become epigonic. Our national art is dead, and we should and must resurrect it."[147]

Though this attempt to revive Russian nationalism met with some criticism, Glazunov, quietly backed by ideological Party Chief Suslov, remained its ardent apologist. In his autobiography, Glazunov freely described his love for everything Russian and explained how he came to understand and value the old Russia of prerevolutionary times. Russian writers, like Vladimir Soloukhin, supported Glazunov's stand in essays about such inherently Russian nationalist painters as Mikhail Vrubel and Vasily Surikov.[148] Well-publicized Moscow exhibits such as *Paintings of Ancient Pskov*[149] added fuel to the growing interest in early Russia. Finally, the one-hundredth anniversary celebration of the *Peredvizhniki* (Wanderers) at the Bolshoi Theater on December 1, 1971, boldly proclaimed the true origins of Soviet art. Even conservative officialdom recognized the contributions of the *Peredvizhniki*. Minister of Culture Yekaterina Furtzeva addressed the guests, saying "... the best traditions of the *Peredvizhniki* continue in the art of Socialist Realism," and stressing that "Russian national art" was an inspiration to all Soviet artists.[150]

As Russian artists examined their heritage, the various republics of the Soviet Union became concerned about the preservation of their individual artistic identity. To call attention to the multinational aspect of the arts in the Soviet Union, several exhibitions opened in Moscow in the late sixties.[151] The art of each republic began to reflect national characteristics, and there were fewer artworks of the "happy peasant and worker" kind. Nevertheless, art officials insisted that "Socialist Realism reasserts the ideological unity and diversity of Soviet multinational art."[152]

Whereas the Khrushchev era was punctuated by vociferous arguments over the merits and demerits of the Russian avant-garde of the 1920s, during the Brezhnev period there were more and more avant-garde exhibitions and growing acceptance of this earlier Soviet art phenomenon. The real turning point in official recognition came in February–March 1966, when two hundred avant-garde works went on exhibit at the Institute of Physical Problems.[153] The exhibit was organized by the internationally renowned physicist Pyotr Kapitsa, head of the institute and a dedicated supporter of abstract art. There was no official interference with this exhibit. Some art historians felt that government leniency was due to efforts to regain popularity lost during the February Sinyavsky-Daniel case, when writers Andrei D. Sinyavsky and Yuli M. Daniel were convicted and sentenced to hard labor for smuggling their writings to the West and publishing so-called anti-Soviet propaganda under the pseudonyms of Abram Tertz (Sinyavsky) and Nikolai Arzhak (Daniel).[154]

Despite occasional setbacks, avant-garde artists persisted in their efforts to gain recognition. In March 1966, the Ministry of Culture organized an exhibition of paintings, gouaches, and watercolors by Alexander Tyshler, one of the artists who had been condemned at the Manezh exhibit in 1962. Tyshler is unique in that he bridged the old avant-garde and the new. In his 1920s abstract paintings he experimented with light and shadow, and he was one of the first to convert verbal images into plastic shapes, as in *I Don't Hear, I Don't See, I Don't Speak* (Colorplate 80). The show, which opened at the Pushkin Museum in Moscow, was Tyshler's first one-artist exhibit in forty years, and it was scheduled to travel to Paris,[155] raising artists' hopes that the Russian avant-garde was becoming officially acceptable. Realizing the sensitivity of the situation, Tyshler said in an interview that he selected the art himself and omitted certain paintings,[156] implying that he served as his own censor. To underscore Tyshler's newfound official approval, the Ministry's publishing house, Sovetskii Khudozhnik, released Flora Syrkina's book about the artist.[157]

Encouraged by the implications of the Tyshler exhibit, the Soviet arts community attempted to gain further ground. Liberal art critic V. Zimenko called for a reevaluation of all periods of art.[158] Even proponents of Russian nationalism, such as Ilya Glazunov, who opposed the art of the 1920s on aesthetic grounds, insisted that the works of Kandinsky, Malevich, and others of that period should be made accessible.[159] Interest in the Russian avant-garde continued to build as the Moscow Union of Artists opened a posthumous Robert Falk show in October 1966,[160] and Moscow's Tretyakov Art Gallery lent an El Lissitsky exhibit to the Grosvenor Gallery in London.[161] The official view was expressed by Minister of Culture Furtzeva, who pronounced Chagall, Malevich, and Kandinsky "magnificent artists" and blamed inadequate exhibition facilities for limited showings of their works in the past.[162]

The regime remained cautious throughout 1967—the fiftieth anniversary of the Soviet State—fearing that the showing of previously banned paintings would fuel the conflict between liberals and conservatives and mar the jubilee celebration.[163] By 1969 books on Cubism and abstract art were being published;[164] an exhibit of Futurist drawings by Vasili Chekrygin was on view at the Pushkin Museum in Moscow;[165] and George Costakis was permitted to lend a limited number of his paintings to Western exhibitions.[166] A previously aborted exhibition of the Cubist painter Aristarkh Lentulov was opened by the Moscow Union of Artists in 1971, and in 1973 Chagall was present at the opening of an exhibition of his works at the Tretyakov Art Gallery.[167] The Russian avant-garde, both historical and contemporary, was thus finally receiving well-deserved attention, and its place in world art was being affirmed. Though Soviet officials were less than enthusiastic, the government steadily increased its exposure of avant-garde artworks. It would be another five years, however, before the Soviet Union would again open its museum reserves, this time for *Paris-Moscow: 1900–1930*, the historic retrospective of the early Russian avant-garde.[168]

Unofficial artists, too, were heartened by the changes taking place in the official art world. Not only did they become more active in organizing exhibitions for scientific research institutes and local clubs, but in the spring of 1965 and through 1966 they participated in a series of group shows at Leningrad University and at the Leningrad House of Culture.[169] Unofficial art was also being exported, more than likely due to the efforts of the Soviet intelligentsia, who helped foreign diplomats in Moscow transfer the art abroad. Moscow artist Anatoli Zverev had an exhibition in Paris and Geneva,[170] and Oskar Rabin had a show in London. Since these exhibits were not attacked in the Soviet press, some Western observers felt that the prospects for freedom in the arts were good. One year later, however, Rabin's work and his participation in the London show were severely denounced because his subject matter, which came to be known as "barracks art," was thought to be too depressing and therefore a misrepresentation of Soviet art abroad.[171]

Just as the fiftieth anniversary of the Soviet state in 1967 had postponed the recognition of the avant-garde, it also affected unofficial artists. Twelve artists, among them Zverev, Vladimir Nemukhin, and Edik Shteinberg, were to exhibit fifty abstract and surrealist works for three days at the Druzhba Labor Union Club on the outskirts of industrial Moscow,[172] but shortly after the guests arrived for the opening a club official pronounced the exhibit closed; the space, he said, was needed for a film screening. It was not known whether government officials had closed the exhibit or whether bureaucrats from the Moscow Union of Artists were responsible,[173] but one day after the exhibit was cancelled, Yekaterina Belashova, secretary of the USSR Union of Artists, complained that artists were straying from Socialist Realism and giving "too much time and energy to empty formalistic exercises."[174] Apparently, the union remained a jealous guardian of its power, and still regarded artistic innovation as a threat.

The Druzhba artists did not give up, however. They sent a letter to the Central Committee protesting the closing and demanding an open discussion of their work. They denied being "abstractionists" and cited comments in their favor by leading supporters.[175] Because the exhibit had been attended by foreign diplomats and journalists, it was viewed as a political as well as an artistic event. Certainly the show marked an important change in atmosphere since the Khrushchev era. For the first time, artists had ventured a public exhibition on their own. Whatever else the show had done, it attracted the intense interest of the Party and the union in the affairs of the unofficial art movement.[176] In May, the Moscow City Party Committee stipulated that any exhibitions planned in the capital had to be approved by the Moscow Union of Artists.[177] In spite of such measures, the unofficial artists' movement could no longer be suppressed. A sign of its widespread recognition was the publication in the United States of *Unofficial Art in the Soviet Union*, by Paul Sjeklocha and Igor Mead, the first book to discuss the artists in detail.[178]

Soviet artists were not only participating in what the authorities interpreted as undesirable art exhibits; some were engaging in dissident political actions as well. In 1968 Boris Birger, a leftist member of the Moscow Union of Artists, was expelled from the Communist Party for signing protests against the 1967 trial of dissident Alexander Ginsberg.[179] Nikolai Andronov, another union member, whose paintings had been criticized by Khrushchev at the 1962 Manezh exhibit and who had also protested the Ginsberg trial, was scheduled to be brought to "strict Party account" for the same offense.[180]

The Party continued to be sensitive about its image abroad. In February 1970, the Soviet press singled out Alexander Glezer, a poet and organizer of three disrupted unofficial art shows, accusing him of being anti-Soviet. Glezer, the press said, was aiming "to gain a reputation as a patron of unrecognized talents" to attract the attention of "unscrupulous wretches and correspondents of various foreign newspapers"[181] so that he could profit by his art sales. The major objection, however, was that Glezer's actions gave the West a false perception of Soviet art.

Indeed, the Soviet policy toward unofficial artists remained ill-defined. During the summer of 1974, artists were unable to judge whether an activity would be condemned or simply ignored. Thus the first ten years of the Brezhnev regime were characterized by uncertainty in government policy, as officials struggled to come to grips with new challenges from the multiple spheres of the Soviet art world, and artists continued to test their options. A dogmatic approach to art was avoided, although certain conservative officials and artists were always ready to launch out against liberalization. At the end of the first decade of Brezhnev's regime, officials were again organizing a conservative campaign. Nevertheless, the challenge from young artists, national art groups, and the unofficial art movement had resulted in the expansion of official criteria of acceptability beyond strict Socialist Realism.

THE SURFACING OF UNDERGROUND ART

The "Bulldozer Incident"

The frustration caused by the inability of unofficial artists to exhibit freely finally precipitated a confrontation between the government and the artists. According to Oskar Rabin, by this time internationally recognized as the leader of the unofficial movement in Moscow, the artists wanted their works to be viewed by a larger public, but local authorities had repeatedly failed to grant them use of exhibition halls. In desperation, thirteen artists—among them Evgeni Rukhin, Vladimir Nemukhin, and the now-celebrated New York artists Vitaly Komar and Alexander Melamid—organized an outdoor exhibit. The *First Autumn Open-Air Exhibition* was scheduled from noon to 2:00 p.m. on September 15, 1974, at "the end of Profsoyuznyi Street, at the intersection of the Ostrovityanova Street in the Moscow suburb of Semenovskoe in the Cheremushki district."[182] The artists acknowledged that their exhibit would probably not transpire without incident, but they did not expect a calamity. Their motives for choosing to exhibit outdoors were not purely artistic but more in the nature of a protest against the government's denial of permission for unofficial exhibits in public buildings. The artists' actions, therefore, were political and, in a sense constituted an anti-government demonstration, with art as the vehicle. The government responded with bulldozers and water trucks, destroying some artworks and confiscating others, according to reports.

City officials denied that works had been confiscated, insisting that the artists had abandoned them in their haste to leave the site. The event exploded into an international incident. Adolph Dubs, charge d'affaires at the American Embassy in Moscow, protested "the failure of police to protect American correspondents from being manhandled."[183] A. M. Rosenthal, the managing editor of *The New York Times*, sent a letter to Anatoly F. Dobrynin, the Soviet Ambassador to the United States, protesting the assault on his Moscow Bureau Chief Christopher S. Wren. Thirty foreign correspondents living in Moscow signed a letter of protest addressed to the Ministry of Foreign Affairs. Sir Norman Reid, director of the Tate Gallery in London, cancelled a trip to Leningrad to confirm plans for a J. M. W. Turner exhibition at the Hermitage, saying: "If I had gone to Russia, ... the artists might have thought that I was completely insensitive to what just happened."[184] While the "bulldozer incident," as it came to be called, was receiving front-page treatment in Western newspapers, the Soviet news agency TASS denounced the exhibition itself as a "cheap provocation" and warned the West:

> As for those who seized upon this incident to sling more mud on the USSR cultural policies, they have miscalculated again. It is the Soviet government that provided the people of the USSR, once illiterate in their majority, with a real and genuine possibility of mastering the best of culture and becoming connoisseurs of art. No matter how the enemies of our country strive to prove the opposite, nothing will come of it.[185]

Broadly speaking, the events of September 15, 1974, reflected the enduring insecurity of the Soviet leadership and the continuing efforts of the bureaucracy to impose conformity on artists. At a time when the government was attempting to improve its image abroad, it seems inexplicable that authorities would decide to mount a major offensive against an unofficial art show. On the other hand, if the artists had been permitted to hold their exhibition, conceivably a precedent would have

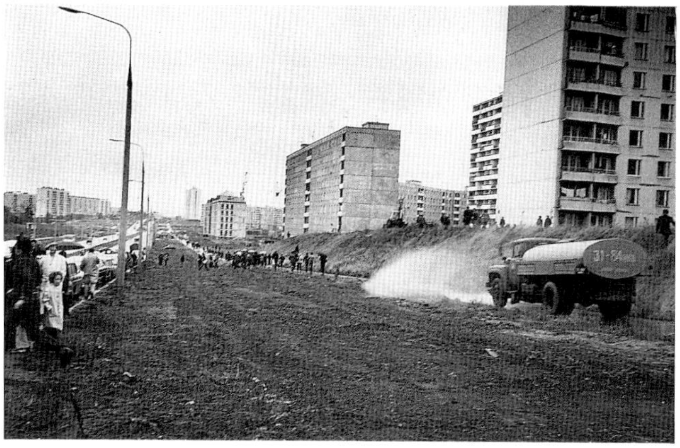

Moscow, September 15, 1974: Water truck continues to spray water in the direction of fleeing men, women, and children as Soviet police break up an unauthorized outdoor exhibit of abstract paintings. Some paintings were burned and at least six artists and an unknown number of bystanders arrested. Police also manhandled Western newsmen and diplomats. UPI/Bettmann Newsphotos

been set for future unauthorized actions by members of Soviet society. As it was, the exhibition of September 15 followed other precedent-setting occurrences, such as the reemergence in April of the most influential Soviet dissident journal, *The Chronicle of Current Events*, which had been suppressed in 1972. In June, ballet dancers Galina and Valery Panov were given exit visas to Israel. In August, Simas Kurdika, a Lithuanian seaman who tried unsuccessfully to defect to the United States, and Silva Zalamanson, one of the Jews arrested during a hijack attempt in 1970, were released early from prison camp as a gesture to speed up American Senate negotiations for a U.S. Trade Act that would be more favorable to the Soviet Union. And in early September, conductor Gennady Rozhdestvensky was permitted to begin a three-year contract with the Stockholm Philharmonic.[186] As in times past, the moves toward liberalization would almost certainly be followed by counter moves. A show of authority was almost inevitable, but violence was unexpected. Some speculated that the decision to disrupt the exhibit was made by the Moscow City Party Committee without the approval of Party officials at a higher level. Others suspected that the attack was orchestrated to embarrass the pro-Western faction of the leadership. In any case, the authorities' subsequent handling of the affair revealed their sensitivity to world criticism of repressive actions. Because Soviet leaders were anxious to prove their credibility at the Geneva talks on cooperation and security in Europe, they moved quickly to make amends and concessions.

The Second Autumn Open-Air Exhibition

Several days after the *First Autumn Open-Air Exhibition*, the artists who exhibited were invited by the cultural administration of the Moscow City Council to discuss a site for a second exhibit. After some negotiation, the organizers of the *Second Autumn Open-Air Exhibition* were issued an exhibition permit and asked only to guarantee that the works would not be offensive to official standards. Such implicit approval of art that was not Socialist Realism was a victory for the artists.

For the Moscow City Council a second exhibit was an opportunity to tell the Soviet and Western news media that authorities did not oppose the paintings[187] so much as the artists' rejection of official art unions. To give the *Second Autumn Open-Air Exhibition* a semblance of legality, the Council arranged the exhibit with the cooperation of the Moscow Graphics Union. The Graphics Union was chosen because it was more receptive to the efforts of unofficial artists than the Moscow Union of Artists, whose members felt that unofficial artists were infringing on their rights. Continuing its hardline position concerning unofficial artists, the Moscow Union of Artists forbade its members to participate in the show. Not all member artists complied.

Thus on September 29, 1974, after a decade of increasingly repressive Soviet control, more than sixty unofficial artists[188] exhibited approximately one hundred fifty paintings, ranging from Pop to realism to pure abstraction to surrealism to the garish acid colors of psychedelic art. The show took place in Izmailovo Park from noon to 4:00 p.m. and attracted more than ten thousand viewers. For the first time, artists were their own censors in the organization of a public exhibit. Reviewing the exhibit, the poet Yevtushenko said: "I see some good pictures, some bad ones, and some mediocre ones, but the most important fact is that they are here in the first place."[189]

Because it took place without the formal auspices of any official organization but with official permission, the *Second Autumn Open-Air Exhibition* was a substantial departure from the usual practice. Artists were trying to reestablish the flexibility that characterized the Khrushchev era. As a foremost Moscow unofficial artist, Vladimir Nemukhin, said: "We are not avant-garde in our art, only in our behavior in trying to stage a public show."[190] The exhibits of September 15 and 29, 1974, showed that the Soviet system had its gray areas in which guidelines were vague and officials uncertain. On these occasions people with skill and courage demonstrated that they could test and sometimes extend the boundaries that limit personal freedom. Brezhnev took care not to commit the same mistake Khrushchev had made in his attacks at the Manezh exhibition in 1962. He made no public comments about the exhibition.

Articles in the Soviet press, however, indicated that the government had not reconciled itself to the existence of modern art. During October and November, nonconformist artists were accused anew of being "hostile to reality and to Russian national culture."[191] Then came the unexpected death of Minister of Culture Furtzeva and her replacement by Petr N. Demichev, a high-level change of command which raised hopes that cultural repression would end. But speculation about artistic freedom came to a halt on November 10, 1974, when Soviet President Nikolai Podgorny gave a speech to commemorate one hundred fifty years of the Maly Theater. Podgorny stated emphatically: "The slightest departure from our principles is inadmissible in any kind of art."[192] The Politburo's ideological chief, Mikhail Suslov, reiterated this policy one day later at the jubilee reception for the USSR Academy of Arts at the Manezh.[193]

The Unofficial Art Movement

Artists and authorities again seemed to be on a collision course. Moscow artists charged that authorities had begun a campaign to break up their group. The government attempted to integrate some artists into official organizations, invited others to join the youth section of the Moscow Union of Artists, and yet others, like Vladimir Nemukhin and Dmitri Plavinsky, to submit paintings for the annual Graphics Union exhibit. Some unofficial artists accepted invitations to join the official system.[194] Others remained silent about the government crackdown, hoping for permission to have a new exhibit. But rigid official conditions for such an exhibit, combined with divisions within their own circle, led the artists to turn down the opportunity for an indoor exhibit when it was offered by the Moscow City Council on December 4, 1974.

In Leningrad unofficial artists proved to be more successful in exhibiting toward the end of 1974. Led by Rukhin and Yuri Zarkikh, they succeeded in holding an exhibit in a local palace of culture. The four-day exhibit, which opened on December 22, marked the first indoor exhibition of its kind in the Soviet Union since the 1920s. Fifty-two artists exhibited approximately two hundred works. Several thousand people attended.[195] The Leningrad authorities had met nearly all the artists' wishes, banning only three canvases—and those on religious grounds.

During 1975, the government policy toward modern art alternated between tolerance and an attempt to curb exhibition activities. In February, unofficial Moscow artists were allowed to mount an indoor exhibit, but Leningrad artists were prohibited from participating in the Moscow show, from showing their paintings elsewhere, and from holding a press conference in a private Moscow apartment. These examples seem to reflect either government uncertainty concerning the treatment of unofficial artists or a deliberate attempt to nourish hostility between the Moscow and Leningrad groups. But despite its limitations, the Moscow exhibit was an important milestone in government tolerance of unofficial art shows. It meant that, in Moscow at least, a number of unofficial artists were displaying under official auspices. Not all artists were satisfied with the conditions, however; some refused to participate because they felt that agreeing to any official censorship meant compromising their principles of free expression. Nevertheless, after the exhibit, unofficial artists felt freer to organize shows without government approval, and they did so in spite of government warnings.

Once again, initiatives by the artists were threatening to get beyond effective government control. Officials did their best to reassert their authority. The Soviet press, in order to discourage popularizing unauthorized exhibits of unapproved works, continued to belittle modern art. The government, which had permitted some unofficial exhibits in order to avoid development of an organized protest movement, grew more conservative in its handling of artists as officials made plans for the Twenty-fifth Communist Party Congress in 1976. In an article in *Novy mir*, Vladimir Yagodkin, the Moscow Party secretary for cultural and ideological affairs, explained that literature and art were not a private matter but a concern of all the people and the entire Soviet state. In the ideological struggle between socialism and capitalism, Yagodkin wrote, no artist could remain neutral toward politics or avoid the task of Communist education.[196]

No significant changes in cultural policies resulted from the meeting of the Twenty-fifth Communist Party Congress. Instead, the Congress reaffirmed previously set standards for art. Nikolai Ponomarev, Chairman of the USSR Union of Artists, summarized the Party's cultural policies: "Our times demand... offensive struggle with tendencies... alien to the practice of Socialist Realism, which ideological opponents from abroad endeavor to impose on us."[197] Few would agree that the origins of so-called dissident art were "from abroad." Rather, many unofficial artists saw themselves as followers of the Russian avant-garde of the 1920s.

After the Party Congress, in May 1976, official and unofficial artists exhibited their works jointly in Moscow apartments in what became known as "Apt-Art" exhibits, and a small number of government-selected unofficial artists were officially invited to exhibit in Moscow. In addition, some of the artists who had participated in the *First Autumn Open-Air Exhibition* were exhibiting publicly under the auspices of the local Graphics Union, first in Moscow, and later in Leningrad.

While unofficial artists were being appeased by the government, they were also involved in activities that challenged government authority. Some united to create their own artists' union—separate and distinct from the union sponsored by the government. In Leningrad, artists planned to gain public attention by floating twenty canvases down the Neva River. The death of one of their leaders, Rukhin, motivated the Leningrad artists to organize an exhibit in his honor, but authorities prevented them from doing so.

Nevertheless, government acceptance of unofficial art gradually increased. Artists were free to experiment with form and color as long as their works remained inoffensive to the government. In August 1976, the

Moscow Union of Artists held a ten-day exhibit of non-Socialist Realist art. Two months later the government made a significant departure from its normal practice and invited unofficial artists in Moscow and Leningrad to become members of a newly formed painters' section of the Graphics Union. The government, in other words, was attempting to bring unofficial artists and previously unaccepted forms of art within the existing bureaucracy of government-controlled organizations.

Developments in modern Soviet art were brought about not only by dynamic tensions within the USSR but also by irresistible international forces. It is widely held that the *Second Autumn Open-Air Exhibition* was the result of international protests touched off by the violent disruption of the *First Autumn Open-Air Exhibition*. In allowing the second show, it was believed, the Kremlin sought to ease the embarrassment felt by some leaders at the image of bulldozers and vigilantes ripping up paintings. Moreover, at the time of the first show, the Soviets were engaged in negotiations involving human rights on at least two fronts: with the United States, in regard to "trade concessions linked to immigration," as embodied in the Jackson Amendment to the U.S. Trade Act; and with thirty-five nations represented at the European Security Conference meetings in Geneva and Helsinki from 1973 to 1975, in which demands were made for better cultural relations with Soviet bloc countries. The suppression of painters made the Soviet position less credible in both cases, giving rise to the claim that the violence of the *First Autumn Open-Air Exhibition* may have been plotted by an ideologically conservative faction within the government to embarrass the prodetente faction of the Soviet leadership.[198] Thus the politics of detente appear to have induced the Soviet government to be more tolerant of artistic freedom than it might have been otherwise. Chairman of the USSR Union of Artists Nikolai Ponomarev said: "We foresee further adjusting of creative ties with artists in developing countries, as well as capitalist countries. In the spirit of the Helsinki Agreement—we are prepared for this exchange, its improvement and expansion."[199]

The uneasy relationship between Soviet officials and unofficial artists underwent a noticeable change between 1974 and 1976. Unofficial artists were not a group of radicals out to do violence to the Soviet system. Most were apolitical—their chief goal being aesthetic freedom. Their work, in their view, was not a challenge to Socialist Realism but rather a new dimension in Soviet art. Most showed a willingness to work within the framework of Soviet society: they joined official unions, sold their art to the Ministry of Culture, and accepted government assignments for art projects. In response, the Soviet government showed that its fundamental policy was to keep dissident activity within an acceptable level. Some of the means of dealing with unofficial artists included co-optation of the artists by the unions, greater union participation in unofficial activities, and selective harassment and appeasement of artists. The official encouragement of the emigration of unofficial artists in the mid- to late 1970s was one of the most successful methods of diffusing the impact of the movement. Many of these artists were able to leave the Soviet Union because of their Jewish heritage. Thus Jerusalem, along with the customary major art centers of Paris and New York, became a new pocket of Russian emigré art activities, adding another dimension to contemporary Soviet art.

The period 1974–1976 marks both the pinnacle of the unofficial art movement and its end. The dialogue began with dogma, threats, and violence. Then came a period of uncertainty in government policy, as officials struggled to come to grips with this new challenge from artists. Finally, the government and artists reached an uneasy accommodation. Though the outlook for the relationship remained unclear, there were grounds for optimism. Artists hoped that relaxation of East-West tensions would induce the Soviet government to relax ideological dictums. It was also expected that the public's desire to become educated in new currents of art, combined with artists' insistence on the right to experiment, would lead the government to even greater tolerance. Officials, on the other hand, grew confident of their ability to cope with dissent.

THE YOUTH MOVEMENT

The decade of the seventies marked a change in the membership profile of the USSR Union of Artists brought about by the emergence of a strong "youth movement" within unions throughout the country. These younger artists, who although official were nonconformist, became known as the *Semidesyatniki* ("those of the seventies"). They freely mingled with unofficial artists and developed their own original approach to art. As a result, their activities contributed to a more flexible interpretation of Socialist Realism.

The seventies artists were influenced by the artists of the sixties, especially those who inaugurated the Severe Style, a reaction to the obligatory saccharine optimism of twenty years of the personality cult. Among other artists, one in particular stands out as the mentor of the seventies artists: Dmitri Zhilinsky, the leading member of the left movement within the Moscow Union of Artists, a member of the USSR Academy of Arts and the boards of the USSR Union of Artists and the art magazine *Tvorchestvo*, and a much admired professor at the Surikov Art Institute. Zhilinsky rejected the art of the 1930s and 1940s and found his stylistic sources in the Russian icon tradition, with its flat treatment of subject matter and perspective based on the perceived importance of elements rather than their position in pictorial space. By applying the icon style to intimate scenes such as *Man with Slain Dog* (Colorplate 90), a self-portrait, Zhilinsky encouraged students to depict the fruits of their own introspection.

Others, like Viktor Popkov, whose artistic searches led them to folk art sources, influenced the new generation with metaphoric paintings such as *Northern Chapel* (Colorplate 60), in which peasant Russia is supported by the pillar of youth and an angelic trinity. Popkov's effect on future generations was insured by his untimely death on November 12, 1974, at the age of forty-two, shortly after unofficial Soviet art had begun to make unprecedented inroads into establishment art. Many artists on all sides of the spectrum rallied around his art and his favorite issues dealing with questions of human destiny.

A few loners also influenced the seventies artists, among them Anatoli Nikich, who gained a reputation as the "poet of the city" for his constructivist landscapes and still lifes. One of the artist's signatures, the treatment of drapery, as seen in *Ceremonial Still Life* (Colorplate 52), introduced classic forms to the art of the seventies artists.

By the mid-sixties, other artists who were to influence the future generation had turned away from machine and factory imagery and had fled to the countryside, where they created nostalgic scenes of old Russia. One of these is Andrei Tutunov, whose depiction of *View of Pafnutiev Monastery* (Colorplate 78) emphasizes a love for Russia during the time of the Old Believers, a seventeenth-century religious sect that was expelled from the official church for holding to the traditions of the Greek Orthodox Church against the wishes of Russian nationalists. Here we see a town built by the Old Believers with small wooden churches and underground escape passages. The rainbow expresses the hope of humankind for the freedom of religious convictions. Tutunov is reminding Russians not to give up in despair.

Evgeni Rastorguev, who works in Moscow but concentrates his creative endeavors on the simple pleasures of his hometown Gorodets, in *Provincial Anecdotes* (Colorplate 63) and *Dance around the Samovar* (Colorplate 62) has captured the heart of Russian folk art on canvas. His quest for the beauty of the Russian folk tradition—images of Russian fairs and peasant humor—are to this day unsurpassed in Soviet art and a clear influence on many seventies artists.

Zaven Arshakuni and Valeri Vatenin pushed the limits of official dictums in the sixties. Arshakuni brought some of the qualities of stage design to his paintings—in particular bright, cheerful colors. The theatrical quality of his works was especially attractive to the seventies artists. His themes of fantasy and his expressive use of colors lend a festive mood to pictures such as *The Bride* (Colorplate 3). Vatenin, much like Popkov, became a martyr image due to his unexpected death in a motorcycle accident. His multi-figured compositions, like *The Evacuation* (Colorplate 83), were innovative in their interpretation of the whole as a totality of numerous thoroughly elaborated particulars and details. His fragmentation of detail, also exemplified in *The Painter Vatenin's Life Story* (Colorplate 82), was later reflected in paintings by the seventies artists.

The seventies artists gained popularity in the Soviet Union by actively participating in major exhibitions. Their style was first observed in 1967 at the *Seventh Moscow Exhibit*. The all-union exhibitions of 1972, 1976, and 1978 established the artists with their public, and in

1979, Anna Dekhtiar's book *Young Painters of the Seventies*, a detailed essay and pictorial account of the struggles of emerging artists, became the first publication to deal with the subject. These artists who developed their signature styles from the seventies into the eighties solidified their reputations in the 1981 *Exhibition of 23*, which featured the works of thirteen painters, five printmakers, and five sculptors from Moscow. Although the exhibition at the Central House of Artists of the USSR Union of Artists was limited to only a few Moscow artists, the diversity of style and subject matter astounded Soviet art critics. It seemed that the artists had passed beyond Socialist Realism into a new world of post–Socialist Realism which, while still largely realistic in style, had strong elements of surrealism, of irony, and of social criticism. The artists' interpretation of key themes, and their surprising mixtures of tradition and stylistic innovation, have had an impact on creativity that has lasted into the nineties.

In their quest for self-expression the new generation explored man's vast accumulation of cultural and spiritual experiences. Some artists expressed a reverence for the past, while others described the technological world, and yet others poeticized the impact of technology on human existence. Symbolism and allusions abounded as artists attempted to reconcile the turmoil of daily life with the traditions of a humanistic culture. They posed the recurring questions: what is? what was? what will be? From the "heroic people of the Revolution" in the 1950s to "we, the workers" in the 1960s, Soviet art had evolved to concentrate on "me, the individual." In the artists' perception, the scientific and technological revolution was threatening traditional moral values and man's relationship to nature. The artists' mission, therefore, was to create a "thinking hero" to contemplate the origins of humankind. In contrast to their 1960s predecessors of the Severe Style, who showed man in the midst of life and generalized his suffering, the seventies artists concentrated on individual personality, explored the inner soul, and placed humankind in a metaphysical universe.

The diversity of the seventies artists was manifested in their range of styles and subject matter—from the naive to portraiture, from historical to surreal. Often artists combined two or three approaches to arrive at a personal creative signature. The simplicity of folk art and its fresh expression can be seen in the works of artists such as Arkadi Petrov, Natalia Nesterova, and Elena Figurina, who combined the poetic quality of anonymous Russian folk art (especially the popular print, or *lubok*) and peasant crafts with the primitive searchings of the early twentieth century as seen in the works of Marc Chagall, Mikhail Larionov (1881–1964), Niko Pirosmanashvili (1863–1918), and Henri Rousseau (1844–1910).

Arkadi Petrov is a master at using decorative elements as well as text to express ideas from simple irony to biting sarcasm. He creates a fairytale environment in which toy-like creatures come alive much as they do in the tales of E. T. A. Hoffmann. Petrov's world is populated with saccharine-sweet, stylized, picture-postcard images: rosy-cheeked beauties, eternally happy lovers, smiling cats, and doves bearing good tidings. "Kitsch" has been elevated to an art form in which contemporary life becomes the idyllic state in which one would prefer to find oneself. Petrov's *Greetings from Donbass* (Colorplate 59), in which the Russian words appear at the top of the painting in postcard style, is a poetic scene from provincial life. Petrov's use of symbols speaks of his nostalgia for the yesteryears of his childhood in the coal mining town where he grew up, and his use of pastel hues emphasizes the light-hearted imagery. The slightly deformed figures and exaggerated objects are typical of naive art. In *Scarecrow* (Colorplate 57) he combines trite Communist Party declarations and popular songs to create a form of criticism with humor. As Petrov includes elements of *Sots* Art (a Soviet version of Pop Art) in more recent works, it becomes evident that his creativity is steeped in complicated feelings and an equally complex painterly system.

Natalia Nesterova, one of the seventies artists best known in the West, concentrates on daily life. Instead of confronting the broad social issues of the 1960s, Nesterova describes common people in familiar activities: eating spaghetti in a garden terrace (Colorplate 49), holding lengthy conversations in restaurants, relaxing on park benches, strolling through the city, lying on a beach, or silently standing in an endless line. The scenario is always simple and without sentimentality, staged in a puppet-theater fashion that was new to

Soviet art. Despite her status as a member of the Union of Artists, her paintings did not find immediate favor with officialdom. In time, however, observers began to appreciate that the world Nesterova stages is, in its simplicity, full of paradox and, in fact, depicts the complexity of life in the contemporary world. In her canvases, layered with heavy paint, people, nature, and architecture flow into each other, as in *Petrodvorets* (Colorplate 50)—each giving the other expression, each reaffirming the other as eternally alive.

Younger than most seventies artists, yet dealing with the same issues, is Leningrader Elena Figurina, whose naive images beckon viewers to explore their souls. Her intuitive art is inspired by the Russian avant-garde artists Mikhail Larionov and Natalia Goncharova (1881–1962) and the Russian icon tradition. Influences of Matisse and Gauguin, as well as the German Expressionists, are visible in her figures, color, and style. Like other artists of her generation, Figurina does not seek to emulate these sources; they are merely a springboard for her own creations. The strangely pathetic extraterrestrial-looking beings that inhabit her paintings are indeed flesh and blood people trying to escape the objective world. In *Reflections* (Colorplate 22) she shows people against a blue sky, themselves in blue, as if they are already in heaven; while below, their red images solidly place them in the earth, in real life. Clearly Figurina is entranced with such early Russian philosophers of Christian Existentialism as Nikolai Berdyayev and Simon Frank. Though the artist would prefer to show us the harmony in man's soul, Figurina's sad figures reassert that man has been evicted from Paradise. In *Memory* (Colorplate 21), she has captured, as it were, the cognizance of a past life—life before the knowledge of good and evil.

Many seventies artists like to draw on history, expressing the past in choice of painting style and subjects and the use of symbols. Though Tatiana Nazarenko's themes range from everyday life to portraiture, she is best known for her historical paintings. Never pure documentation, they depict contemporary man's interaction with the past. The viewer becomes the witness to a historical event that becomes a lesson for today's world. Nazarenko shows a deep understanding of the masters of the early Renaissance and admires the works of Piero della Francesca, Vittore Carpaccio, Jan van Eyck, Rogier van der Weyden, and Pieter Brueghel. Her monumental painting *Pugachev* (Colorplate 43) is reminiscent of *Histories of Pugachev* by the Russian nineteenth-century poet Alexander Pushkin, which describes how the renowned eighteenth-century Russian general Alexander Suvorov led the rebel Pugachev, locked in a wooden cage, to his death sentence. Two legendary heroes are thus intertwined in a tragic moment of history. The rebel confronts the viewer frontally in a crucifixion stance. The wooden bars of his cage, against the peaceful Russian landscape of the Urals, seem to be dissolving into the sky as though anticipating the victim's ascent after death. Pugachev, the martyr, stands as the symbol of human suffering, as Suvorov marches silently but with dignity forward, resigned to his own destiny. The right-hand panel of this diptych includes a portrait of Catherine II, coldly observing the execution of her orders. The regiment of soldiers may represent the masses of people who have no control over the events of their lives. Perhaps Nazarenko is implicating her fellow citizens, since many rebels were led to their death during the Stalin era. Certainly one leaves the painting convinced that history repeats itself.

The seventies artists are particularly fond of portraiture, but not in the sense of the commissioned academic court or society portrait or the portraits of the noble heroes of the Stalin era. Their subjects are their friends and colleagues, who have well-defined personalities, positive and negative features. The heroes of these portraits are concrete individuals as well as the artist's message bearers. Such heroes abound in Nazarenko's oeuvre. They may also be found in the portraits of fellow Muscovite Elena Romanova. Romanova captures the Russian character of her subjects as well as their unique personal attributes and their cultural background. On the other hand, her *Self-Portrait in a Fur Hat* (Colorplate 67), while describing the artist in great detail, leaves the viewer pondering the psyche behind the physical portrayal. Who is the artist? What is her fate? Personal contemplation is also the underlying theme of *Midday, Summer* (Colorplate 66), in which a mother is cleaning mushrooms under the watchful eyes of her son, who is learning the details of this typical Russian pastime. The pitcher of field flowers and the half-empty glass of milk are intimate details in lives seemingly without worldly concerns.

A trend which truly reflects the urbanization and mechanization of the twentieth century is Photorealism, which became especially popular among Soviet artists after a 1975 exhibit of *Contemporary American Art*, organized by Armand Hammer. The show—the first of its kind in the Soviet Union—made its debut in Moscow and featured such American Photorealists as Chuck Close and Andy Warhol, who impressed the Soviet artists with their sheer accumulation of data and their ability to reproduce reality as literally and uncritically as the camera. Whereas American Photorealism was a direct descendant of Pop Art and the result of a yearning for images after a decade of abstract art in the sixties, Soviet Photorealism was directly stimulated by its American counterpart. In Russia this style, which became known as "Hyperrealism" or "hyper" (*giper*), was particularly associated with Estonian artists and disparagingly labeled "documentalism," or "slideism," or "photographic objectivism." Many Soviet art historians questioned the validity of the art form, which they believed to be merely a technical transference of a photographic image to canvas.

The Hyperrealists, like the American Photorealists, worked from photography and utilized the techniques of montage and airbrush. In its fidelity to the subject, the photographic nature of their work related to the Severe Style of the 1960s. Hyperrealist paintings showed influences of industrial design and the mass media and depicted the technological revolution of the seventies. Marlboro cigarettes, a can of Pepsi, boxes with Western labels, and shopping bags—all coveted items among Soviet consumers—were illustrated on canvas. Then display windows with garish lights, dingy unswept staircases of rundown apartment buildings, and used cars made their debut. Soon there were contemporary faces—images of students, workers, or friends—dealing with personal issues or particular events. Thus the genre of eighteenth-century Western portraits was reborn but without its idealism. In fact, the Hyperrealist portrait showed, even accentuated, the subject's imperfections.

Soviet Hyperrealist artists soon formed groups headed by leading practitioners of the art. Sergei Sherstiuk was a member of the now defunct Group of Six, founded in Moscow in 1980 by the avant-garde painter and philosopher Alexander Tegin (born 1951). In addition to Tegin and Sherstiuk, the group included Sergei Bazilev (born 1952), Sergei Geta (born 1950) and Nikolai Filatov (born 1951) from Kiev, and Igor Kopystiansky from Lvov. From 1980 to 1985, each artist in the group had to produce Photorealistic artworks. If one of the artists failed to do so, he was criticized by other members of the group. At times the Group of Six exhibited jointly with the Sretensky Boulevard group headed by Ilya Kabakov, one of the leaders of the Moscow underground, who believed in giving moral support to fellow artistic innovators.

Sherstiuk, who originally worked from slides, believes that Photorealism destroyed symbolism. In his paintings he prefers to show the impact of human interaction, using close friends and family as his subjects; thus he adeptly switches people in time and space to better understand actual occurrences. Sherstiuk's diptych *Men of One Family, 1941 and 1945* (Colorplate 71) appears to be painted from a photograph, but in fact is based on the stories he heard about his uncles and grandfather. The family portrait before the war is heroic, almost Socialist Realist in the monumentality of its heroes. Seven men are pictured, confident and strong at the outset of war, the burning sky in the background indicating turbulence ahead. The second part of the diptych, after the war, shows three survivors, each injured, each staring bleakly at the viewer. The family patriarch died in Stalingrad in 1943, and a new family head has been chosen, seated at the right in the customary chair of honor. One vacated chair remains as a symbol of loss. Though the sky is now a peaceful blue, it is the only sign of optimism in a scene of family bereavement.

Simon Faibisovich entered the Soviet art scene at a later stage than most Photorealists. He initially pursued a career as an architect, became a member of the Graphics Union in 1978, and began participating in city and all-union exhibitions in 1979. Yet, of all the Soviet Photorealists, he is the best known in the West for his urban street scenes and ordinary people. Mostly, his figures are seen on buses, trains, and subways, reflected in or looking through windows. Works such as *Boy* (Colorplate 19) and *At the Exit* (Colorplate 18) have an unreal quality and multiple dimensions of meaning.

Olga Grechina also deals with elements of photography, using out-of-focus images reminiscent of the reflections in Faibisovich's paintings. Grechina is a narrator of contemporary Soviet life. Her subjects range from the flower vendor on a street corner, to an astronaut in space, to close friends amiably chatting, as in *Reflection* (Colorplate 29). Her vivid, splashy colors belie the humdrum of existence and portray a romanticized, cheerful life. Only the blur of movement, in which subjects appear out of focus, indicates that Grechina's paintings capture mere instants in a life that is rushing by. Yet the stacked impressions of everyday events collected in a single scene show the artist's preoccupation with the continuity of life.

Valeri Lukka, on the other hand, combines photographic elements and parody in his paintings. Like Grechina he deals with daily events, but they are not all equally cheerful. *Unloading Meat on Sadovaya Street* (Colorplate 41) shows a truck with giant slabs of red meat; against the background of a drab Leningrad street, the scene is more surreal than real. Is Lukka taunting the Soviet viewer who is confronted with daily food shortages? Or is he referring to past works such as Pavel Nikonov's *Butcher Shop* of 1968 (Russian Museum, Leningrad)? On the other hand, in *American Swimming* (Colorplate 42), the synchronized swimmers with their toothy artificial smiles are less humorous than meets the eye; the work is a comment on the non-smiling Soviet citizen whose serious taut face permeates all events of Soviet life, including sports and entertainment.

Symbolism—producing signs of reality but not reality itself—and surrealism also characterize works by the seventies artists, for example those of Olga Bulgakova and Alexander Sitnikov. The art of these painters implies that the meaning of one world lies in another and that it is possible to unite the two. Each artist deliberately selects subjects that will stand out against the banality of existence. A dreamlike quality pervades paintings such as *Dream about the Red Bird* (Colorplate 13), by Bulgakova, in which there is a visual layering of imagery. Within the transparent form of a magical red bird, multiple beings intertwine, perhaps representing temperaments of the creative psyche, perhaps depicting a variety of emotions. An impression of despair is created by the open beak of the bird. The bald-headed figures, the thrusting knife, the open scissors, and the predominant red color are traditional dream symbols of anger, despair, and passion. These are countered by the full moon, which appears in other paintings by Bulgakova, and the disembodied eye, dream symbols for liberation from worry and despair. The three canvases—the actual and the two portrayed—as well as the three figures, may refer to the Christian Trinity. Finally, the triangle and moon are female symbols, and the triangle and palette are symbols of an artist, implying that this is the artist's dream. *Transformation* (Colorplate 14) deals with duality, a Dostoevskian theme common in Russian thought. In this work Bulgakova expresses the human desire to discover the key to who we are and what we can become.

Whereas Bulgakova's works are subtle illuminations of her personal philosophy, Sitnikov's are more direct, even visceral. The artist claims Andrei Rublev, Kuzma Petrov-Vodkin (1878–1939), Pavel Filonov, and Pablo Picasso as his spiritual mentors. In his early works, Sitnikov was known for his soft and gentle hues and lyrical themes. By the mid-seventies, he turned to stronger colors, heavily layered, to achieve a prominent relief effect. His themes include myths and allegories told with the visual imagery of bulls, roosters, and dogs. At times these images literally dissolve into the vivid colors, becoming secondary to the paint. Sitnikov's half-animal, half-human creatures intertwine in a half-physical, half-spiritual world. Paintings such as *The Red Echo* (Colorplate 77), with its phantasmagorical composition, show the painter's preoccupation with good versus evil. Like Bulgakova, Sitnikov develops a theme in a series of paintings. His *Shostakovich* (Colorplate 76) shows his admiration for the great Russian composer, Dmitri Shostakovich, a subject that recurs in many of the artist's works. To Sitnikov and other Russians, Shostakovich is the personification of the ideal in the arts, the embodiment of genius, and a direct representation of the creative spirit. In Sitnikov's works he may also symbolize the suffering of the spirit in a stifling system.

Viktor Kalinin is another artist who relies on symbols. Working in an expressionistic style, he strives to enhance narration with elements of the spiritual. His subtle palette and painterly approach combine poetic and concrete ideas. To create his monumental works, the

KASIMIR MALEVICH
Black Square, 1913
Oil on canvas
Tretyakov Art Gallery, Moscow

artist draws on history and tradition, borrowing from Renaissance frescoes, biblical themes, or sketches by the renowned Russian painter Mikhail Vrubel (1856–1910). Like many Soviet artists today, Kalinin claims Malevich's *Black Square* (Tretyakov Art Gallery, Moscow), a Suprematist work of pure abstraction, as one of his sources. Alexander Petrov takes an approach that is similar to Kalinin's, but his two-dimensional figures and objects are more delineated, and his creations are more naive than mysterious.

A discussion of the seventies artists cannot end without mentioning Andrei Gennadiev, who like his contemporaries aims to put the viewer in touch with universal ideas which exist outside the work itself. Gennadiev blends old Russian traditions with modern twentieth-century expression in works that show a range of influences—from the iconography of Byzantine art to the metaphysical concepts of the Leningrad artists who formed the St. Petersburg Group in 1964. Mysticism, which permeates Russian art and thinking, is an important aspect of Gennadiev's work, as it is of Bulgakova's and Sitnikov's. He uses metaphysical symbols from a variety of ancient cultures and eras, from ancient Egyptian astral-occult signs to esoteric Christian symbols. Like most seventies artists, Gennadiev wants his signs to be evocative as visual facts and to stimulate our thinking. He gives familiar objects a surreal treatment and introduces the "I, the observer" element in his self-portraits. Gennadiev captures most of the trends of the decade in his *Self-Portrait with Ladder* (Colorplate 23), as he invites us to go beyond the limits of our world.

GLASNOST

As the seventies artists were making their mark on Soviet art, unofficial artists continued their battle to establish a profile in Moscow and Leningrad. In the words of one of their leaders, Erik Bulatov, known for his use of political slogans and road signs, as in *Stop-Go* (Colorplate 12), which calls attention to ideological ambiguity: "We are afraid to show our work, but we show it. There is no other way for us to go."[200] At the same time, a new generation of artists was graduating from Soviet art institutes and academies. Thus several generations of artists were poised to take advantage of impending changes in all areas of Soviet life. A herald of things to come in the visual arts in the 1980s was the landmark exhibition *Paris-Moscow: 1900–1930*, a joint venture of the Centre Georges Pompidou in Paris and the Ministry of Culture in Moscow, which was shown in both capitals from 1979 to 1980.

In the late seventies, the international political environment grew more turbulent, acerbated by Soviet aggression in Africa and Afghanistan. A new Cold War threatened. Brezhnev's death in November 1982, followed by the succession of Yuri Andropov, promised little change unless for the worse. Andropov was known for his former position as head of the KGB and for his role in the suppression of the Hungarian Revolution in 1956. However, Andropov died unexpectedly in February 1984 and was succeeded by Konstantin Chernenko, a former Brezhnev protégé. Most people believed that the status quo had returned, that the "period of stagnation," as the Brezhnev years were succinctly termed, would continue. But Chernenko died in March 1985, and Mikhail Gorbachev succeeded him. Change was imminent.

As Gorbachev began to assert himself, it became evident that a new philosophy was taking form at the highest levels of officialdom. *Glasnost* and *perestroika* were being introduced. Many events in the arts became indicators of these changes. The new exhibition center of the Tretyakov Art Gallery began to exhibit art of the early avant-garde. A February 1987 exhibition at the Kashirskaya Exhibition Hall, Moscow, and one in December at the Harbor in Leningrad marked the first showings in public exhibition spaces of official and unofficial art. For years union officials had fiercely opposed such exhibits, arguing that members of a professional organization should not hang their art next to that of "unprofessional" artists. Now it appeared that individuals would no longer be censored. The Union of Artists, which largely determined what art could be exported to the West, developed a laissez-faire approach as it approved formerly controversial art. The exhibition of Zhilinsky's painting *The Year 1937: Tribute to the Victims of Repression* (collection of the artist) at the Academy of Arts marked the artistic indictment of the Stalin era by the leader of the left wing of the Moscow Union of Artists. Zhilinsky's painting shows his father being arrested during the height of the Stalin purges. Members of the Soviet cultural elite were testing the boundaries of official acceptability and at the same time questioning if the new openness would last.

Though artists' unions were undergoing internal changes, they were not rushing to embrace the avant-garde. In 1987, works that could be construed as obscene or overly critical of the Soviet government were still restricted from union exhibits. In the fall *Retrospection*, a thirty-year survey of unofficial art, organized by Ermitazh, an informal association of Moscow official and unofficial cultural figures, was heavily criticized for including emigré art, adding another taboo to the list. Despite their conservative stance, the USSR Union of Artists pronounced Socialist Realism an overly dogmatic doctrine at its January 1988 Congress, the first one to be held in the *glasnost* era. Several delegates lobbied for eliminating the term Socialist Realism altogether. Finally they agreed to review the term more closely in the future to determine if Socialist Realism should be replaced by more favored terms such as "humanism" or "realism without borders." Still, it took approval from the newly elected chairman of the Moscow Union of Artists, Oleg Savostiuk, to permit the opening of the exhibition *Labyrinth*, which was organized by many different artists' groups at the Palace of Youth in the summer of 1988. Another exhibition, organized by a liberal association within the Moscow Union of Artists, was to open at a union exhibition hall and was to include non-union artists; the exhibit was prohibited pending a review by the union jury but was later allowed to go on. The freedom to exhibit at will was still being contested as recently as 1988.

One further event was to profoundly affect the lifestyle of Soviet artists. With the cooperation of the USSR Ministry of Culture, Sotheby's, the London-based auction house, held the first international art auction in Soviet history in Moscow on July 7, 1988. Artists like Igor Kopystiansky, who was gaining prominence for his furled canvas technique, as in *Construction* (Colorplate 40), were unsettled by the amount of money their works brought. Although a market for Soviet art already existed, Sotheby's involvement and publicity raised interest to a higher pitch as it introduced Soviet artists to the international art world. The majority of artists represented in the sale, however, were from Moscow, which precluded forming a correct assessment of the national art scene on this occasion.

Receiving hard currency for their paintings from Western buyers shocked the sensibilities of many artists who were used to creating for small groups of friends and admirers. The success of Sotheby's sale motivated Soviet organizations and Western dealers alike to join the bandwagon. As some artists debated the pros and cons of commercialization versus bureaucratization, others took the opportunity to go abroad for one-artist shows. Suddenly, unofficial artists, who had made up a large segment of the Sotheby's sale, were no longer to be found in the Soviet Union. Ilya Kabakov, who had been creating conceptual paintings such as *Path* (Colorplate 33), traveled throughout Europe and the United States, producing installations based on his communal life in Moscow. Edik Shteinberg, whose geometric figures and compositions of interpenetrating planes, such as *Composition December 1976* (Colorplate 72), were rooted in the early Russian avant-garde, traveled to Paris and New York for one-artist shows.

To better understand the issues of commercialization, a three-day conference on "The Economics of Culture: the Basic Facts about Art in the Free Market" was held at the Tretyakov Art Gallery in June 1989. Every effort was made to join the Soviet art world with its international counterparts. Unquestionably, the social status of many members of the Soviet art community was changing, yet the absence of a commercial gallery structure supported by Soviet, not Western, collectors has continued to hamper the development of Soviet artists into the nineties. Many more have left the USSR, creating an "art drain" at home.

As artists of all persuasions, left or right, moderate or radical, were given the opportunity to communicate with the public, young artists—unfettered by the anxieties of their elders who had lived through the personal hardships of a closed society—were particularly active. Initially, Soviet critics accused them of conformity, consumerism, and a lack of self-affirmation—in part because negative criticism seemed to automatically follow any display of innovation. Ironically, such criticism directed some aspiring artists to adopt a controlled or stylized art form based on the traditions of the old masters. Those who radically opposed the trend toward "retrostyle" found it difficult to place their works within the system.

The *XV Moscow Youth Exhibit,* held at the Manezh in 1984, is generally considered the first show to successfully identify the new generation. On this occasion Soviet art critics were less disturbed by innovation in technique than they were by the "philosophy of life" reflected in the works. Artists such as Maxim Kantor (born 1957), Alexei Sundukov (born 1952), and Lev Tabenkin (born 1952) concerned themselves with interpreting the negative events affecting humankind. Their social commentary was directed toward the "period of stagnation" and echoed the demand for social rectification called for at the Twenty-Seventh Communist Party Congress in 1986. Similar creative searchings were evident at the *XVII Moscow Youth Exhibit* and the all-union *Youth of the Nation* exhibits in 1987. One of the exhibiting artists, Evgeni Dybsky, who is noted for his abstract metaphoric "landscape" paintings, showed an extraordinary sense for color, foreshadowing such later works as *Second Meeting #3* (Colorplate 17). Whereas the sixties generation had abandoned the romantic view of the peasant and the worker to celebrate man as a courageous entity dealing directly with the forces of life; and the seventies artists had become introspective and concerned with intimate relationships; now the young generation of eighties artists focused on all of humankind, addressing universal human expectations, frustrations, goals, and hopes.

A new avant-garde was developing in the Soviet Union, one that could openly explore its artistic heritage, from the Constructivism of Malevich to the Conceptualism of Kabakov. In Moscow and Leningrad young artists grouped together in loose associations, often based on friendships. Furmanny Lane, with its tenement buildings in Old Moscow, became the mecca of many young artists in the Soviet Union beginning in 1984. Seven artists—among them Farid Bogdalov—considered themselves to be "the only true locals."[201] These seven grew up under the influence of Moscow's unofficial art circles and first showed together at Apt-Art exhibits. They incorporated text in their works, a feature they adopted from the Conceptualists, many of whom had worked as book illustrators.

Among others who gravitated to Furmanny Lane were the Champions of the World, a group of six artists, including Guram Abramishvili and Andrei Yakhnin.[202] Together they arranged happenings, or conceptual events. They were similar to the Russian Futurists in their behavior, mannerisms, dress style, and self-conscious eagerness to develop a "pose." They painted on such unlikely art materials as rags and plywood, left their artwork unsigned, and often destroyed or incorporated finished works into new works. In 1987 the Furmanny Lane artists were joined by other groups such as the Center Group of about twenty artists who produced works ranging from the naive to the surreal, and A Voluntary Order of National Post-Eclecticism, a group of Kievian artists influenced by the Ukrainian Baroque.

By 1989 economic conditions persuaded most artists to develop their own signature style and produce their own works. The free, unhampered group creativity of Furmanny Lane ended when artists perceived a need to make names for themselves for commercial purposes. Thus the new avant-garde was born. Unlike their elders, the new avant-gardists did not need to discover freedom; they simply declared themselves free and concerned themselves with creating their own identity.

Nearing the end of the twentieth century, the language of the state no longer influences everyday activities or the creativity of an artist. Unofficial art is now a cultural phenomenon to be contemplated by scholars. A new era of post–Socialist Realism has dawned, and it is strongly pervaded by elements of the surreal, of irony, and of social commentary. The term "socartism" has been used to define the sociocultural phenomenon of *perestroika* in eclectic art forms. Artists continue to be fearful of losing their newfound freedom, and as the decade of the nineties begins they must wrestle with the question of what their art means in a global context. To some extent this has led to clashes among artists, similar to those in the twenties when artists' groups vied for supremacy. Ironically, former rebels themselves become intolerant.

As we familiarize ourselves with a newly awakened Russia, emerging from the grip of a totalitarian system, we discover the astonishing pluralism of Russian art and artists—from the militants of Socialist Realism to the advocates of a Russian nationalist art, to the experimenters of several generations of the avant-garde. The Soviet art scene of the nineties promises to be as turbulent as that at the beginning of the century. It would be presumptuous to make predictions. Most of the art of the 1980s bears little resemblance to the art of the 1930s and 1940s. Young Soviet artists have turned toward subjective expression. Most do not believe a new "freeze" is in sight. Yankilevsky, one of the most controversial of the avant-garde Moscow artists, who attempted to join an artists' union in 1970 but was not admitted until 1981, even before *glasnost* was saying: "Our art now belongs to Soviet life just as much as pop music."[203]

The avant-garde of the 1970s has thus become part of the establishment of the 1980s, and new forces are stirring as the nineties begin. In this process of cultural transformation innovative concepts will surely emerge to challenge what has become acceptable.

Notes

1. John E. Bowlt in "Artists of the World, Disunite!" *Russian Avant-Garde: 1908–1922* (New York: Leonard Hutton Galleries, 1971), p. 10, cites the dates 1895–1922. Dagmar Hnikova, *Russische Avant-Garde: 1907–1922* (Bern and Stuttgart: Hallwag Verlag, 1975), p. 4, cites the dates 1907–1922. In the 1980s the dates 1900–1930 were most frequently used by art historians. Though dates vary somewhat according to author, the general time frame is the same.

2. G. V. Plekhanov, *Sochineniya*, ed. D. Ryazanova, vol. 14: "Iskusstvo i obshchestvennaya zhizn" (Moscow: Gosudarstvennoye Izdatel'stvo, 1974), p. 136.

3. *Proletkult* was founded in 1906. It was the first arts organization to formulate the concept of a separate proletarian culture. *Proletkult* did not become effective until 1918, when it held its first convention. Its members had supported the Revolution, believing that artists could not work isolated from society. Other organizations that placed themselves at the service of the Communist regime included the Futurists under the leadership of Vladimir Mayakovsky, and literary groups such as the Smithy and October.

4. V. I. Lenin, *Polnoe sobranie sochinenii*, vol. 41, 5th ed. (Moscow: Gospolitizdat, 1959), pp. 304–305.

5. AKhRR, the Association of Artists of Revolutionary Russia, was renamed AKhR, the Association of Artists of Russia, in 1926. I. M. Gronskii and V. N. Perel'man, comps., "Deklaratziya Assotziatzii Khudozhnikov Revolyutzionnoi Rossii," *Assotziatziya Khudozhnikov Revolyutzionnoi Rossii: Sbornik vospominanii, statei, dokumentov* (Moscow: Izobrazitel'noe Iskusstvo, 1973), p. 289.

6. S. Frederick Starr, Foreword to *Russian Avant-Garde: 1908–1922* (New York: Leonard Hutton Galleries, 1971), p. 8.

7. Alexander Gerasimov, *Pravda*, February 10, 1949.

8. The American realist Rockwell Kent became an Honorary Member of the USSR Academy of Arts in 1960. Khrushchev sent him a personal letter of congratulations on this occasion. "Khronika: Sessiya Akademii Khudozhestv SSSR," *Iskusstvo* 6 (1960), p. 76.

9. "Pyataya sessiya Akademii Khudozhestv SSSR," *Iskusstvo* 3 (1953), p. 3.

10. For additional information about the USSR Academy of Arts see: U.S. Department of State, "Visit to the Leningrad Art Academy," by Heyward Isham, Foreign Service Despatch No. 399, February 5, 1957, pp. 1–3; B. Ioganson, "Sovetskaya Akademiya Khudozhestv," *Iskusstvo* 8 (1957), pp. 13–16; A. Zotov, "200 let Akademii Khudozhestv," *Iskusstvo* 1 (1958), pp. 4–11; and "Akademiya Khudozhestv SSSR," *Iskusstvo* 3 (1961), p. 79.

11. I. M. Gronskii and V. N. Perel'man, comps., "O perestroike literaturno-khudozhestvennykh organizatzii," *Assotziatziya Khudozhnikov Revolyutzionnoi Rossii: Sbornik vospominanii, statei dokumentov* (Moscow: Izobrazitel'noe Iskusstvo, 1973), pp. 329–330.

12. "Novye formy organizatzii tvorcheskoi zhizni," *Iskusstvo* 9 (1967), p. 2.

13. Interview with Vitaly S. Manin, Secretary, USSR Union of Artists, Moscow, USSR, December 15, 1989.

14. R. Zakin, "O razvitii samodeyatel'novo iskusstva v SSSR," *Iskusstvo* 9 (1961), p. 79.

15. G. M. Malenkov, *Otchetnyi doklad XIX S'ezda Partii o rabote TsK VKP(b)*, (Moscow: Gospolitizdat, 1952), p. 73.

16. G. Nedoshivin, "O probleme tipicheskovo v zhivoposi," *Iskusstvo* 1 (1953), pp. 17 and 20.

17. Camilla Gray, *The Russian Experiment in Art: 1863–1922*, revised by Marian Burleigh-Motley (London: Thames and Hudson, 1986), p. 190.

18. Vorob'ev; Nusberg; and Shelkovskii, sostaviteli letopisi. "Letopis' artisticheskovo podpol'ya v SSSR 1946–1966 gody," ("Chronology of the Artistic Underground in the USSR 1946–1966"; mimeographed). The Vorob'ev chronology lists ten artists in this group: Gurvich, R. Vasti, A. Aref'ev, V. Shagin, Sh. Shvarts, V. Gromov, Ye. Rotenberg, O. Sokhanevich, Ye. Mikhnov-Voitenko, and A. Leonov.

19. Ye. Polishchuk, "Problema konflikta v sovetskoi syuzhetnoi kartine," *Iskusstvo* 1 (1954), p. 29.

20. Boris Ioganson, "Temam sovremennosti—dostoinoe reshenie," *Iskusstvo* 3 (1954), p. 5.

21. Belyutin is still active in the nineties. His studio has many members and has received much publicity in the *glasnost* era. Larisa Kashuk, "Zhiva Belyutinskaya studiya!" *Ogonëk* 34 (August 1989) and Nina Moleva, "Recognition at Last," *Soviet Life* (January 1990), pp. 50–53, 60.

22. "Po Sovetskomy Soyuzu," *Iskusstvo* 3 (1956), p. 79.

23. Vorob'ev. Interview with Knut Hammarskjold, President, IATA, Washington, D.C., March 1974. Hammarskjold served in the Swedish Embassy in Moscow in the mid-1950s. He explained that many diplomats were beginning to collect unofficial Soviet art during this period.

24. Boris Ioganson, "Vsesoyuznaya khudozhestvennaya vystavka 1954 Goda: Vsenarodnyi smotr," *Iskusstvo* 2 (1955), p. 10.

25. A. Ginevski, "Nakanune s'ezda," *Iskusstvo* 3 (1956), p. 21.

26. Ibid.

27. Alexander Gerasimov, "Put' nashevo iskusstva," *Sovetskaya kul'tura*, March 27, 1956.

28. Ilya Ehrenburg, *Sobranie sochinenii*, vol. 8: *Lyudi, gody, i zhizn'* (Moscow: Khudozhestvennaya Literatura, 1962–1967), p. 204.

29. Interview with Oskar Rabin and other Moscow artists, Moscow, November 1974 and May 1976.

30. Rabin's original group of followers included Plavinsky, Sveshnikov, Zverev, and Nemukhin. His activities from 1956 to 1965 are best documented in: *Oskar Rabin: Paintings 1956–1965* (London: Grosvenor Gallery, June 10–July 3, 1965).

31. "Khronika," *Iskusstvo* 7 (1956), p. 79.

32. V. M. Molotov, "Vystuplenie V. M. Molotov protiv anarkhii v intellektual'nom proizvodstve," *Sovetskaya kul'tura*, November 20, 1956. After the suppression of the Hungarian Revolution, Molotov in his renewed post as Minister of State Control and official arbiter of Soviet Culture reaffirmed the doctrine of Socialist Realism at the meeting of Soviet writers, artists, and critics.

33. Gyorgy Lukacs, "Gyorgy Lukacs on Stalinism and Art," *East Europe* 13 (May 1964), p. 23.

34. "Pervyi Vsesoyuznyi S'ezd Sovetskikh Khudozhnikov—Tzentral'nomy Komitetu Kommunisticheskoi Partii Sovetskovo Soyuza," *Iskusstvo* 3 (1957), p. 10.

35. Ibid., p. 34.

36. "Khronika—po Sovetskomu Soyuzu," *Iskusstvo* 3 (1957), p. 79; U.S. Department of State, "Some Brief 'Cultural' Impressions of Leningrad," by H. G. Barnes, Jr., Foreign Service Despatch, American Embassy (Moscow) to Department of State, Washington, D.C., declassified, March 15, 1957, p. 3. In March 1957 an exhibition of the works of Alexander Rodchenko was mounted in Moscow, and the Hermitage Museum in Leningrad organized a small exhibition of Russian Expressionist, Cubist, and Futurist paintings.

37. "Pervyi Vsesoyuznyi S'ezd," p. 9.

38. By Deineka in 1933, by Alexander Matveev in 1937, by Vera Mukhina in 1939, and by Alexander Gerasimov in 1940.

39. "Khronika—po Sovetskomu Soyuzu," *Iskusstvo* 2 (1957), p. 79; *Literaturnaya gazeta*, February 21, 1957; and interviews with Ilya and Nina Glazunov, artists, Moscow, January 1978.

40. "Khronika—po Sovetskomu Soyuzu," *Iskusstvo* 5 (1957), pp. 79–80. For a complete list of participating countries, see p. 79.

41. Vadim Polevoi, "Khudozhnik i zhizn: Diskussiya po voprosam khudozhestvennovo tvorchestva na VI Vsemirnom Festivale Molodezhi i Studentov v Moskve," *Iskusstvo* 6 (1957), p. 18.

42. Ibid., p. 33.

43. Ibid., p. 18.

44. "Khronika," no. 5 (1957), p. 79.

45. V. Serov, "Zadachi Orgkomiteta Soyuza Khudozhnikov RSFSR," *Iskusstvo* 8 (1957), pp. 26–27.

46. N. S. Khrushchev, "Za tesnuyu svyaz' literatury i iskusstva s zhizn'yu naroda," *Iskusstvo* 5 (1957), pp. 3–14.

47. Ioganson, "Sovetskaya Akademiya," p. 15; "Khronika—po Sovetskomu Soyuzu," *Iskusstvo* 6 (1957), p. 81.

48. "Obsuzhdenie Vsesesoyuznoi Yubileinoi Khudozhestvennoi Vystavki—kratkii otchet o IV Plenume Soyuza Khudozhnikov SSSR," *Iskusstvo* 4 (1958), p. 3.

49. N. Volkov, "O tzvetovom stroe kartiny," *Iskusstvo* 8 (1958), pp. 19–24. Volkov's article discusses French Impressionism and shows reproductions of such well-known paintings as Matisse's *Still Life with Goldfish* (1911).

50. N. Dmitrieva, "Vystavka proizvedenii N. K. Rerikha," *Iskusstvo* 8 (1958), p. 31.

51. Vorob'ev.

52. Alexander Glezer, "20 let spustya," *Kontinent* 6 (February 4, 1976), p. 391.

53. Vorob'ev.

54. Interview with Evgeni Rukhin, Leningrad, November 1974. The information was corroborated by Oskar Rabin in Moscow in May 1976.

55. N. Mikhailov, "Sovetskie khudozhniki-bortzi za kommunizm," *Iskusstvo* 6 (1959), p. 8.

56. "Khronika—po Sovetskomy Soyuzu," *Iskusstvo* 8 (1959), p. 78.

57. N. Zhukov, "Iskusstvo i sovremennost," *Literaturnaya gazeta*, January 17, 1959; U.S. Department of State, "Lecture on Abstract Art," by Morris Rothenberg, Foreign Service Despatch, American Embassy (Moscow) to Department of State, Washington, D.C., declassified, May 25, 1959, pp. 1–4; and S. Rappoport, "Abstraktnye formy v dekorativno-prikladnom iskusstve i abstraktzionizm," *Iskusstvo* 9 (1959), p. 42.

58. N. Volkov, "Protiv deformatzii," *Iskusstvo* 10 (1960), p. 27.

59. V. Gaposhkin, "Obsuzhdaem aktual'nye problemy sovetskovo iskusstva: Protiv estetizatzii besobraznovo," *Iskusstvo* 4 (1961), p. 33.

60. "Khrushchev Attends French Art Exhibit," *New York Herald Tribune*, September 5, 1961.

61. A. Il'f and N. Nedbaeva, eds. *Soyuz Khudozhnikov SSSR* (Moscow: Sovetskii Khudozhnik, 1978), pp. 16–17.

62. "Pervomu S'ezdu Khudozhnikov RSFSR," *Iskusstvo* 8 (1960), p. 6.

63. N. S. Khrushchev, "Toward New Successes in Literature and Art," *Kommunist*, May 10, 1961; and for a list of the Party leaders who attended the meeting, see: "Khronika—po Sovetskomu Soyuzu," *Iskusstvo* 10 (1960), p. 78.

64. Interview, Rabin; and Alexander Glezer, "Die Wiedergeborene Kunst und die Sowjet-Inquisition—Die Non-konformistischen Maler Russlands," *Frankfurter Allgemeine Zeitung*, May 24, 1975.

65. Interview with George Costakis, art collector, Moscow, May 1976. This information was corroborated by Hammarskjold.

66. Lydia Masterkova, who was associated with the Rabin group in Paris, had a retrospective of her abstract paintings at the Shalyapin House in 1961. That same year an exhibit of young Moscow nonconformists was held at the Moscow Union of Artists. And the VI Youth Festival in Moscow saw the participation of many young innovators.

67. Vorob'ev.

68. "Khronika—po Sovetskomu Soyuzu," *Iskusstvo* 12 (1961), p. 77.

69. Works by Evgeni Bachian and Anatol Brusilovsky were represented at an exhibition in the offices of the magazine *Molodaya gvardiya*. Mikhail Grobman, "Pervyi naibolee polnyi spisok vystavok moskovskikh khudozhnikov avangardistov" ("The First Most Complete List of Exhibitions of Moscow Avant-Garde Artists"), Jerusalem, October 10, 1972 (mimeographed).

70. Arsen Pohribny, Peter Spielman, and Helmut Zumbro, eds. *Progressive Strömungen in Moskau, 1957–1970* (Bochum: Heinrich—Druckerei GmbH, 1974).

71. Vorob'ev. Grobman.

72. "Resheniya XXII S'ezda i zadachi Moskovskikh khudozhnikov," *Iskusstvo* 2 (1962), p. 78.

73. "I See the Sun," *Newsweek*, May 14, 1962, p. 103.

74. Vladimir N. Turbin, *Tovarishch vremya i tovarishch iskusstvo (Comrade Time and Comrade Art)* (Moscow: Gosudarstvennoe Izdatelstvo Iskusstvo, 1961).

75. U.S. Department of State, "Khrushchev, Modern Art, and Rebellious Intellectuals," American Embassy (Moscow) Airgram A-817, December 11, 1962, p. 2.

76. Ernst Neizvestny, "Otkryvat' Novoe!," *Iskusstvo* 10 (1962), p. 10.

77. Eli Belyutin, "Khrushchev i Manezh," unpublished manuscript, Moscow, 1970, p. 65; Seymour Topping, "Khrushchev Views Abstract Art, then Lectures Russian Painters," *New York Times*, December 3, 1962; "Sophie Schiller and 'The Belyutin School,' " *Ely Belyutin, Sophie Schiller: Paintings and Monotypes from Moscow and Boston*, ed. Norton T. Dodge (St. Mary's City: The Enterprise, 1977); Vorob'ev.

78. Grobman.

79. Belyutin, pp. 4–5. The Manezh (or Manege, which is French for riding school) was constructed in 1817 by Czar Alexander I to serve as a riding academy and indoor exercise course for the nobility, officers of the guards regiments, and distinguished members of Moscow's foreign community. In 1957 the Manezh became the Central Exhibition Hall and was opened to art exhibitions. The exhibition area is seven thousand square meters. To date it is used for major all-union exhibitions. For further information see: "Khronika—po Sovetskomu Soyuzu," *Iskusstvo* 8 (1962), p. 78.

80. "Khronika—po Sovetskomu Soyuzu," *Iskusstvo* 1 (1963), p. 77.

81. Ibid.

82. "Ko Vtoromu S'ezda Khudozhnikov SSSR: Bol'shim, soderzhatel'nym, iskaniyam–shirokuyu dorogu!," *Iskusstvo* 12 (1962), p. 2.

83. Among other art officials explaining the exhibition were: the Secretary of the Board of the Artists' Union of the RSFSR, Ye. F. Belashova and the Chairman of the Moscow Union of Artists, D. K. Mochal'skii.

84. "Khrushchev on Modern Art," *Encounter* 20 (April 1963), pp. 101–103.

85. "Vysokoe prizvanie sovetskovo iskusstva—sluzhit' narodu, delu kommunisma," *Iskusstvo* 11 (1962), p. 2.

86. Ibid.

87. Ibid.

88. Ibid., p. 4.

89. Ibid.

90. Belyutin, p. 10.

91. Ibid.

92. "Vysokoe prizvanie," p. 4. Though it is not known if Khrushchev was aware of it, the "donkey" reference relates to a hoax perpetrated by the Parisian comic journal *Fantasio* in 1910. The editors submitted a canvas painted by a brush tied to a donkey's tail to the *Salon des Indépendants* and fooled some of the critics. The same story had caused the Russian avant-garde artist Mikhail Larionov to name his exhibition group the *Donkey's Tail* in 1912; Gray, p. 278.

93. Priscilla Johnson and Leopold Labedz, eds. *Khrushchev and the Arts: The Politics of Soviet Culture: 1962–1964* (Massachusetts: The MIT Press, 1965), p. 102.

94. Topping, p. 1.

95. "Sturm auf die Gemäldeausstellung in Moskau: Du Narr, du weisst ja nicht, was Kunst ist," *Die Welt*, December 10, 1962.

96. Ibid.

97. Belyutin, pp. 3, 13–14, 17–18, 37, 71, 83–84.

98. "Ko Vtoromu S'ezdu," p. 2; "Za ideinuyu chistotu sovetskovo izobrazitel'novo iskusstva," *Iskusstvo* 2 (1963), p. 3.

99. Johnson, *Khrushchev*, p. 8.

100. Editorial, *Iskusstvo* 12 (1962), p. 4.

101. Ibid., pp. 4–5.

102. Vorob'ev.

103. Grobman.

104. Ralph Blum, "A Reporter at Large: Freeze and Thaw: The Artist in Russia—I," *The New Yorker*, September 4, 1965, p. 17.

105. N. S. Khrushchev, "Vysokaya Ideinost' i khudozhestvennoe masterstvo—velikaya sila sovetskoi literatury i iskusstva," *Iskusstvo* 3 (1963), pp. 2–15.

106. Johnson, *Khrushchev*, p. 203.

107. David Miller, "Soviet Sculptor Says Artists Ought to Do Manual Labor," *The Herald Tribune*, April 2, 1963.

108. "Vtoroi Vsesoyuznyi S'ezd Khudozhnikov: Za konsolidatziyu izobrazitel'novo iskusstva na osnove nezyblemykh printzipov sotzialisticheskovo realizma," *Iskusstvo* 6 (1963), p. 16.

109. Ibid., pp. 2 and 8.

110. Ibid., p. 3.

111. Katharine Kuh, "An American Critic Reports on Art in the Soviet Union," *Saturday Review*, August 24, 1963, pp. 17–26.

112. John Canaday, "Modern Artists Are Still at Work in the Soviet Union," *New York Times*, International ed., October 3, 1963.

113. Sydney Gruson, "Soviet Art Is Set for London Sale," *New York Times*, May 7, 1963.

114. Denys Sutton, "Russian Vitality," *Financial Times*, June 9, 1964; and Charles S. Spencer, "Soviet Show in Britain Avoids Propaganda," *New York Times*, June 9, 1964.

115. Interview with Evgenia Kaplan, widow of Anatoli Kaplan, Leningrad, USSR, December 19, 1989.

116. Yurii Bychkov, "Obshirnaya zametka," *Sovetskaya kul'tura*, June 16, 1964.

117. Kim Selikhov, "Obkom v oborone," *Kommunist* 11 (1963).

118. Belyutin, p. 155; Vorob'ev; Grobman.

119. Interviews with Evgeni Rukhin, Moscow, Leningrad, and Tallin, May 1976.

120. "Moscow Public to Judge 'Decadence' of Painter," UPI, Moscow, June 15, 1964.

121. Theodore Shabad, "Controversial Soviet Artist Gets Show," *New York Times*, European ed., June 16, 1964; and idem, "Decadent Wins a Skirmish in Moscow Art War," *New York Times*, June 16, 1964. The information was confirmed during interviews with Ilya Glazunov in New York and Moscow in March 1980.

122. Strobe Talbott, trans. and ed., *Khrushchev Remembers: The Last Testament* (Boston: Little, Brown and Co., 1974), p. 73.

123. Editorial, *Pravda*, January 9, 1965.

124. "Ioganson," TASS, no. 5-4 (January 1965); and "Ioganson Elected First Secretary of the Board of the Union of Artists USSR," *Survey of the Soviet Press*, no. 393 (January 29, 1965), p. 31.

125. "Sessiya Akademii Khudozhestv SSSR," *Pravda*, March 2, 1966.

126. "Pered velikoi datoi," *Pravda*, March 13, 1966.

127. Tair Salakhov, "V serdtze vedushchii urok," *Pravda*, September 28, 1966.

128. Tretii S'ezd Soyuza Khudozhnikov SSSR, "Tzentral'nomu Komitetu Kommunisticheskoi Partii Sovetskovo Soyuza," *Izvestiya*, November 30, 1968.

129. Other Party leaders reported present were: Kirilenko, Pelshe, Ustinov, Kapitonov, Ponomarev, and Solomentzev.

130. Tzentral'nyi Komitet KPSS, "Tret'emu S'ezdu Khudozhnikov SSSR," *Pravda*, November 27, 1968.

131. "Moscow Officials Charged with Corruption," *New York Herald Tribune*, March 17, 1965.

132. A. Sukontzev, "Vokrug sladkovo piroga," *Pravda*, May 15, 1969.

133. Ibid.; "Slovo za Soyuzom Khudozhnikov," *Pravda*, August 20, 1969.

134. A. Zis', "Modernizm—vrag tvorchestva," *Pravda*, March 3, 1970.

135. Ibid.

136. Nikolai Tomskii, "S pozitzii sotzialisticheskovo realizma," *Kommunist* (September 1970), pp. 91–105.

137. O. Butkevich, "Zametki o diskussii vokrug VIII Moskovskoi Vystavki Molodykh Khudozhnikov," *Sovetskaya kul'tura*, March 1, 1969.

138. Tair Salakhov, "Ekzamen na zrelost', " *Pravda*, September 14, 1972; and B. S. Andreev, "Byt' bortsom," *Komsomol'skaya pravda*, August 18, 1972.

139. Yurii Nekhoroshev, "Dorogi molodykh," *Literaturnaya Rossiya*, September 15, 1972.

140. "Vmeste s Partiei, vmeste s narodom," *Pravda*, May 16, 1973.

141. N. Ponomarev, "Ob ideino-vospitatel'noi rabote s molodymi khudozhnikami," *Iskusstvo* 1 (1973), p. 4.

142. N. Ponomarev, "Sovestkii khudozhnik—aktivnyi uchastnik stroitel'stva kommunisticheskovo obshchestva," *Iskusstvo* 8 (1973), p. 5.

143. N. Ponomarev, "Glavnaya politika," *Sovetskaya kul'tura*, June 8, 1973.

144. Ibid.

145. Ibid.

146. "Solschenitzyn im Westen," *Der Spiegel*, February 18, 1974, pp. 66–78.

147. Leonid Likhodeev, "Otrazhennaya giperbola," *Komsomol'skaya pravda*, June 20, 1965.

148. V. Soloukhin, "Pisem iz Russkovo Muzeya," *Molodaya gvardiya* 10 (1966).

149. "Moskva," *Iskusstvo* 3 (1971), p. 74.

150. "Gordost' russkoi kul'tury," *Pravda*, December 22, 1971.

151. In February 1966 an exhibit of 3,500 works of the Baltic republics opened at the Manezh exhibition hall. The 1967 *All-Union Youth Exhibit* and the *All-Union Jubilee Art Exhibit* also demonstrated the growth of national schools.

152. "Sovetskoe mnogonatzional'noe izobrazitel'noe iskusstvo v stroitel'stve kommunisticheskovo obshchestva," *Pravda*, November 27, 1968.

153. Peter Grose, "Soviet Scientists Back Modern Art," *New York Times*, February 25, 1966.

154. Max Hayward, ed. and trans., *On Trial* (New York: Harper and Row Publishers, 1966), pp. 1–38.

155. Peter Grose, "Modern Artist, 67, Gets Soviet Show," *New York Times*, March 9, 1966.

156. Ibid.

157. F. Syrkina, *A. G. Tyshler* (Moscow: Sovetskii Khudozhnik, 1966).

158. V. Zimenko, *Sovetskaya kul'tura*, quoted by Raymond H. Anderson in "Soviet Critic Urges Relaxation of Curbs on Art," *New York Times*, March 23, 1966.

159. Soloukhin.

160. Raymond H. Anderson, "Muscovites See Once-Banned Art," *New York Times*, November 21, 1966; and Hermann Pörzgen, "Was Man Uns Noch Alles Verbirgt ... ," *Frankfurter Allgemeine Zeitung*, November 28, 1966.

161. Charles S. Spencer, "London Sees Lissitzky's Art," *New York Times*, October 4, 1966.

162. Victor Zorza, "Art for the Foreigners' Sake," *Manchester Guardian*, October 28, 1967.

163. Victor Zorza, "Tighter Hand on Soviet Artists," *Manchester Guardian*, February 15, 1967.

164. O. Semenov, "Kategoriya vremeni i prostranstva v kubizme i abstraktsionizme," *Iskusstvo* 9 (1969), pp. 41–47.

165. Jindrich Chalupecky, "Moscow Diary," *Studio International*, February 1973, p. 88.

166. George Costakis, "Collecting Art of the Avant-Garde," p. 74, in Angelica Zander Rudenstine, gen. ed., *The George Costakis Collection: Russian Avant-Garde Art* (New York: Henry N. Abrams, 1981); Hermann Pörzgen, "Privatmuseum in Moskau," *Frankfurter Allgemeine Zeitung*, May 13, 1972; A. Astrachen, "Artistic Detente," *Washington Post*, October 25, 1973.

167. Henry Kamm, "Emotional Return to Russia Buoys Chagall," *New York Times*, June 18, 1973.

168. *Paris-Moscou: 1900–1930* (Moscow: Le Ministère de la Culture de l'URSS and Paris: Le Centre Pompidou, 1979).

169. Interview with Evgeni Rukhin, Leningrad, November 1974.

170. John Ashbery, "Soviet Avant-Garde Painter Zverev Has His First Exhibition in Paris," *New York Herald Tribune*, February 23, 1965.

171. V. Olshevskii, "Dorogaya tzena chechevichnoi pokhlebki," *Sovetskaya kul'tura*, June 14, 1966; and interview with Oskar Rabin, Moscow, May 1976. Rabin explained that the term "barracks art" developed because of the old houses and depressing apartment scenes he used in the background of most of his paintings. "Barracks art" was also a play on the term Baroque art.

172. Invitation, "U nas v gostyakh moskovskie poety i khudozhniki," Moscow, January 22, 1967. The artists who participated in the exhibit were: N. Vechtomov, Vorob'ev, A. Zverev, V. Kropivnitzkaya, E. Kropivnitzkii, L. Kropivnitzkii, L. Masterkova, V. Nemukhin, D. Plavinsky, O. Potapova, O. Rabin, and E. Shteinberg.

173. "Show of Abstract Red Art Shut Quickly in Moscow," *Washington Post*, January 23, 1967; Raymond H. Anderson, "Moscow Art Show Shuts After an Hour," *New York Times*, January 23, 1967; and Evgeny Yevtushenko, quoted in "Yevtushenko Lauds Exhibit Which 'Bureaucrats' Closed," *Washington Post*, January 27, 1967.

174. "Belashova Remarks," TASS International Service in English, 1444 G.M.T., January 23, 1967.

175. Edmund Stevens, "Counter-attack of Red Artists Hints New Era," *Baltimore Sun*, February 1, 1967.

176. "Massregelung von Künstlern in der Sowjetunion," *Neue Züricher Zeitung*, February 6, 1967; P. Lebedev, "Propaganda sovetskovo izobrazitel'novo iskusstva za rubezhom," *Sovetskaya kul'tura*, February 4, 1967.

177. Alexander Glezer, "Soviet 'Unofficial' Art," *Index on Censorship* 4 (1975), p. 36.

178. Paul Sjeklocha and Igor Mead, *Unofficial Art in the Soviet Union* (Berkeley and Los Angeles: University of California Press, 1967).

179. "CP Expelled Moscow Painter," Reuters, Moscow, April 12, 1968; *Moskovskii Khudozhnik*, April 4, 1968, cited in "Several Moscow Painters Expelled," Reuters, Moscow, April 4, 1968.

180. "CP Expelled."

181. Alexander Glezer, "Dvadtzat' let spustya," *Kontinent* 6, February 4, 1976, p. 403; and interviews, Rabin.

182. Invitation, "Pervyi osennii prosmotr kartin na otkrytom vozdukhe," Moscow, September 15, 1974. The thirteen artists who organized the exhibit were: Oskar Rabin, Alexander Rabin, Evgeni Rukhin, Vladimir Nemukhin, Nadezhda El'skaya, Yuri Zarkikh, Borukh Shteinberg, Alexander Melamid, Vitaly Komar, Vasily Sitnikov, Valentin Vorob'ev, Igor Kholin, and Lydia Masterkova. A total of twenty-four artists expected to exhibit their works.

183. Roger Leddington, "Artists," AP, Moscow, September 16, 1974.

184. "Briton Cancels Visit," *New York Times*, September 21, 1974; and "The Bulldozers Lose the Battle against Nonconformist Art," *Human Rights in the USSR* (September/October 1974), p. 21.

185. "Art Show," AP, Moscow, #V179 NL, September 18, 1974; Konstantin Andreev, "Instead of 'Sensation'—a Flop," TASS International Service in English, 1745 G.M.T., September 23, 1974; and Peter Osnos, "TASS Defends Disruption of Exhibit," *Washington Post*, September 19, 1974.

186. "The KGB Just Isn't Itself These Days," *The Economist*, September 21, 1974, p. 38.

187. "Moscow Press Conference on Art Show," TASS (in Russian), September 28, 1974.

188. Alexander Glezer, Yuri Zarkikh, comps., "Katalog vtorovo osennevo pokaza zhivopisi i grafiki," exhibition catalogue, Moscow, September 29, 1974 (mimeographed). Catalogues for this exhibition vary. One version lists fifty-two entrants, one of which is crossed out. An addendum lists six additional names in handwriting, making a total of fifty-eight entrants. Another version includes an addendum with an added fourteen entrants (typed) and one additional entrant (handwritten) for a total of seventy-two participants. The exact number is difficult to determine, since the *Dvizhenie* group, which included Francisco Infante, is listed as one entry, the entire exhibit could have included as many as eighty artists.

189. Peter Osnos, "Soviets Allow Unofficial Art Show in Park," *Washington Post*, September 30, 1974.

190. Hedrick Smith, "Modernist Art in Soviet a Legacy of Khrushchev," *New York Times*, September 23, 1974.

191. Fedor Reshetnikov, "Letopis' zhizni narodnoi," *Vechernyaya Moskva*, October 18, 1974. Also see: Yurii Nekhoroshev, "Khudozhestvennye poiski ili dukhovnyi perelom," *Moskovskaya pravda*, October 20, 1974; and N. Rybal'chenko, "Kak rasseyalsya mirazh," *Vechernyaya Moskva*, October 23, 1974.

192. Nikolai Podgorny, "Gordost' sovetskovo iskusstva," *Pravda*, November 11, 1974.

193. Hermann Pörtzgen, "Die Modernen bleiben draussen," *Frankfurter Allgemeine Zeitung*, November 13, 1974. Politburo members in attendance were: M. A. Suslov, V. V. Grishin, A. P. Kirilenko, K. T. Mazurov, A. Ya. Pel'she, A. N. Shelepin; and the candidate members P. N. Demichev, B. N. Ponomarev, M. S. Solomentzev, and V. I. Dolgykh.

194. El'skaya, A. Rabin, and Igor Kholin were invited to join the Moscow Union of Artists, Youth Section, provided they would abide by the rules.

195. The number of viewers who attended the exhibit varies considerably in each report. Some write only one thousand people attended. Others cite as many as eight thousand people.

196. Vladimir Yagodkin, "Ideologiya, politika, i literaturno-khudozhestvennaya rabota," *Novy mir* (October 1975), pp. 6–7.

197. Nikolai Ponomarev, "Glavnaya politika," *Sovetskaya kul'tura*, June 8, 1976.

198. Unofficial artists were conscious of the impact of foreign interest in their search for aesthetic freedom. Early in 1977, several artists reportedly attempted to form a Moscow group to monitor the success of the Helsinki Agreement. Their aim was to elicit foreign reaction to any repressive measure that might be applied to fellow artists.

199. Ponomarev, "Glavnaya politika."

200. *New York Times*, October 7, 1986.

201. The other seven artists were Yurii Albert, Sven Gundlakh, Vadim Zakharov, Konstantin Zvezdochetov, the brothers Volodia and Sergei Mironenko, and Andrei Filipov. Larisa Kashuk, "Furmanny Lane," *Furmanny Lane* (Polish Modern Art Foundation, November 1989).

202. Other members were Konstantin Zvezdochetov (their leader), Konstantin Latishev, Boris Matrosov, and Igor Zaidel.

203. Wolfgang Nagel, "Rot ist nicht mehr die Farbe der Hoffnung," *Stern* (May 1982), p. 60.

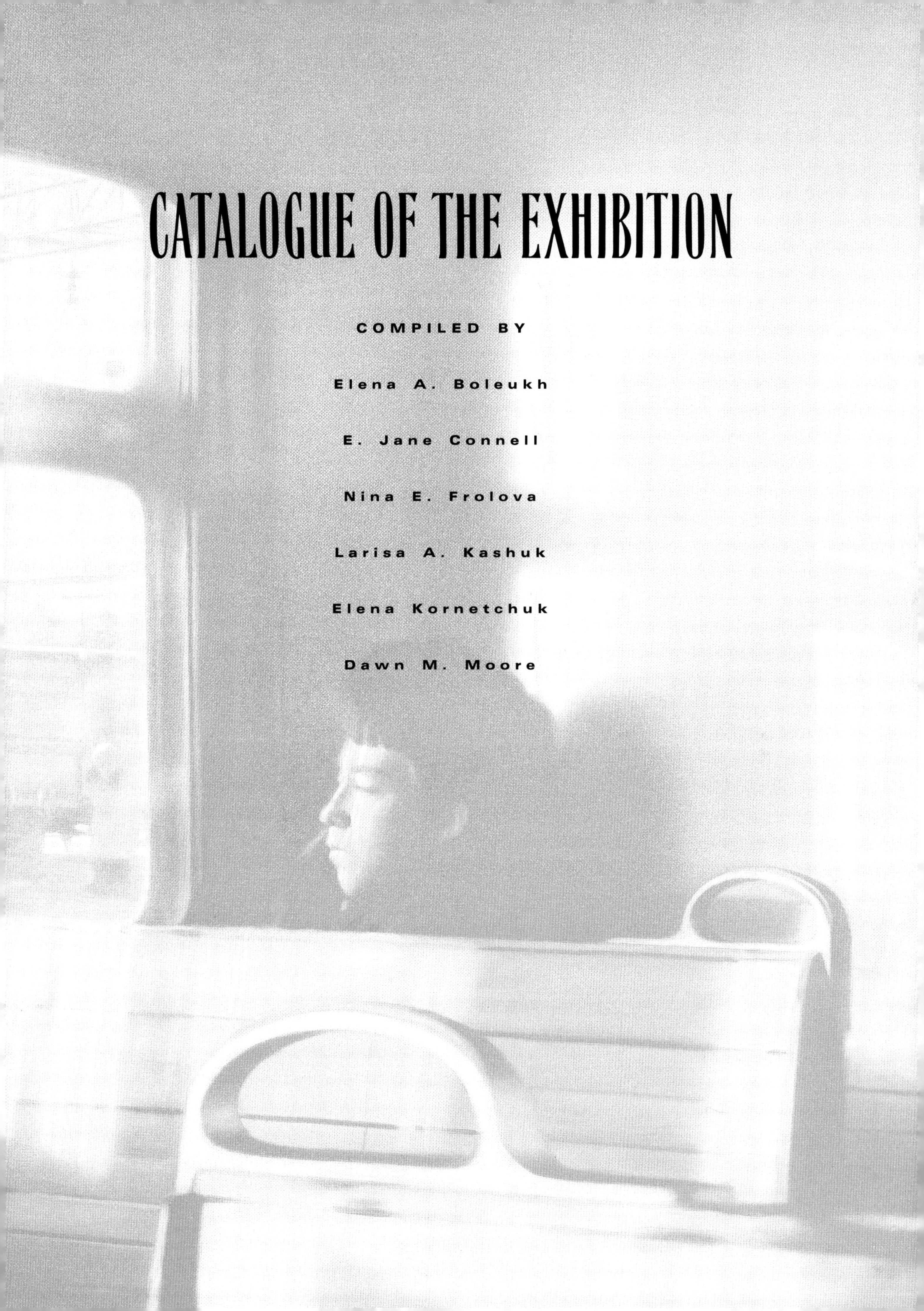

CATALOGUE OF THE EXHIBITION

COMPILED BY

Elena A. Boleukh

E. Jane Connell

Nina E. Frolova

Larisa A. Kashuk

Elena Kornetchuk

Dawn M. Moore

Guram Abramishvili

BORN 1966

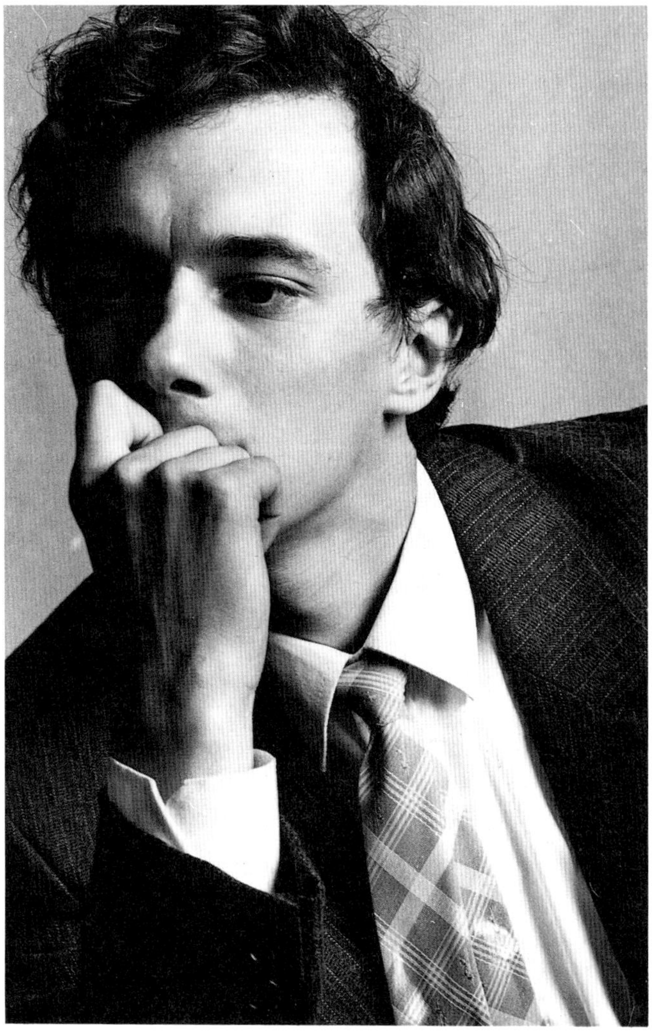

Once in the morning I awoke and saw in front of myself an elderly citizen who held in his hands a small refrigerator. Having noticed my confusion he politely excused himself, placed the refrigerator on the table and left. I cautiously opened the door of the refrigerator and saw a small gray hare there.

"How did you get here?" I asked him.

The hare attentively looked at me and answered:

"A good person always will find a pastime for himself."

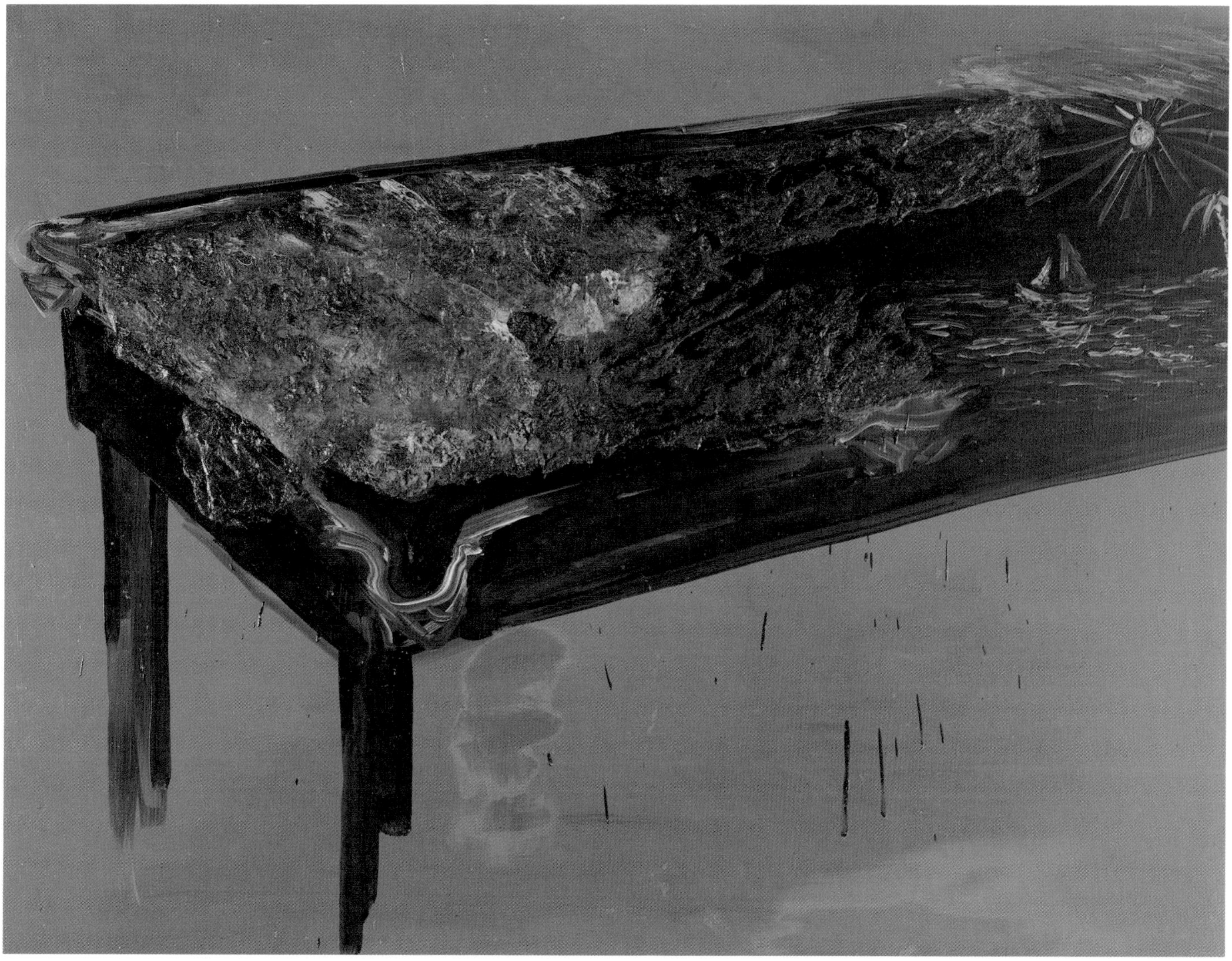

Pl. 8 *The Game,* 1988
Oil, mixed media on canvas, $51^{1}/_{4} \times 69$ inches (130 × 175 cm)
Courtesy of the Artist

GLEB BOGOMOLOV

BORN 1933

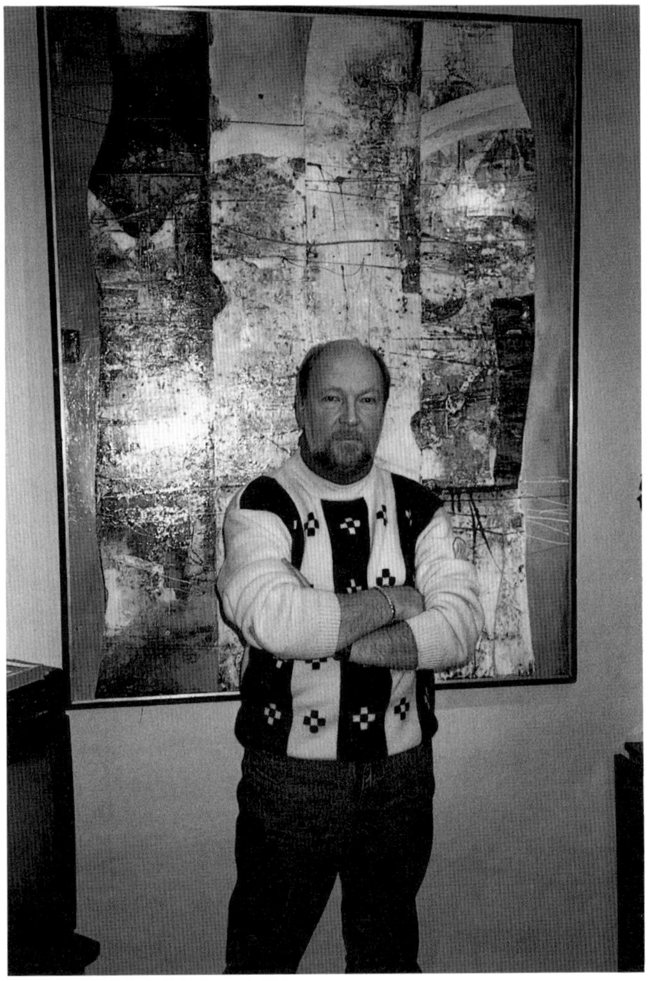

I perceive art as a multifunctional sphere of human activity. Within this multifunctionality I distinguish the following:

a) the function of the cognition of the world, including the transcendental world

b) the function of "forming" the world.

I pay special attention to the avant-garde. I accept the equality of [the present and former] styles as equal in essence. That is why I easily combine the features of ancient art with modern art.

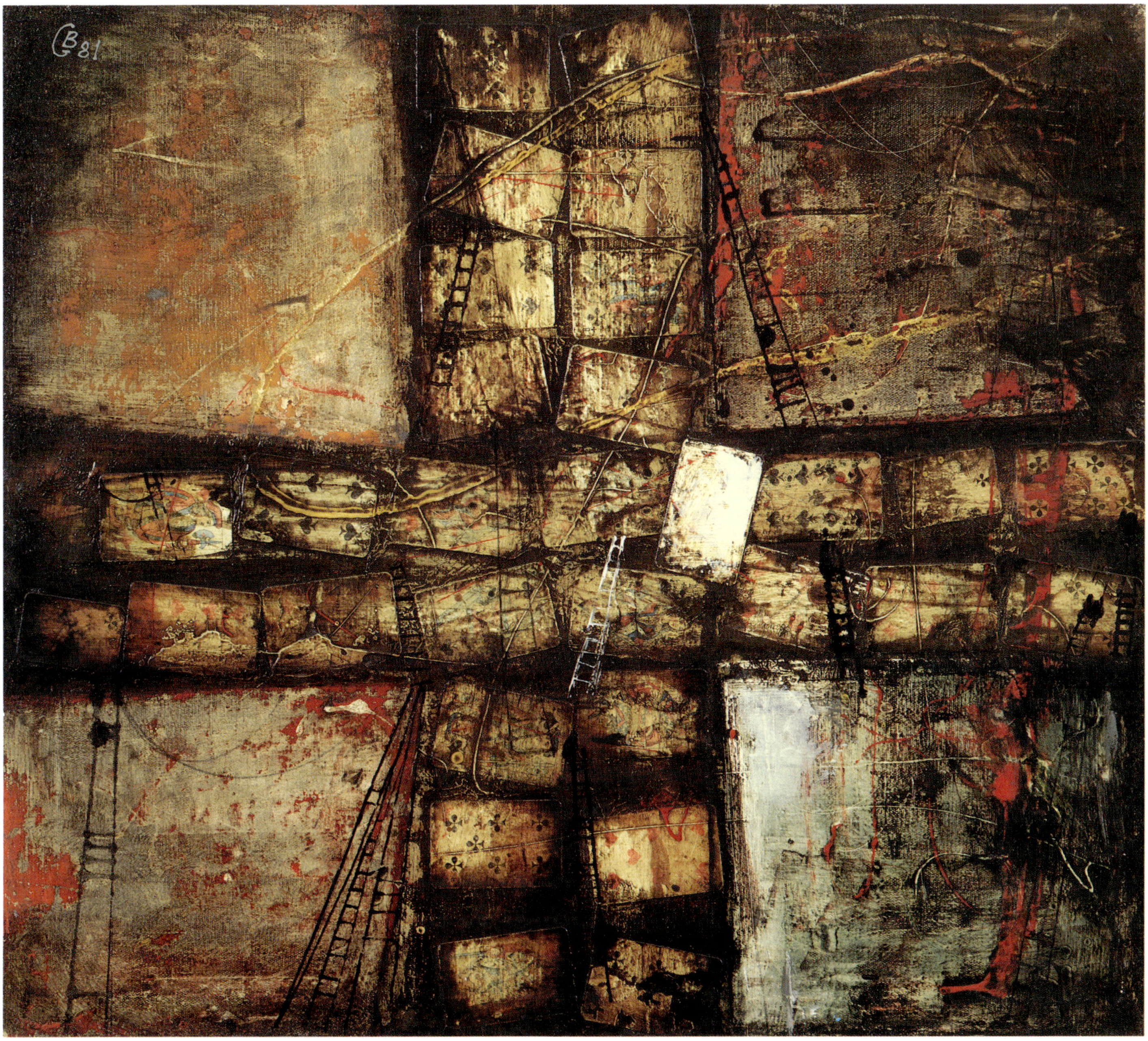

Pl. 9 *The Cross*, 1981
Mixed media, $27^1/_2 \times 32$ inches (68.8×80 cm)
Courtesy of the Artist

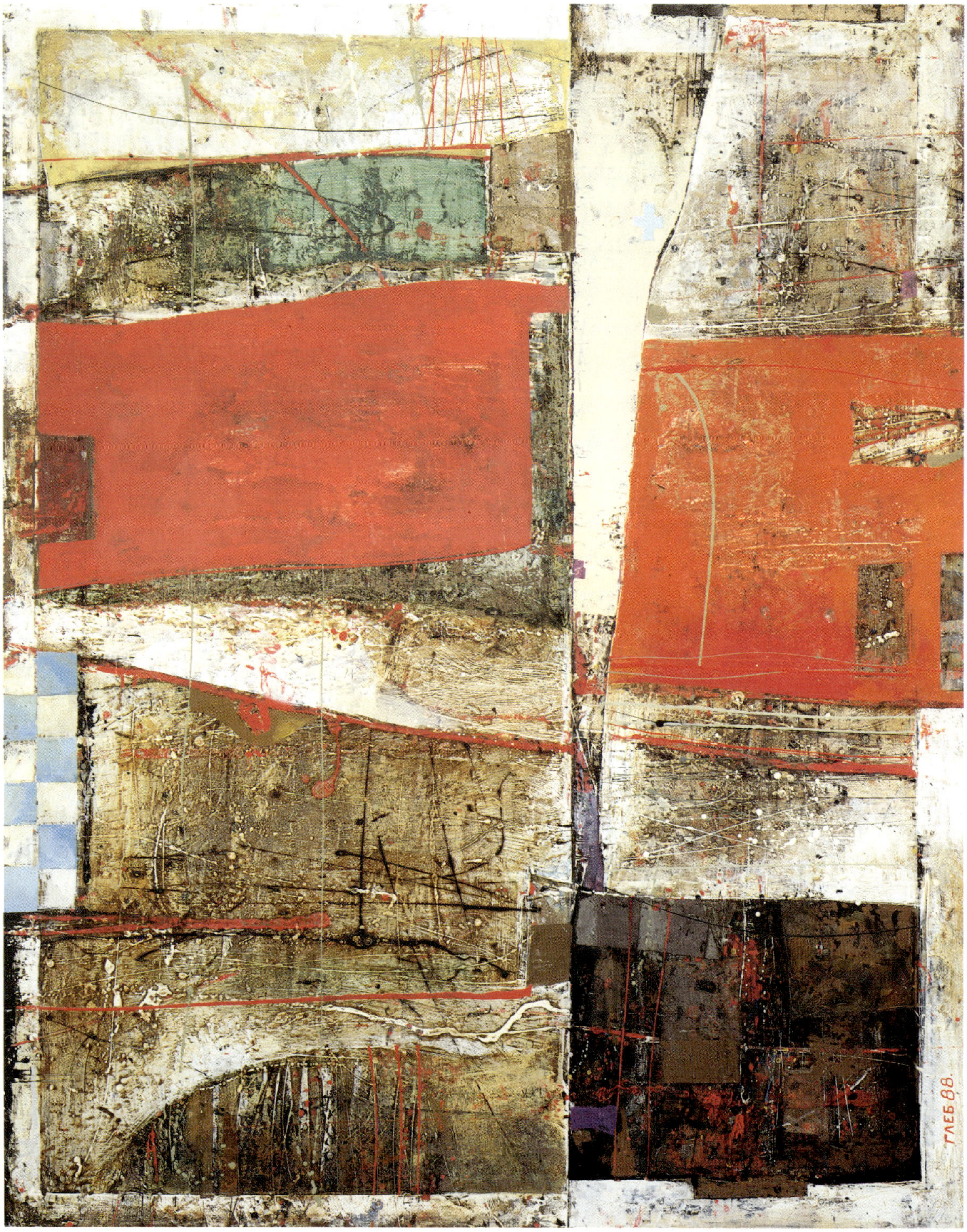

Pl. 10 *The Shadow of Spartacus*, 1988
Tempera, oil, and gold foil on canvas, 59 × 47 1/4 inches
(150 × 120 cm)
Courtesy of the Artist

GLEB BOGOMOLOV

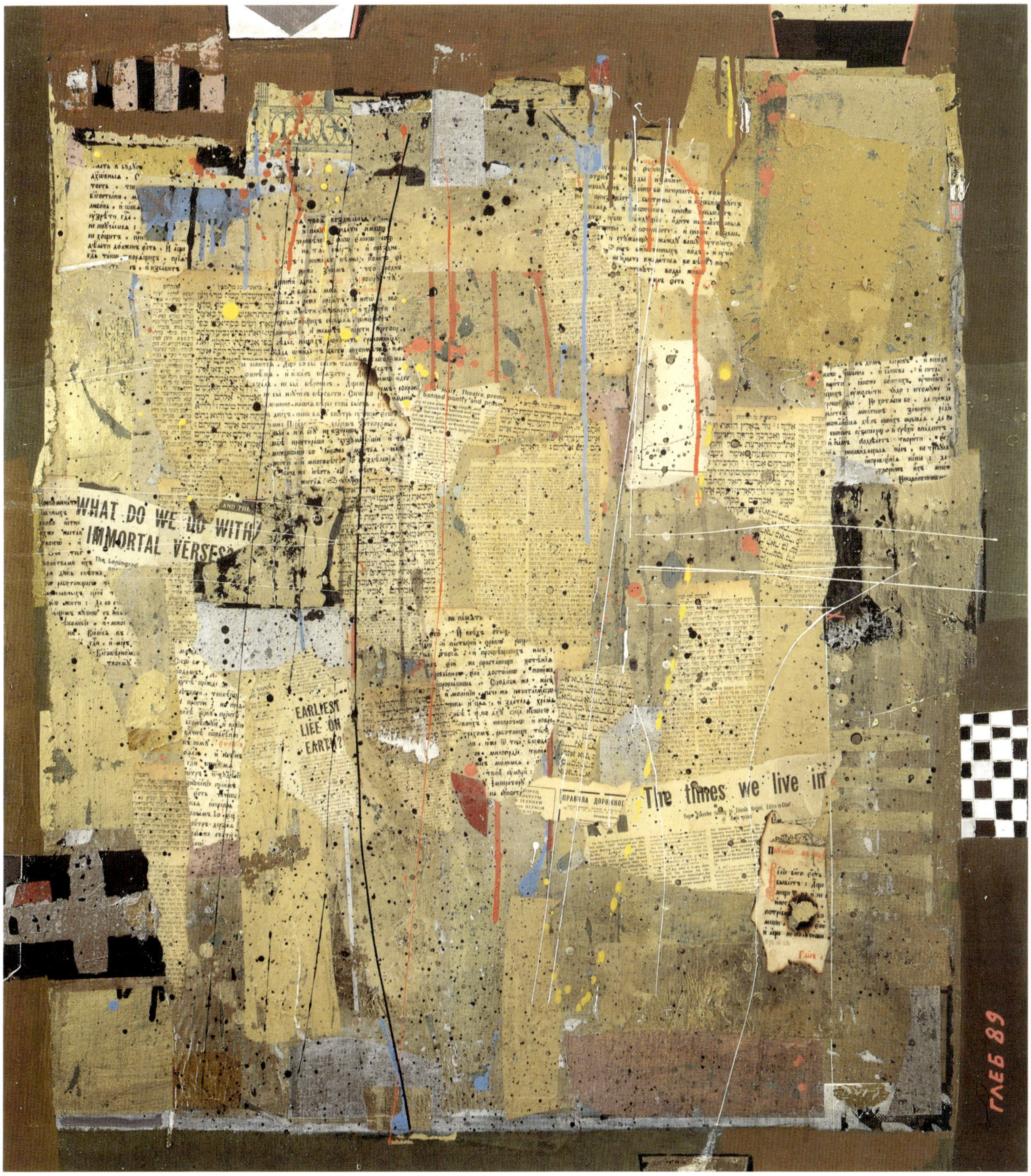

Pl. 11 *Texts*, 1989
Collage, gold foil, and mixed media on canvas,
$39\frac{1}{2} \times 39\frac{3}{8}$ inches (100.3×99.7 cm)
Courtesy of the Artist

Erik Bulatov

Born 1933

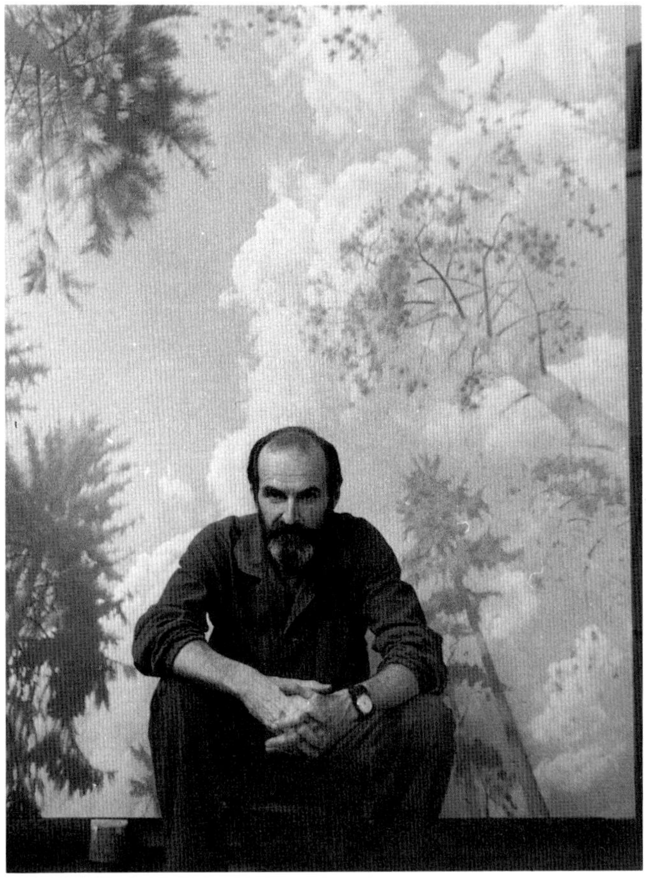

Art is a rebellion of man against the everyday reality of life. Colors, forms, space—these are an artist's sensations, his thoughts, his "reality," through which he manifests his contact with the world. That is why art is so changeable and so eternal in its quests. Probably that is why art is always current, always living, and always inside a man.

A picture interests me as some kind of system, not hermetically sealed, but opening into the space of my everyday existence. A picture illuminates that space, making it visible and clear—not only the space, but myself in it as well.

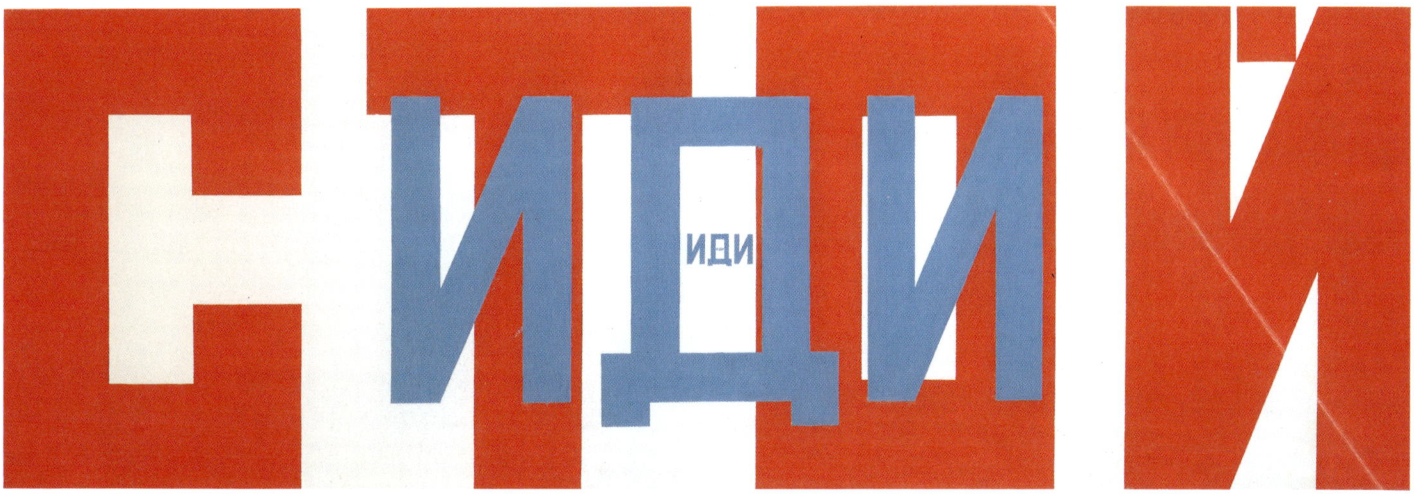

Pl. 12 *Stop-Go*, n.d.
Oil on canvas, $31^{1}/_{2} \times 94^{1}/_{2}$ inches (80×240 cm)
Collection of Nancy and Norton Dodge

Olga Bulgakova

BORN 1951

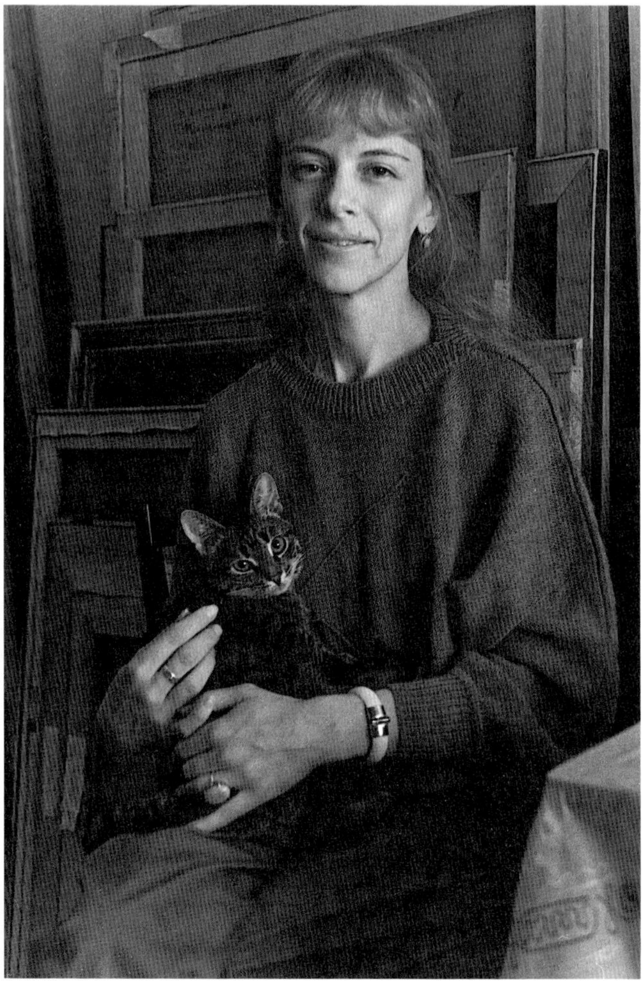

The most important theme for me is the interrelation of creative work and life. White and black, good and evil, wise and stupid, creation and destruction, always and unavoidably exist in the world like the necessary opposite poles of a magnet.

The musings that precede creation, when concepts are born from reality, already exist independently and are interwoven with the work as an equal part of it.

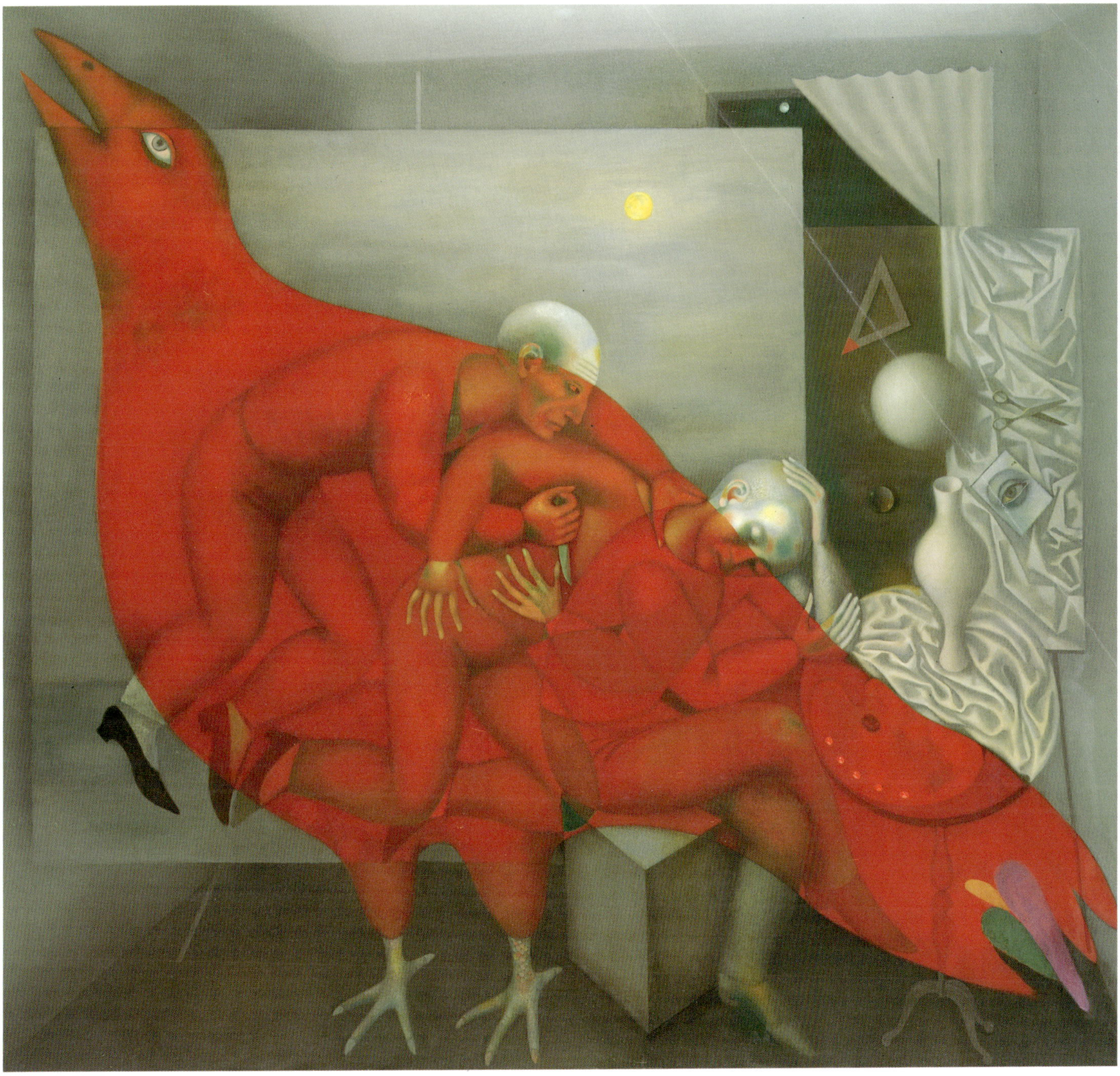

Pl. 13 *Dream about the Red Bird*, 1989
Oil on canvas, 67 × 72½ inches (170 × 184 cm)
Courtesy of the Artist

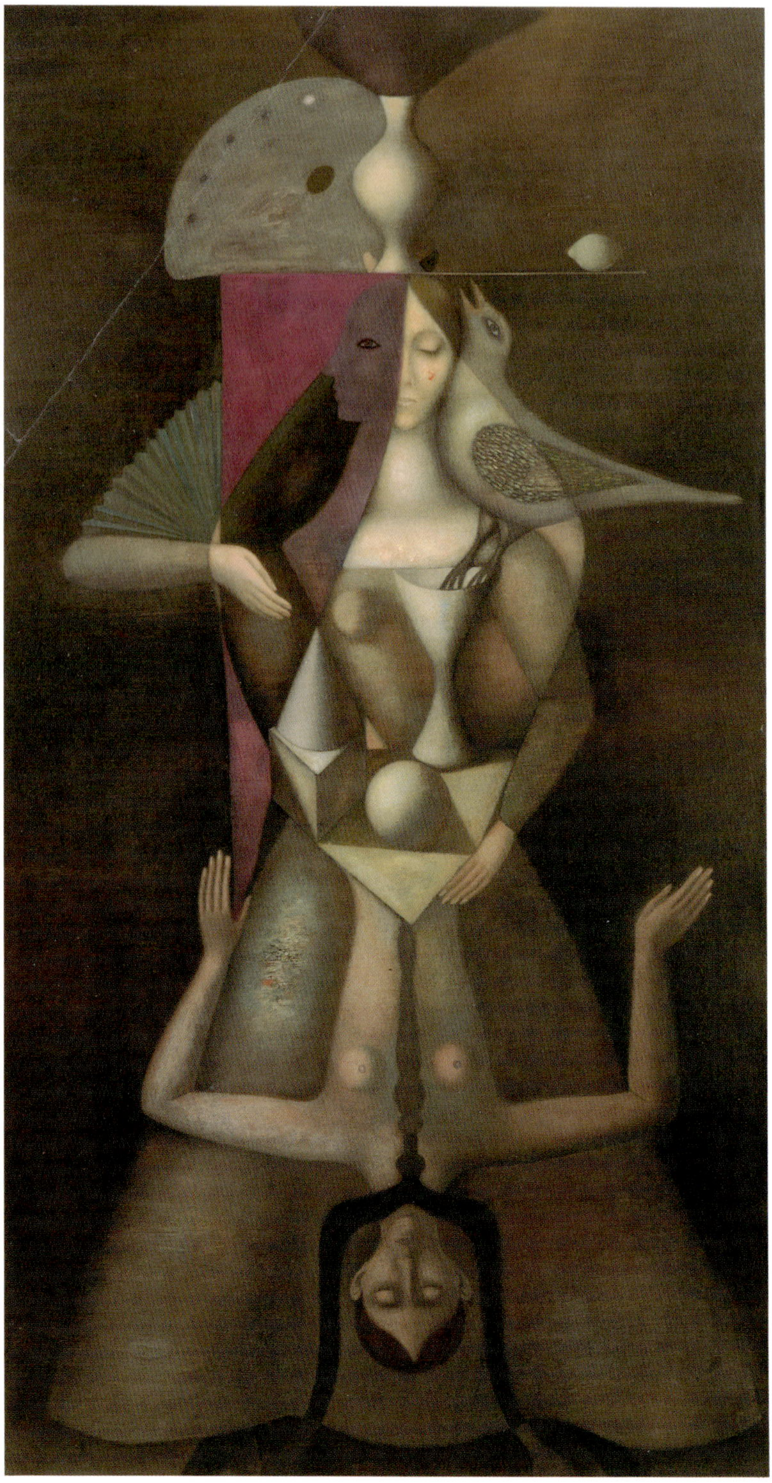

Pl. 14 *Transformation*, 1989
Oil on canvas, 59 × 33½ inches (150 × 85 cm)
Courtesy of the Artist

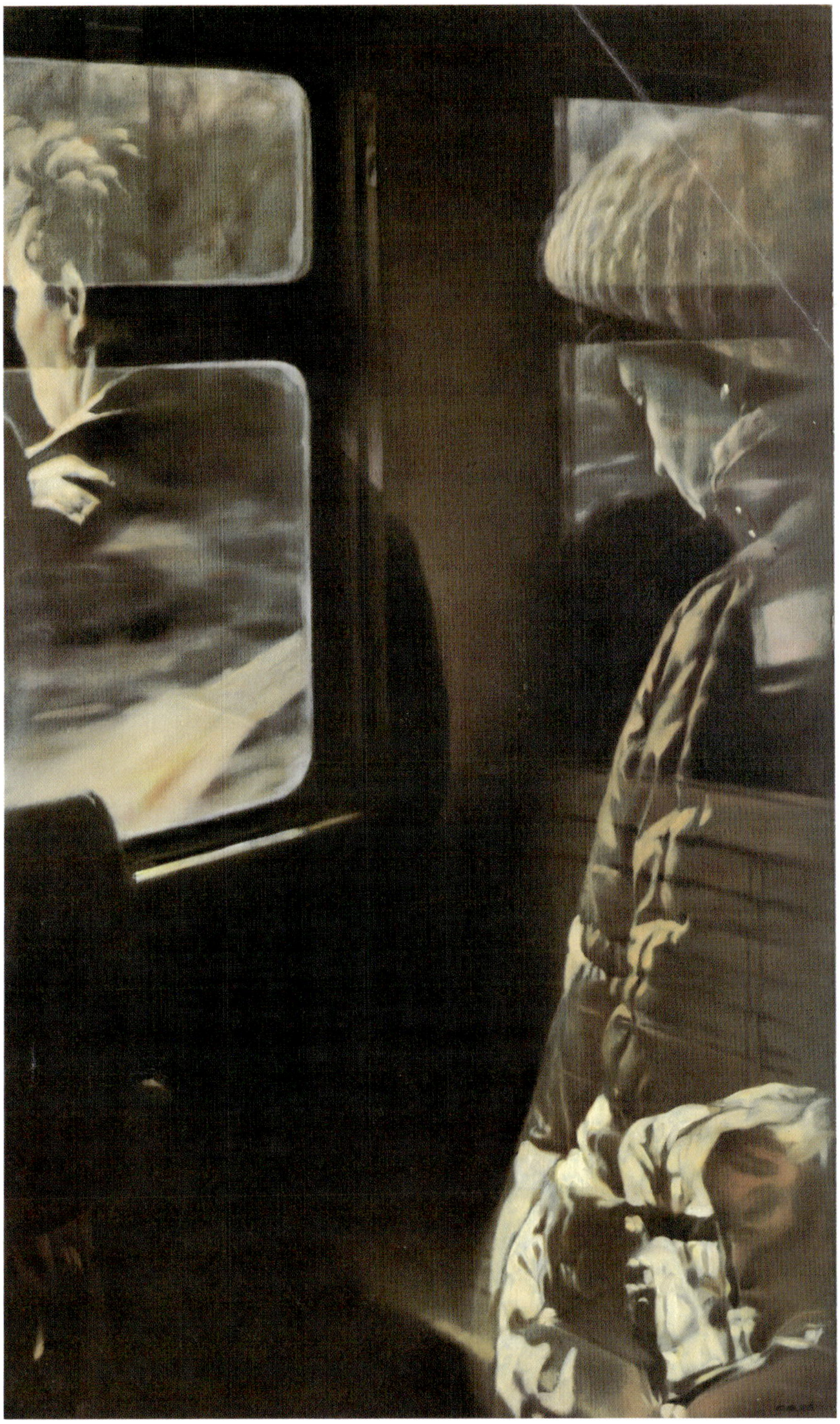

Pl. 18 *At the Exit,* 1986
Oil on masonite, 55 × 33½ inches (140 × 85 cm)
Collection of Nancy and Norton Dodge

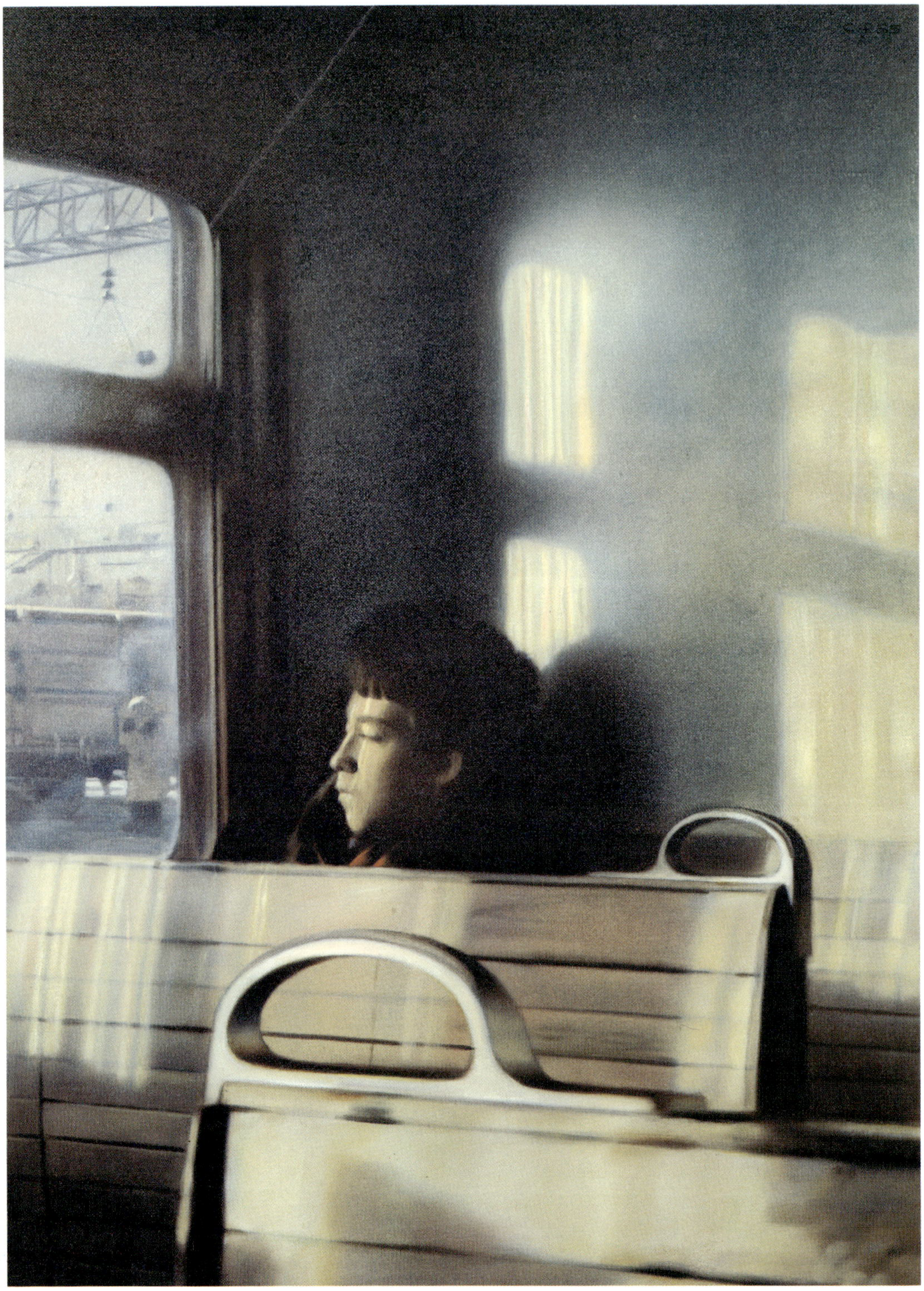

Pl. 19 *Boy* (from the series Moscow Suburban Electric Trains), 1985
Oil on masonite, 51 × 39½ inches (130 × 100 cm)
Collection of Nancy and Norton Dodge

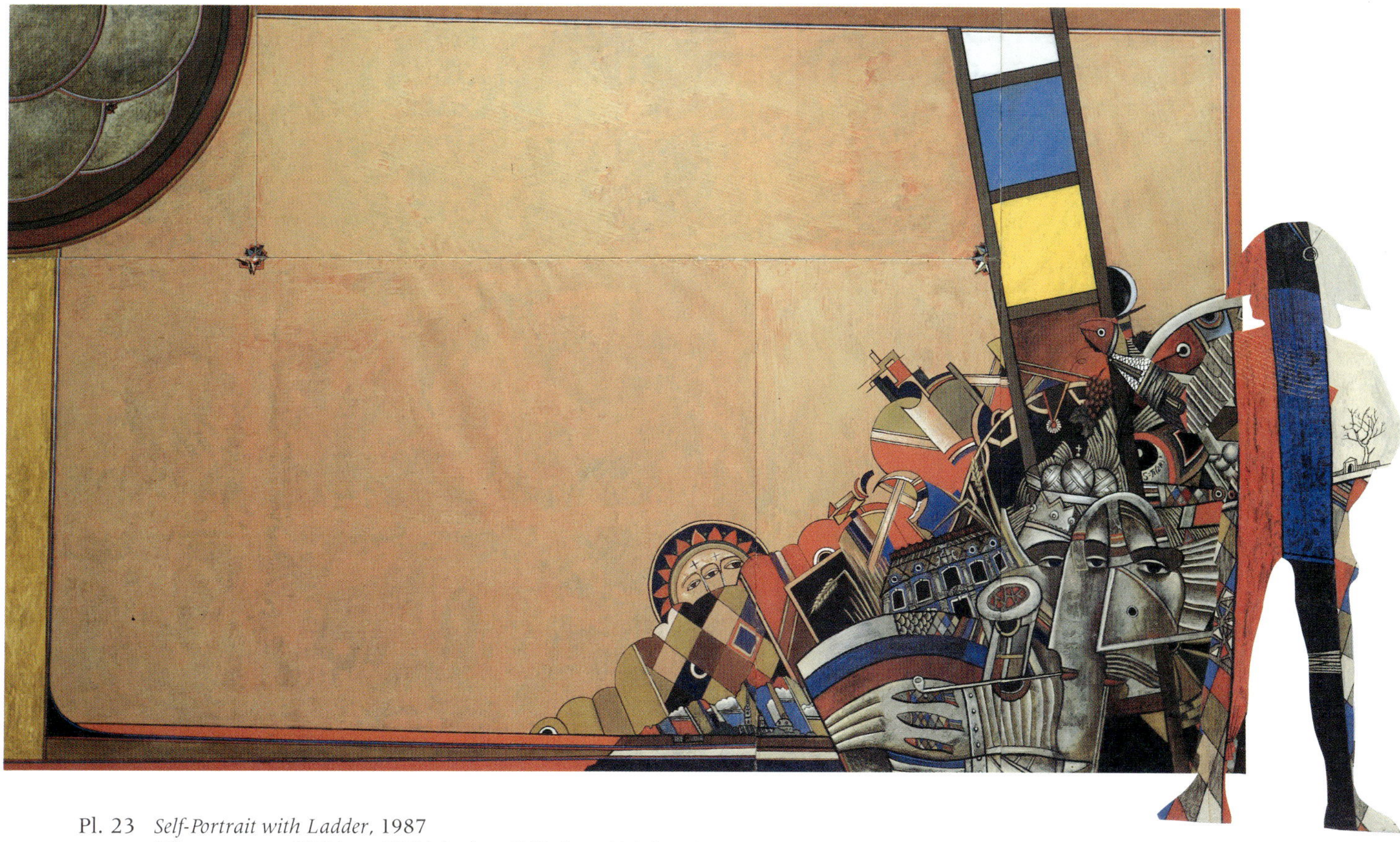

Pl. 23 *Self-Portrait with Ladder*, 1987
Oil on canvas, 117½ × 195½ inches (298.5 × 496.5 cm)
polychrome wooden figure, H. 84 inches (213.5 cm)
Private Collection

Ilya Glazunov

BORN 1930

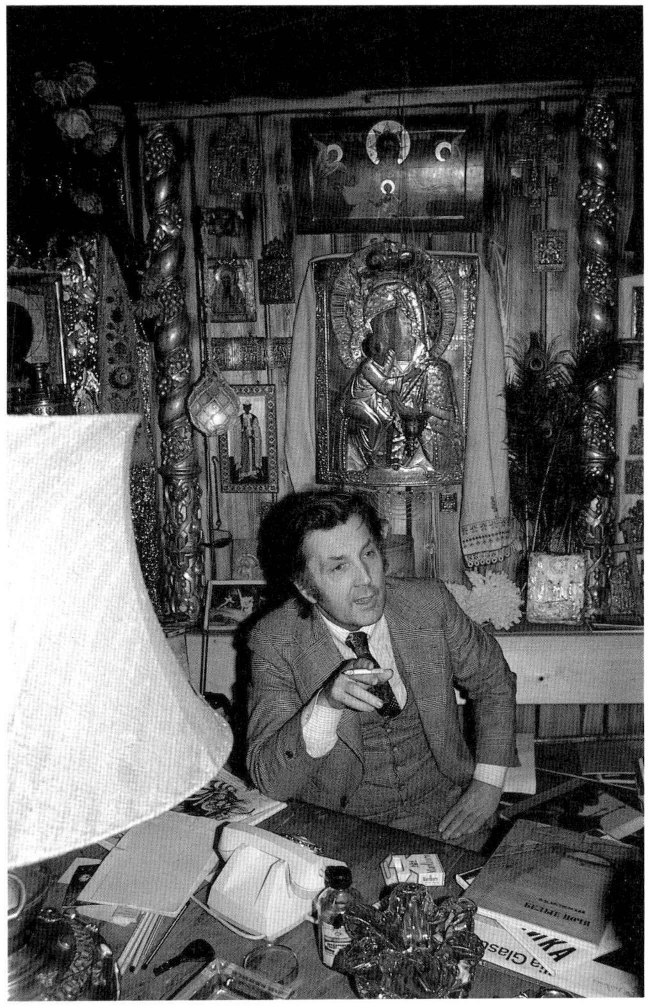

God and my conscience are my mentors.

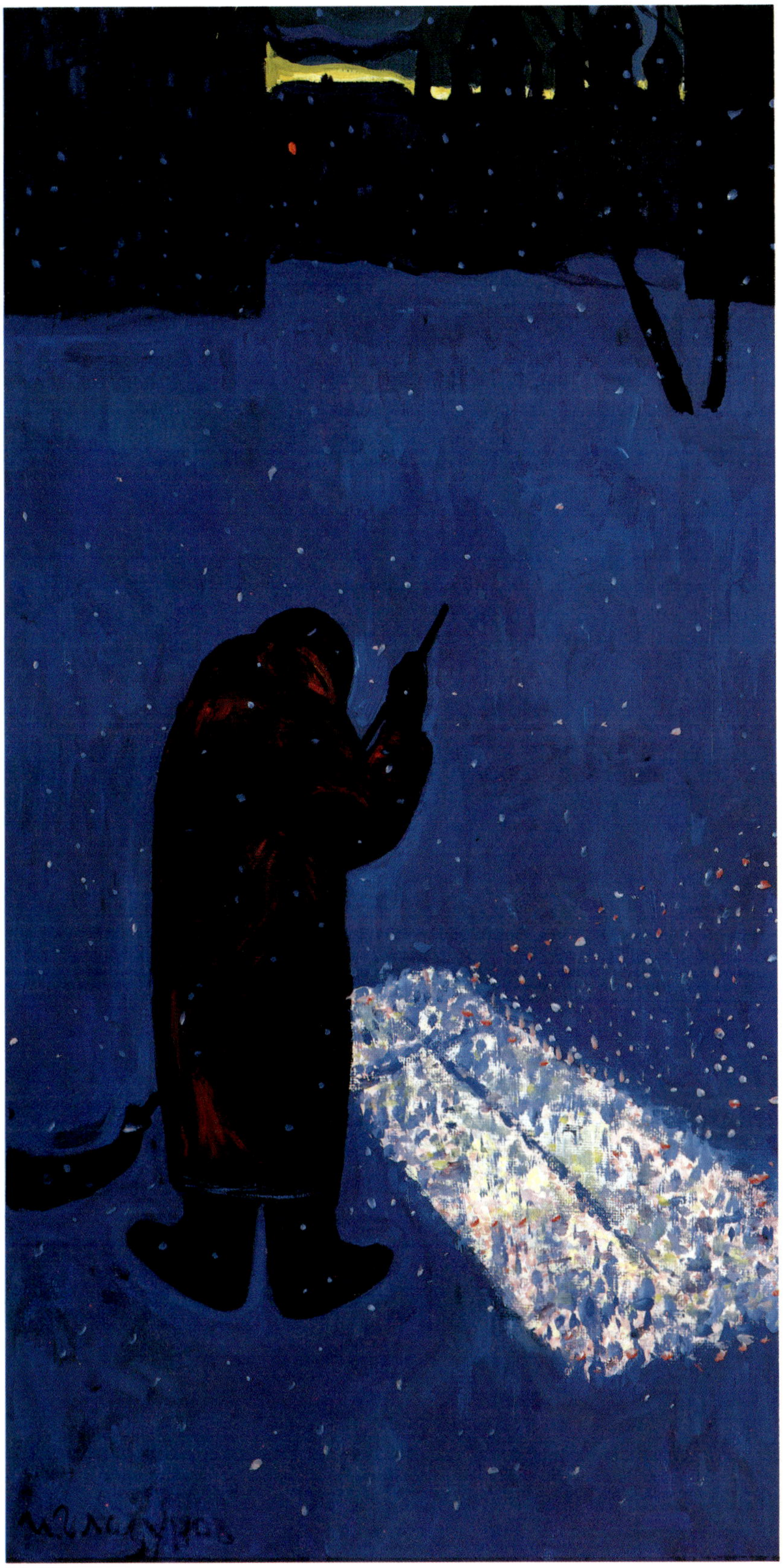

Pl. 24 *New Year's Morning*, 1978
Oil on canvas, $31^{1}/_{2} \times 16$ inches (80×40.6 cm)
Dr. Michel and Victoria Hersen

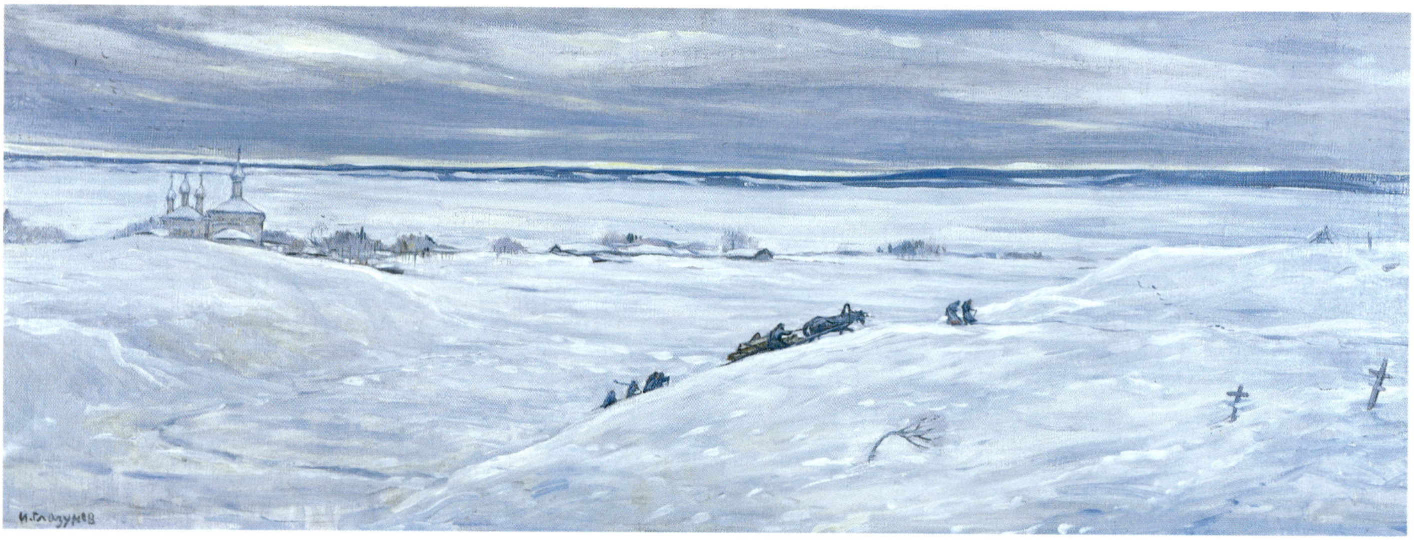

Pl. 25 *The Procession*, 1978
Oil on canvas, $21^{1}/_{8} \times 55^{3}/_{4}$ inches (53.6 × 141.6 cm)
Collection of The Menninger Foundation, gift of Mr. and Mrs. Robert McCullough of St. Charles, Illinois

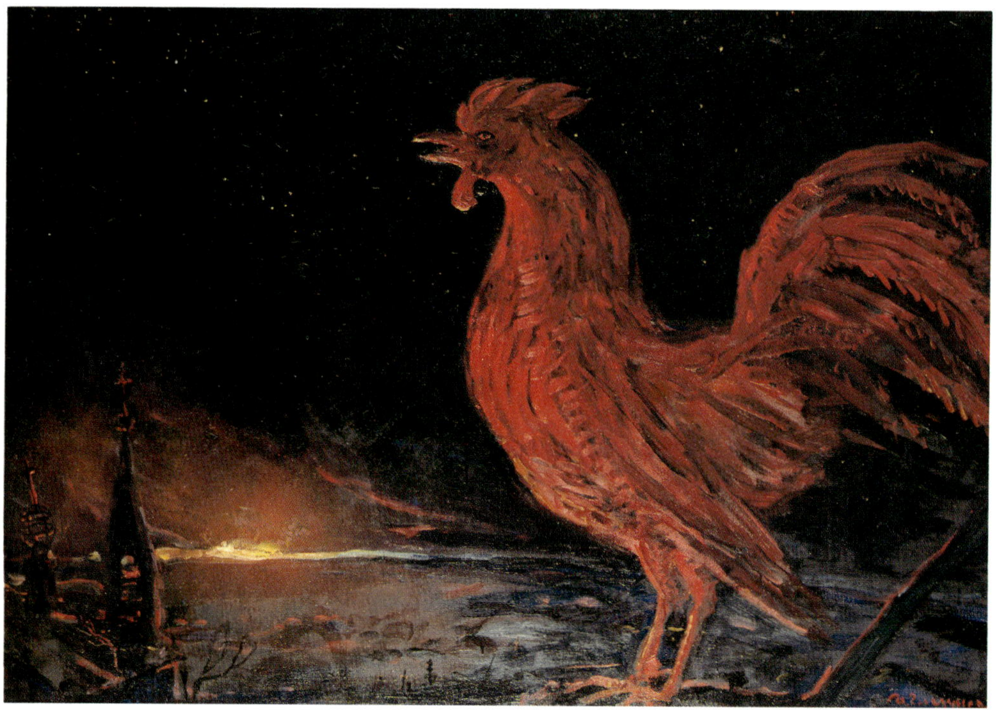

Pl. 26 *The Third Cock*, 1987
Oil on canvas, $39^{3}/_{8} \times 57^{1}/_{8}$ inches (99.7 × 144.8 cm)
Bernard and Miriam Landman

Francisco Infante

BORN 1943

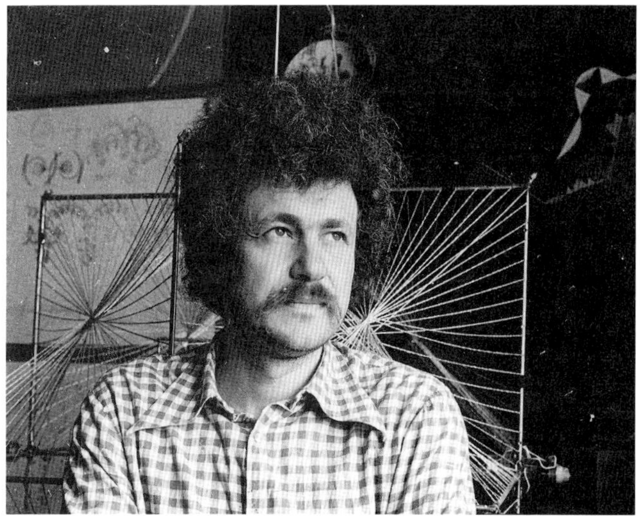

Art is necessary in order for us to have an opportunity to straighten ourselves out, to become vertical. And this is whether you are a creator or a consumer. Because to see a picture, for instance, requires one's own effort, as it requires one's own effort to create a picture.

The artistic nature of the creator helps to establish the language of art and thereby gives a metaphysical dimension to life, through art.

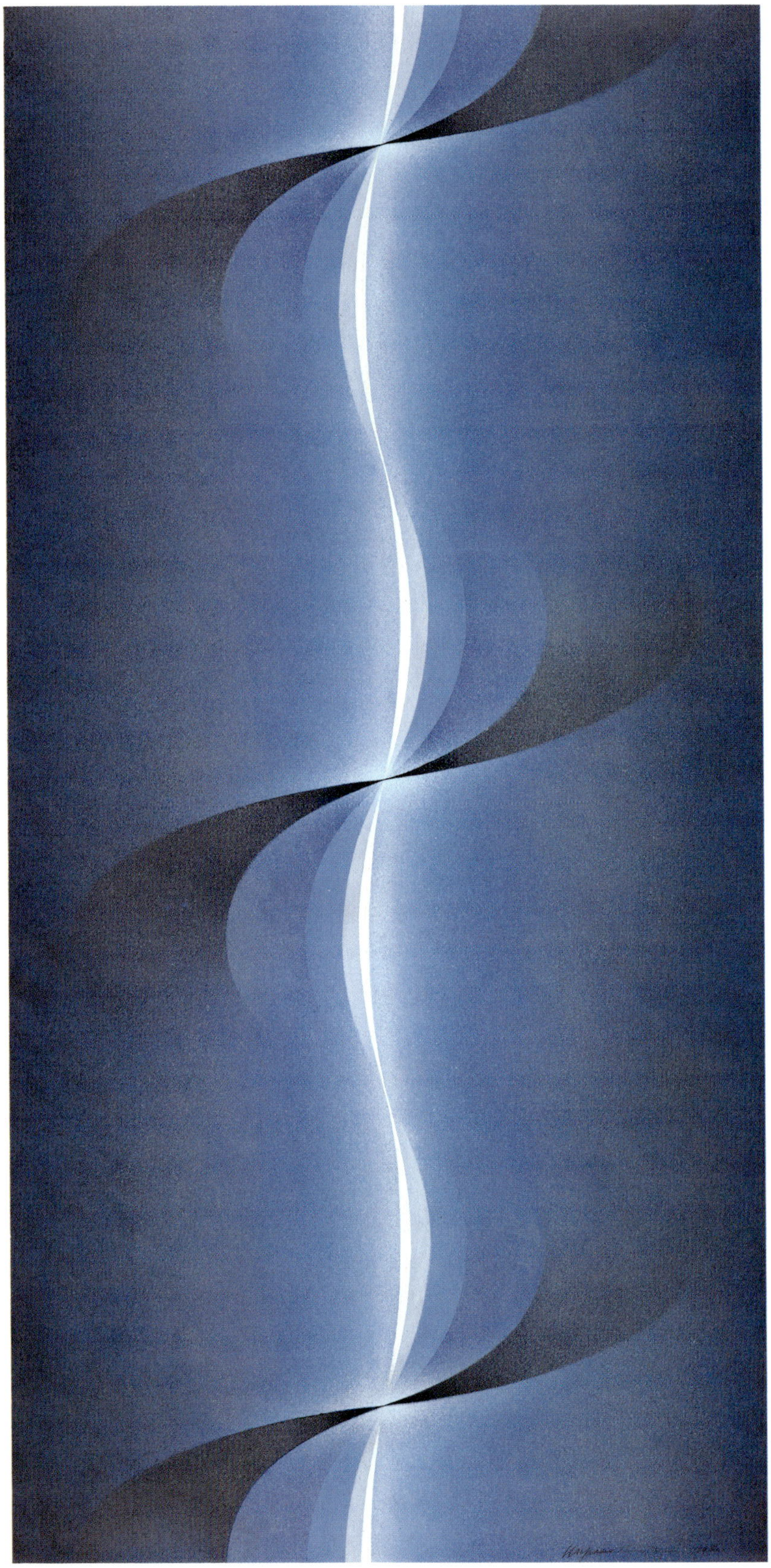

Pl. 30 *Spirals*, 1965
Tempera on paper, 40¾ × 20¼ inches (103.4 × 51.6 cm)
Private Collection

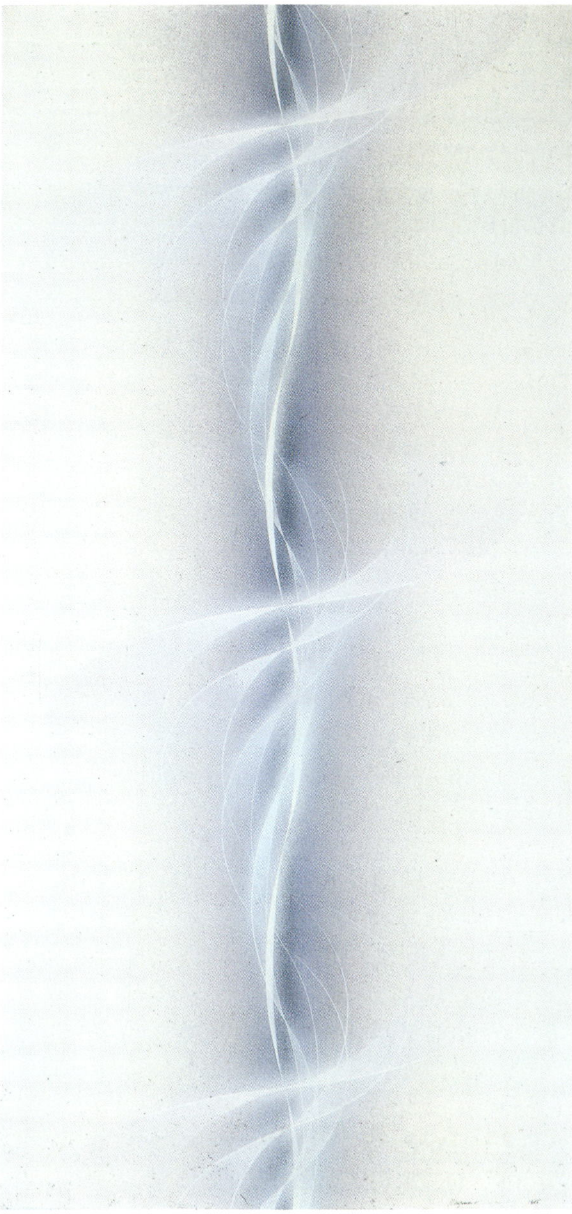

Pl. 31 *Spirals*, 1965
Tempera on paper, $40^{1}/_{4} \times 20^{1}/_{8}$ inches (102 × 51 cm)
Private Collection

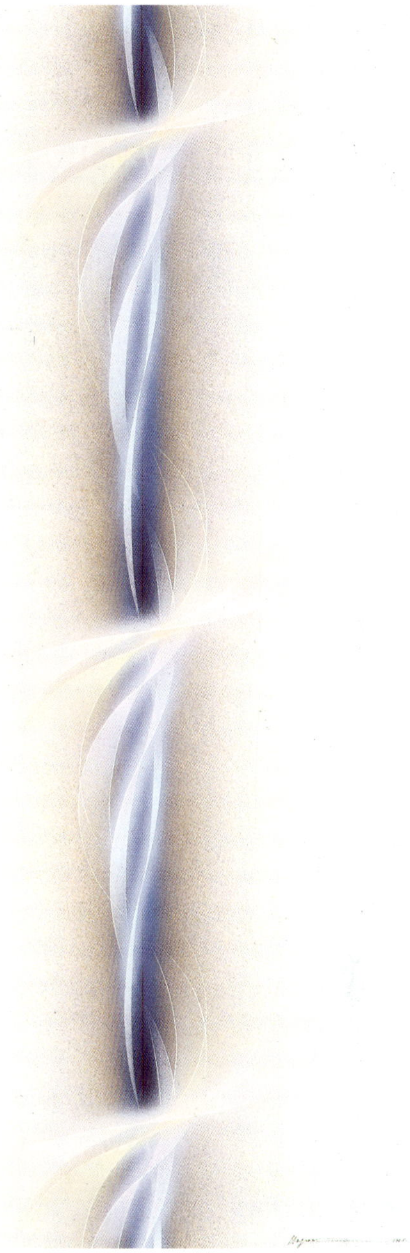

Pl. 32 *Spirals*, 1965
Tempera on paper, $40^{1}/_{2} \times 20^{1}/_{4}$ inches (103 × 51.5 cm)
Private Collection

Ilya Kabakov

BORN 1933

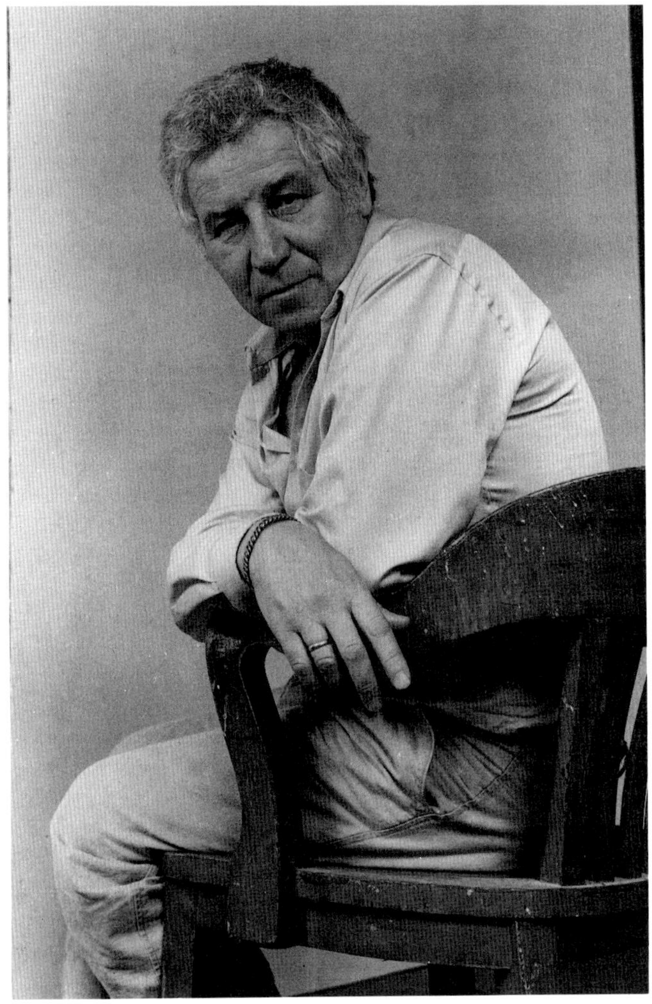

I do not see the world in images. For me in everything that happens the important thing is its meaning, its reason or absurdity, the paradox of this or that phenomenon, or perhaps something else which I as yet do not quite understand.

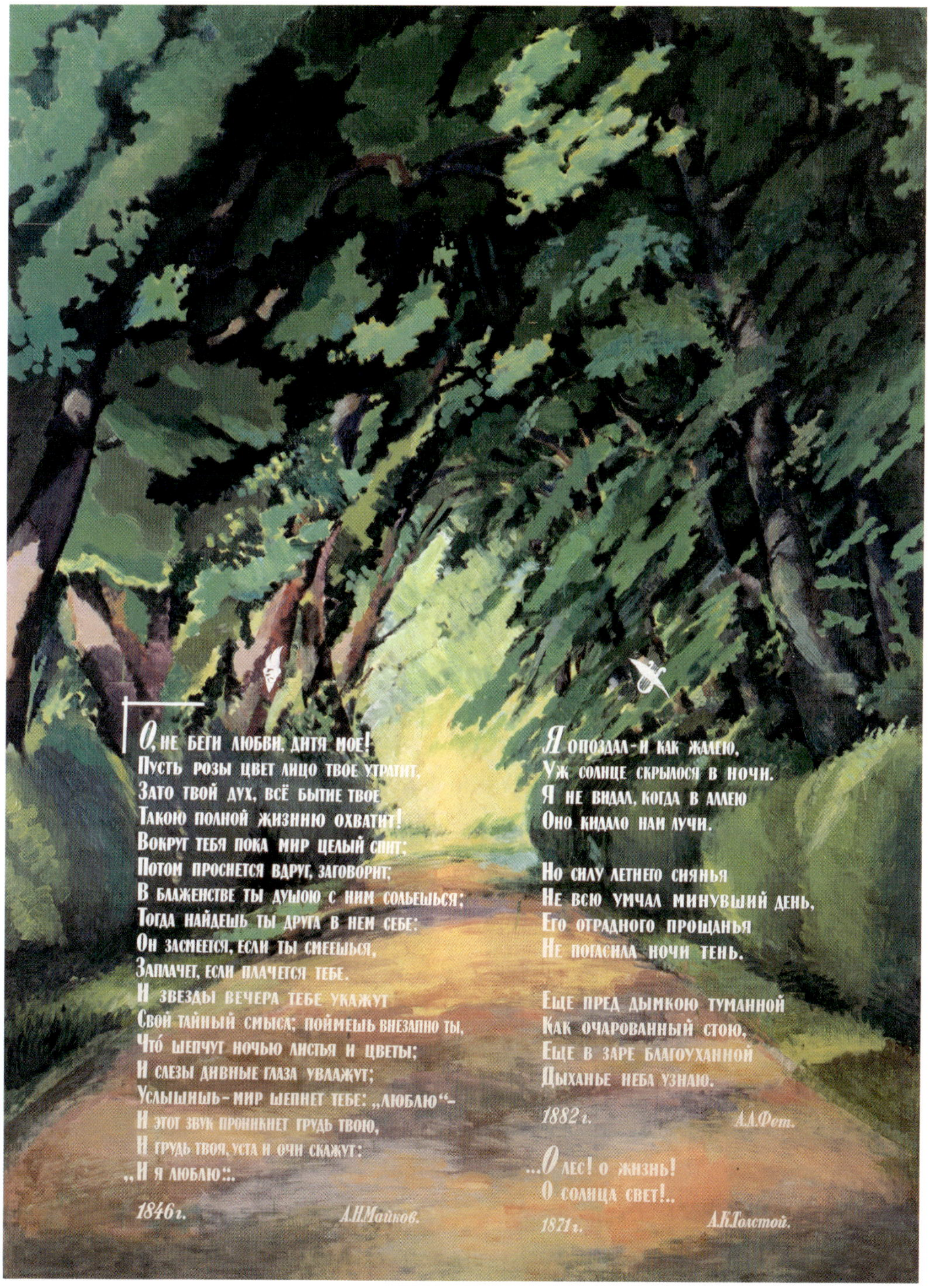

Pl. 33 *Path*, 1982
Enamel paint on cardboard, $74^{3}/_{4} \times 102^{3}/_{8}$ inches (190 × 260 cm)
Mireille Levy, Lausanne, Switzerland

Viktor Kalinin

BORN 1946

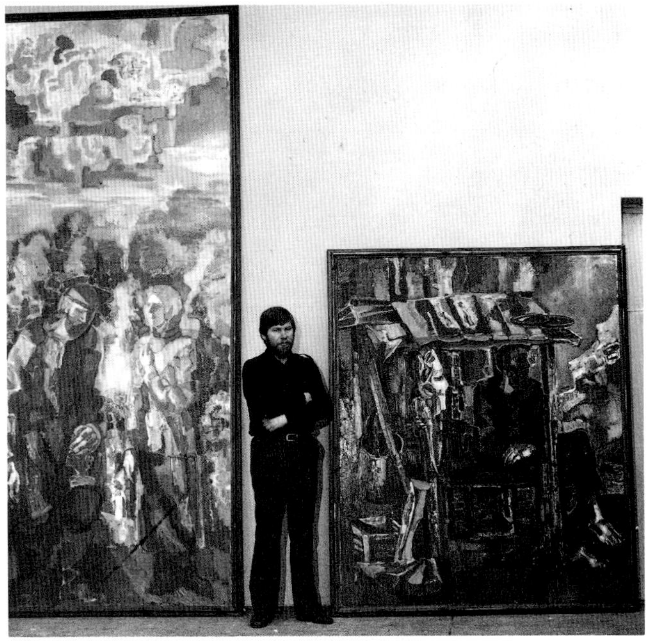

I imagine the space of a picture as an ancestral nest. The characters of my pictures sometimes experience an attraction towards [the picture], sometimes strive to get away from it. This determines the thematic, plastic, and color structure of one or another of my works. The motifs of the road, bridge, gate, home, hearth, are important to me.

The degree of closeness among people and the degree of their dissociation; the striving to confide in someone wiser, more enlightened; and to find the inner strength for an independent step; reflection before making a choice—these comprise the schematic list of states which I would like to express in my works. In order [for me] to enter these states, not only do special signs and orientations acquire importance but also the dream state and reminiscence, in which man finds anew that which seemed to have been lost forever.

I love to paint large groups of people, seeing others off, welcoming them back, and in processions. I want to express the creative restlessness of people in their search for harmony and justice, and also their illuminations, their losses, and their hopes along the way.

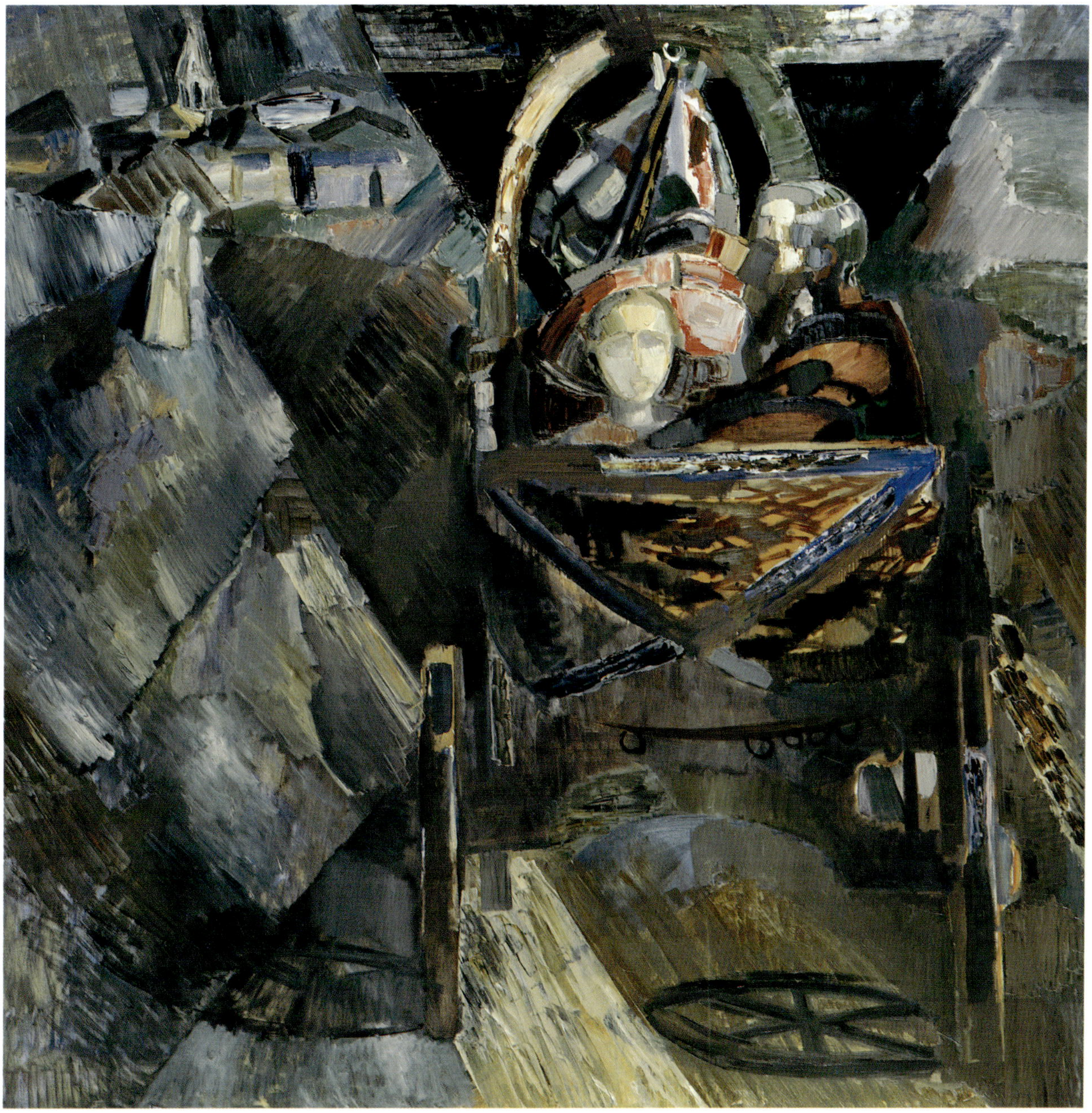

Pl. 34 *The Return,* 1988
Oil on canvas, 78¾ × 78¾ inches (200 × 200 cm)
Courtesy of the Artist

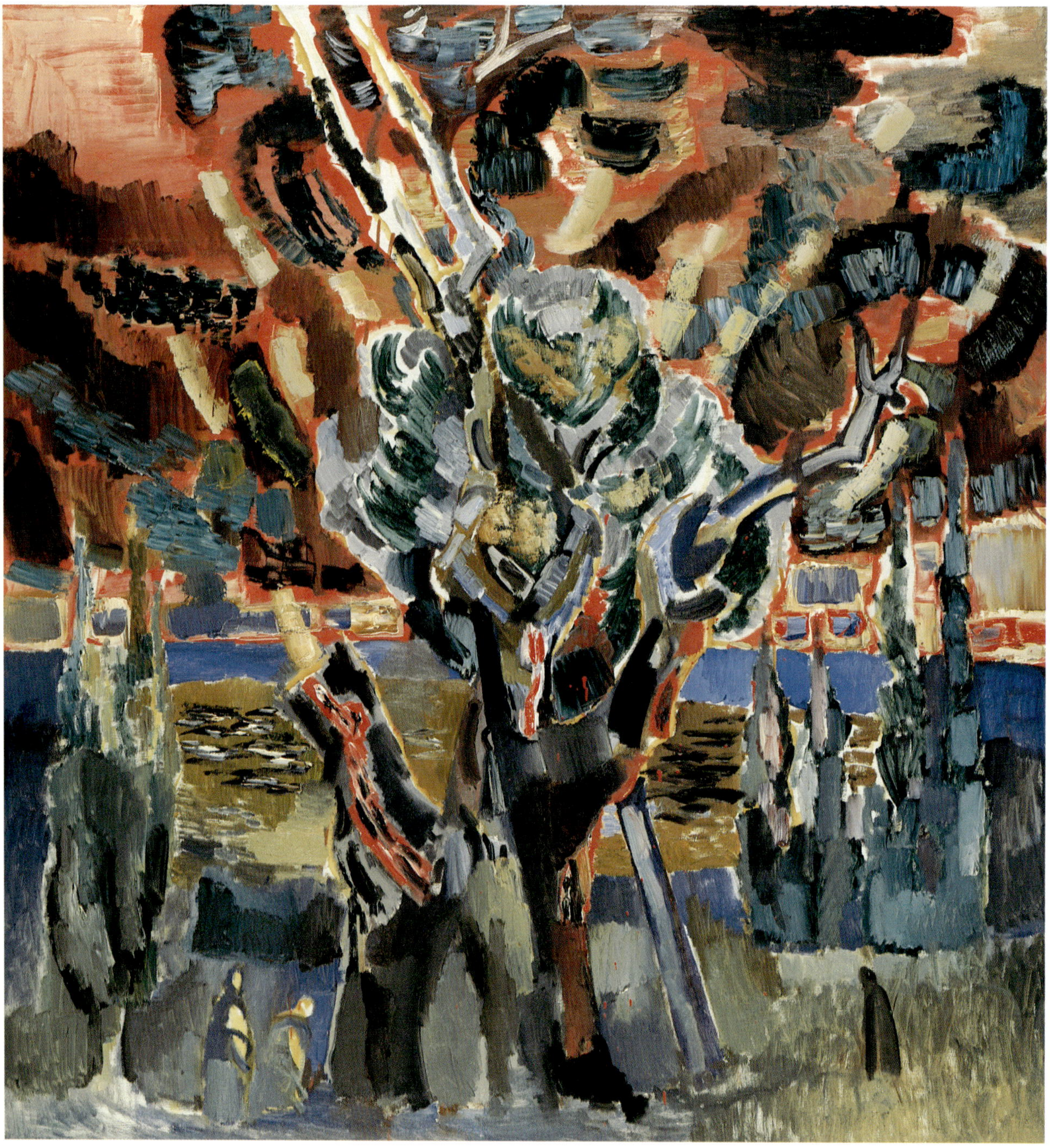

Pl. 35 *Tree (Oak of Mamre)*, 1989
Oil on canvas, 70 3/4 × 67 inches (180 × 170 cm)
Courtesy of the Artist

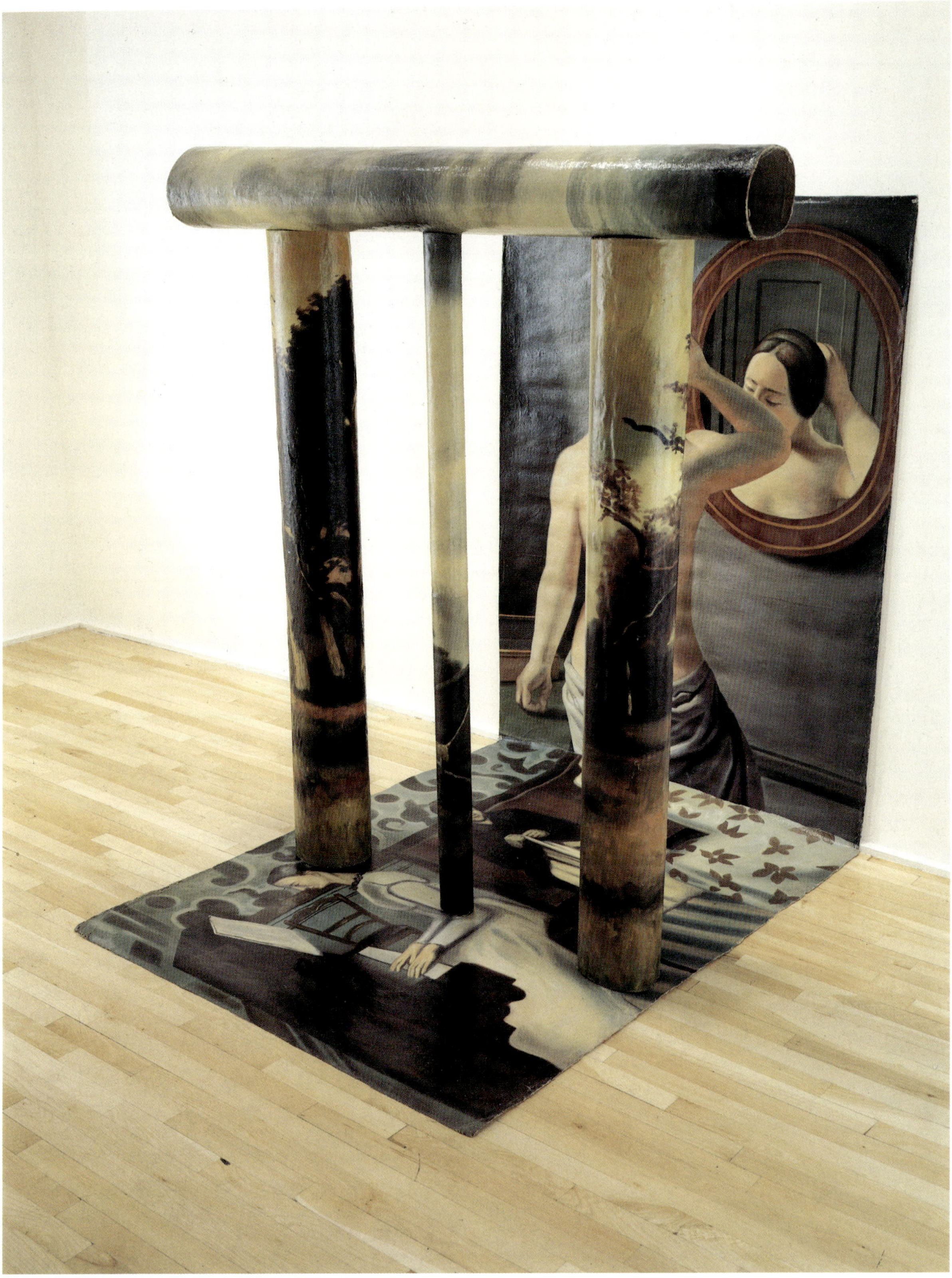

Pl. 40 *Construction*, 1985–1986
Oil on canvas, 72 × 96 × 72 inches (180 × 240 × 180 cm)
Collection of Nancy and Norton Dodge

Igor Kopystiansky

Valeri Lukka

Born 1945

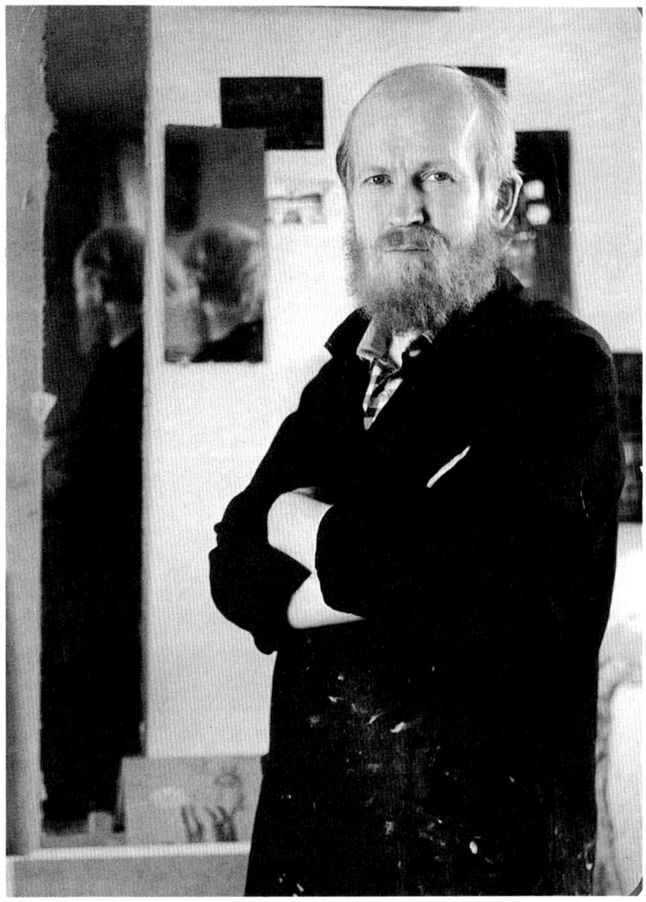

Today the situation in our art reminds one of a ball of thread which is torn apart: it doesn't matter which end you pull, it is torn.

It is a paradox, but our present [art] is not determined by the past. We have neither form nor style (and, after all, form is the artist's fate). Moreover, we have neither memory nor history. And God help us to connect the torn-apart ends or at least throw our stone into the sleepy surface of the swamp. It is important to make ripples on the surface.

If there is any meaning at all to what we are doing, it is more than anything in the intonation of that muttering or shouting which echoes from our pit and which cannot be made up or faked. However, that is a category that more likely is moral, rather than aesthetic.

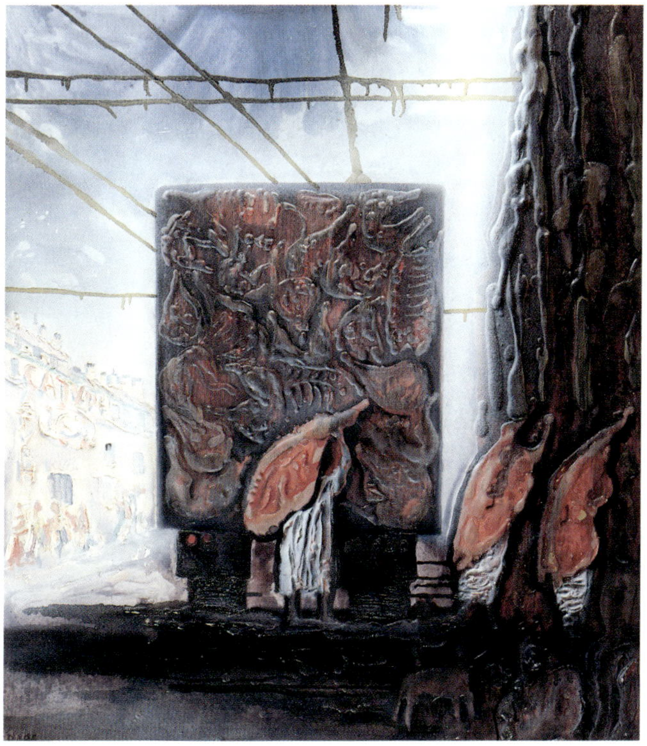

Pl. 41 *Unloading Meat on Sadovaya Street,* 1985
Oil and tempera on masonite, $36^{1}/_{2} \times 32^{1}/_{4}$ inches (93 × 82 cm)
Courtesy of the Artist

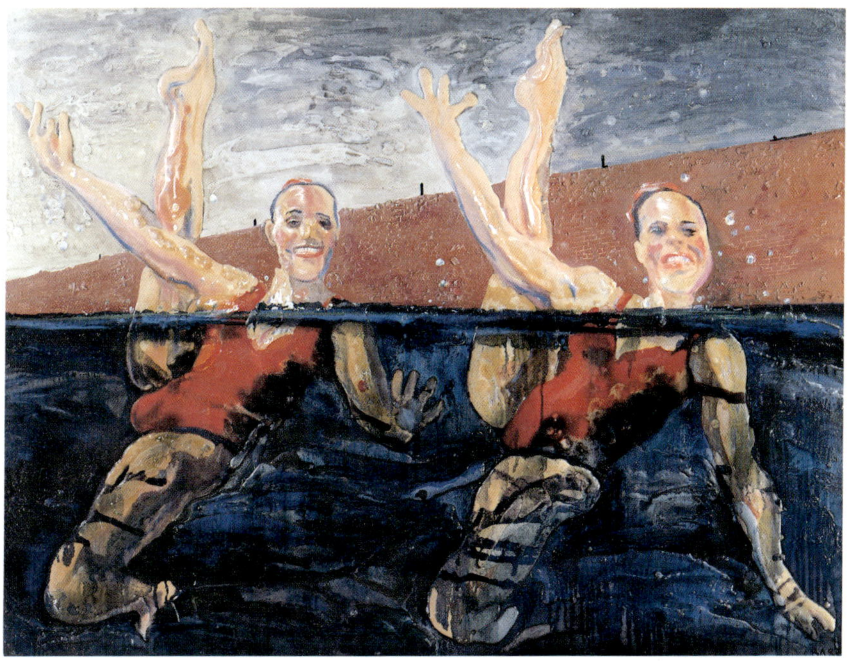

Pl. 42 *American Swimming,* 1987
Oil and tempera on masonite, $36^{1}/_{2} \times 48$ inches (92.5 × 122 cm)
Courtesy of the Artist

Tatiana Nazarenko

Born 1944

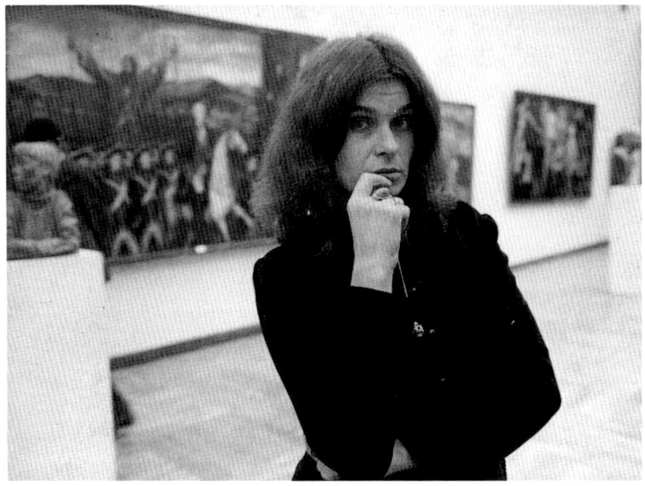

F. Tyutchev's lines are dear to me: "Know to live within yourself. A whole world is in your soul." It is precisely that "whole world" which I try to express in my paintings. I do not like to explain my goals, my intentions, my philosophy. All that can be found in my work—despair, the experience of old age, loneliness, betrayal—these are the main themes of my work. My strongest impressions are of our difficult reality.

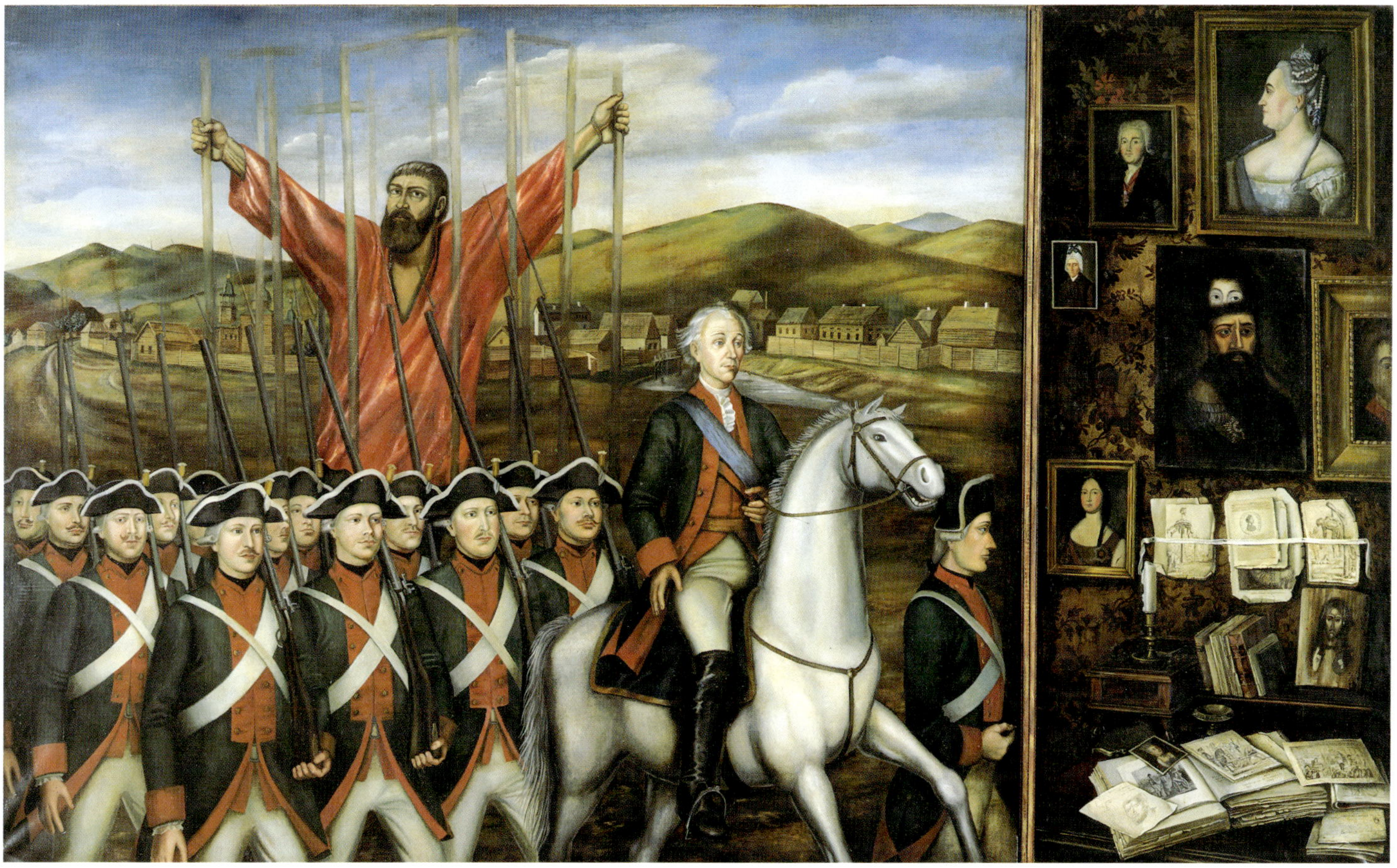

Pl. 43 *Pugachev,* 1980
Oil on canvas, 71 × 118 inches (180 × 300 cm)
Courtesy of the Artist

Vladimir Nemukhin

Born 1925

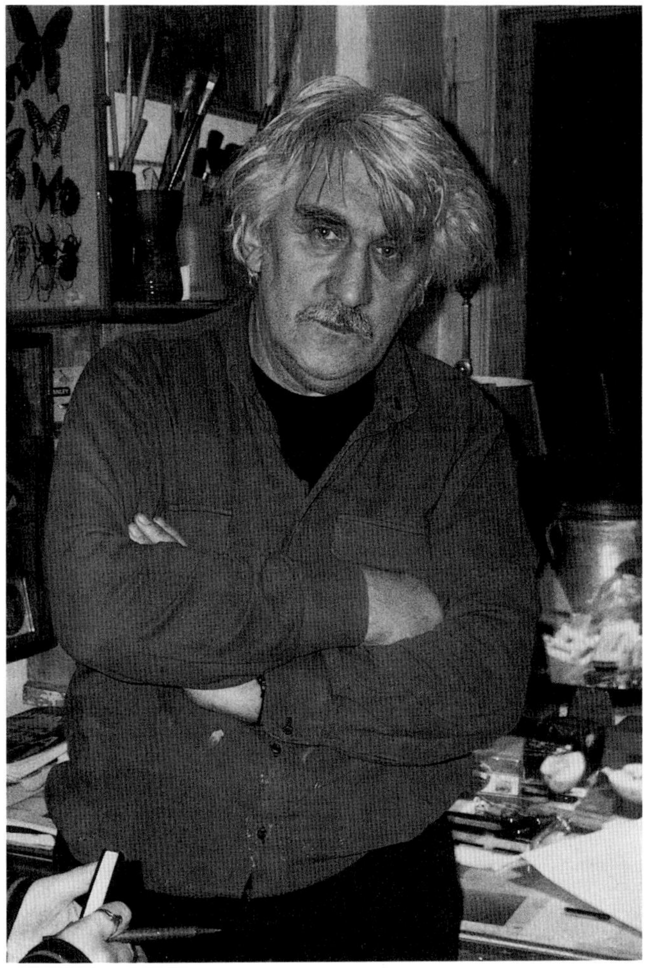

I did not choose the playing card; rather, the playing card chose me. The card, which is the object of the game and the imagination, cuts through the plane of a picture and imparts motion to the painting surface, evokes recollections.

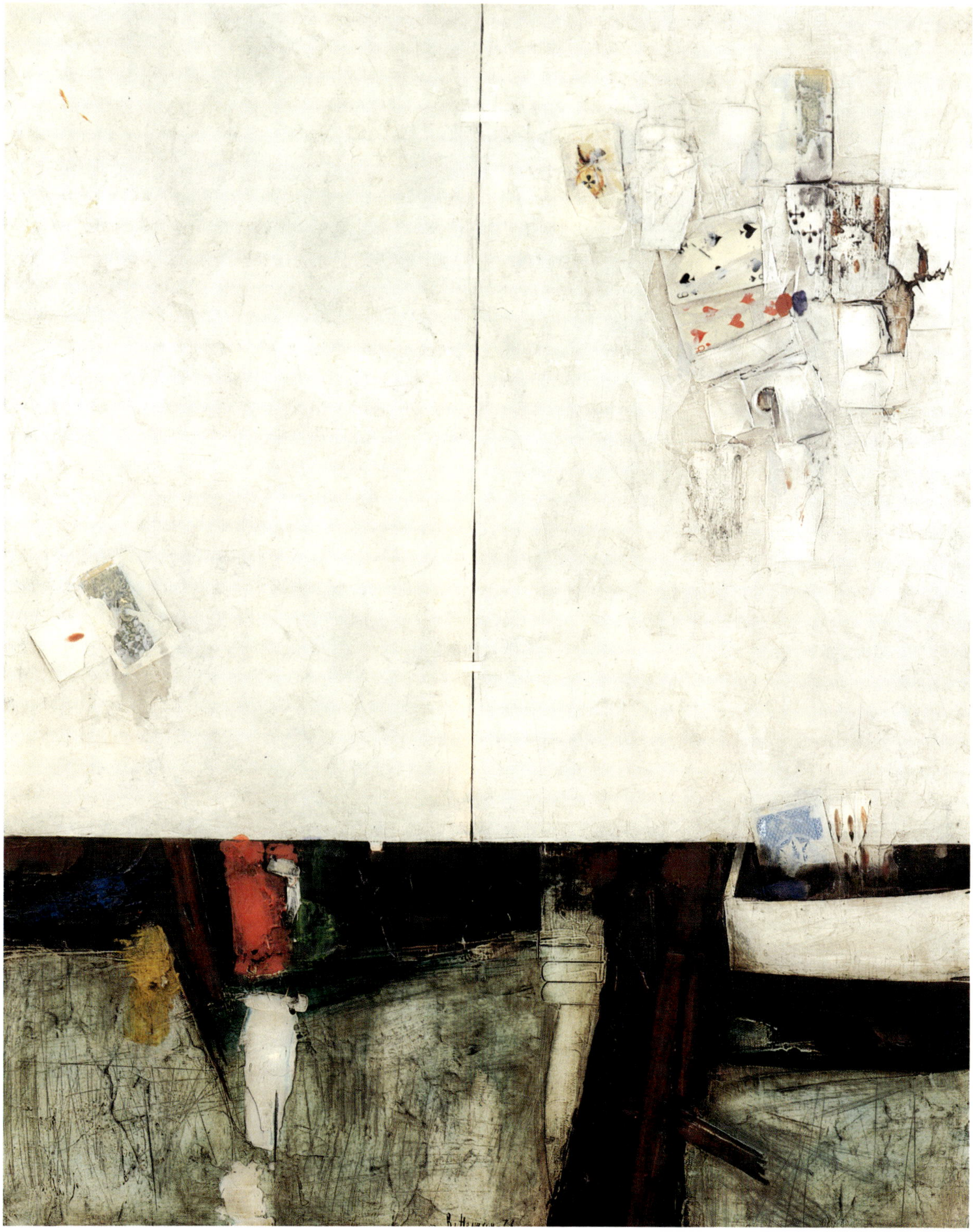

Pl. 44 *Card Table 4*, 1973
Mixed media, $39^{1}/_{2} \times 31^{1}/_{2}$ inches (100.3 × 80 cm)
Collection of Nancy and Norton Dodge

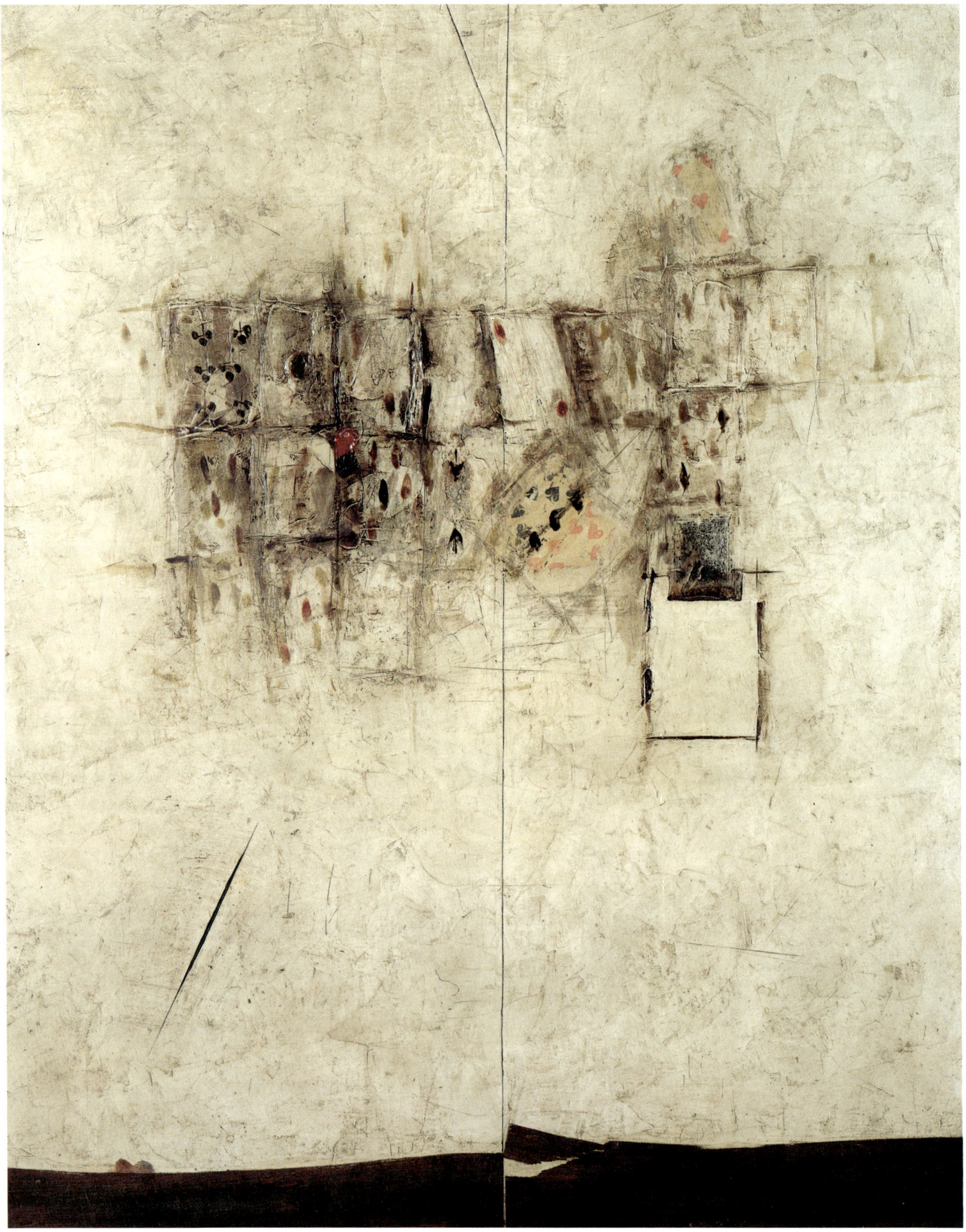

Pl. 45 *Patience*, 1974
Mixed media, 39 1/2 × 31 1/2 inches (100.3 × 80 cm)
Collection of Nancy and Norton Dodge

Vladimir Nemukhin

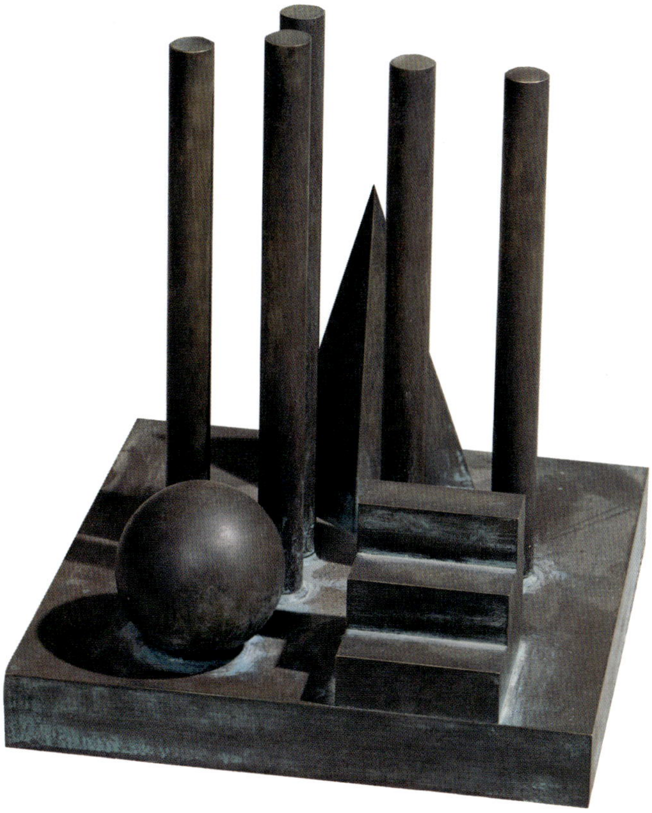

Pl. 46 *Dedicated to Weisberg*, 1986
Bronze, $10^1/_2 \times 11 \times 11$ inches ($26 \times 27 \times 27$ cm)
Courtesy of the Artist

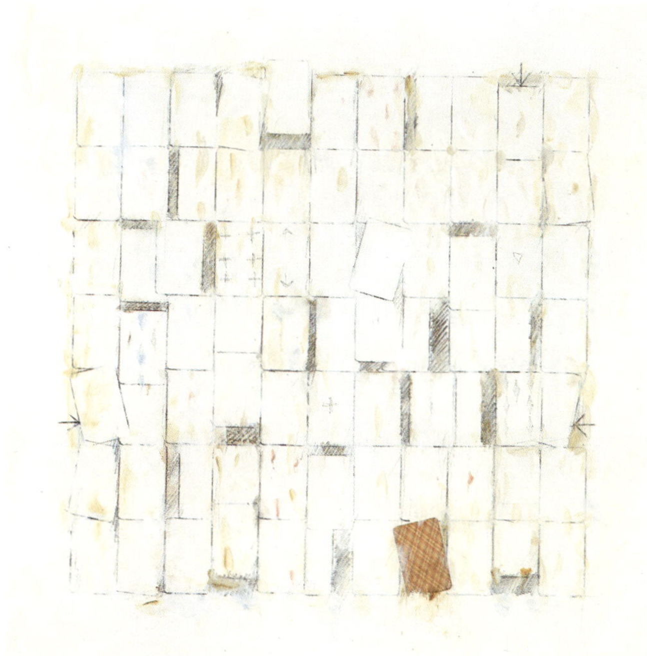

Pl. 47 *Patience*, 1989
Mixed media on canvas, $39^3/_8 \times 39^3/_8$ inches (100×100 cm)
Courtesy of the Artist

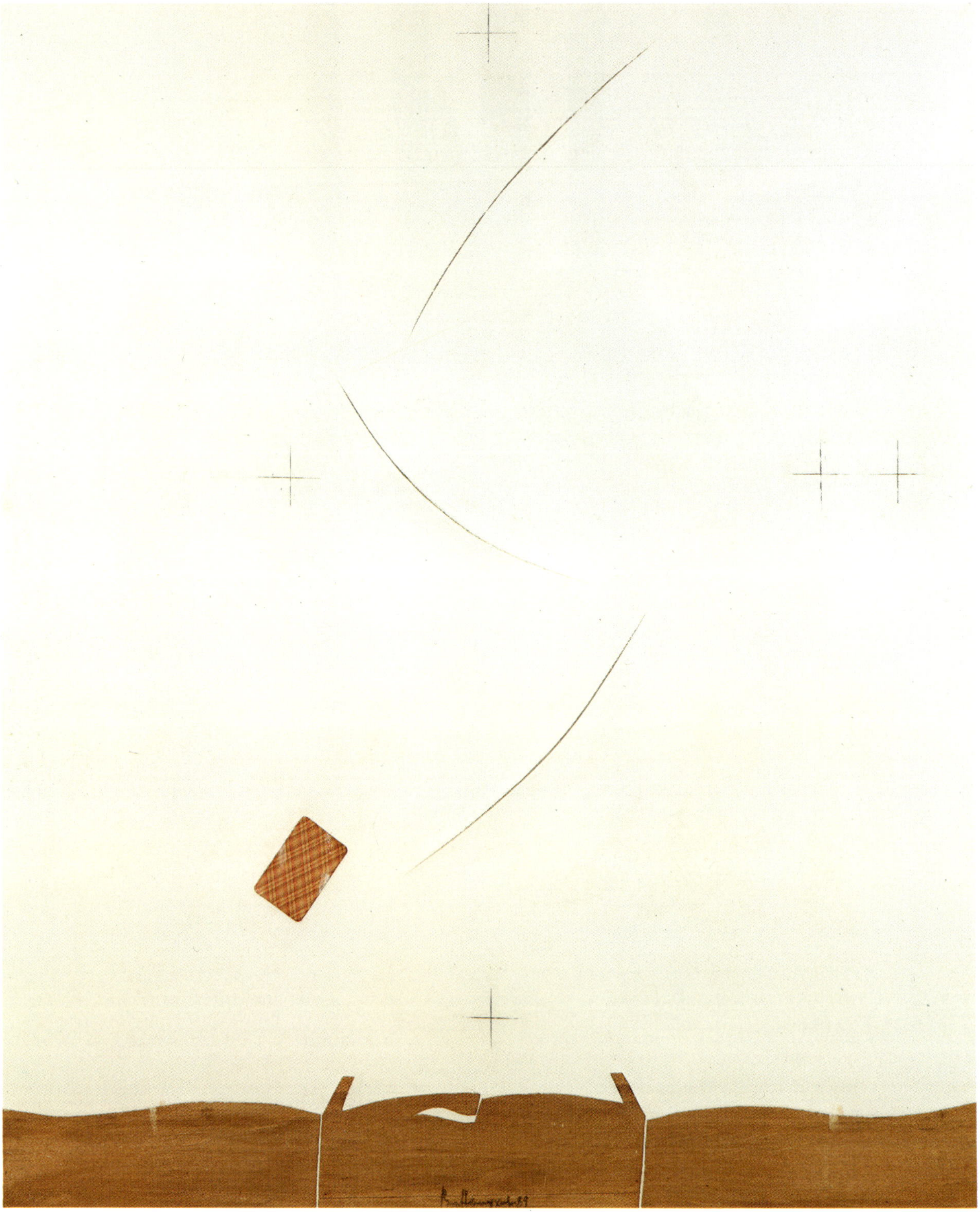

Pl. 48 *Still Life with Card*, 1989
Mixed media on canvas, 47 1/4 × 39 3/8 inches (120 × 100 cm)
Courtesy of the Artist

VLADIMIR NEMUKHIN

NATALIA NESTEROVA

BORN 1944

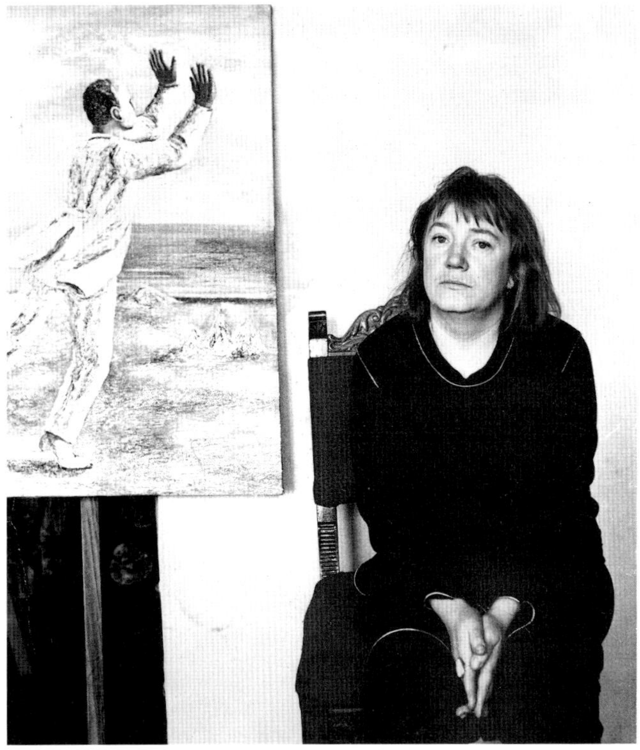

Natalia Nesterova has said the poem "The Appeal" by Rudyard Kipling best expresses her feeling about her art.

If I have given you delight
  By aught that I have done,
Let me lie quiet in that night
  Which shall be yours anon:

And for the little, little, span
  The dead are borne in mind,
Seek not to question other than
  The books I leave behind.

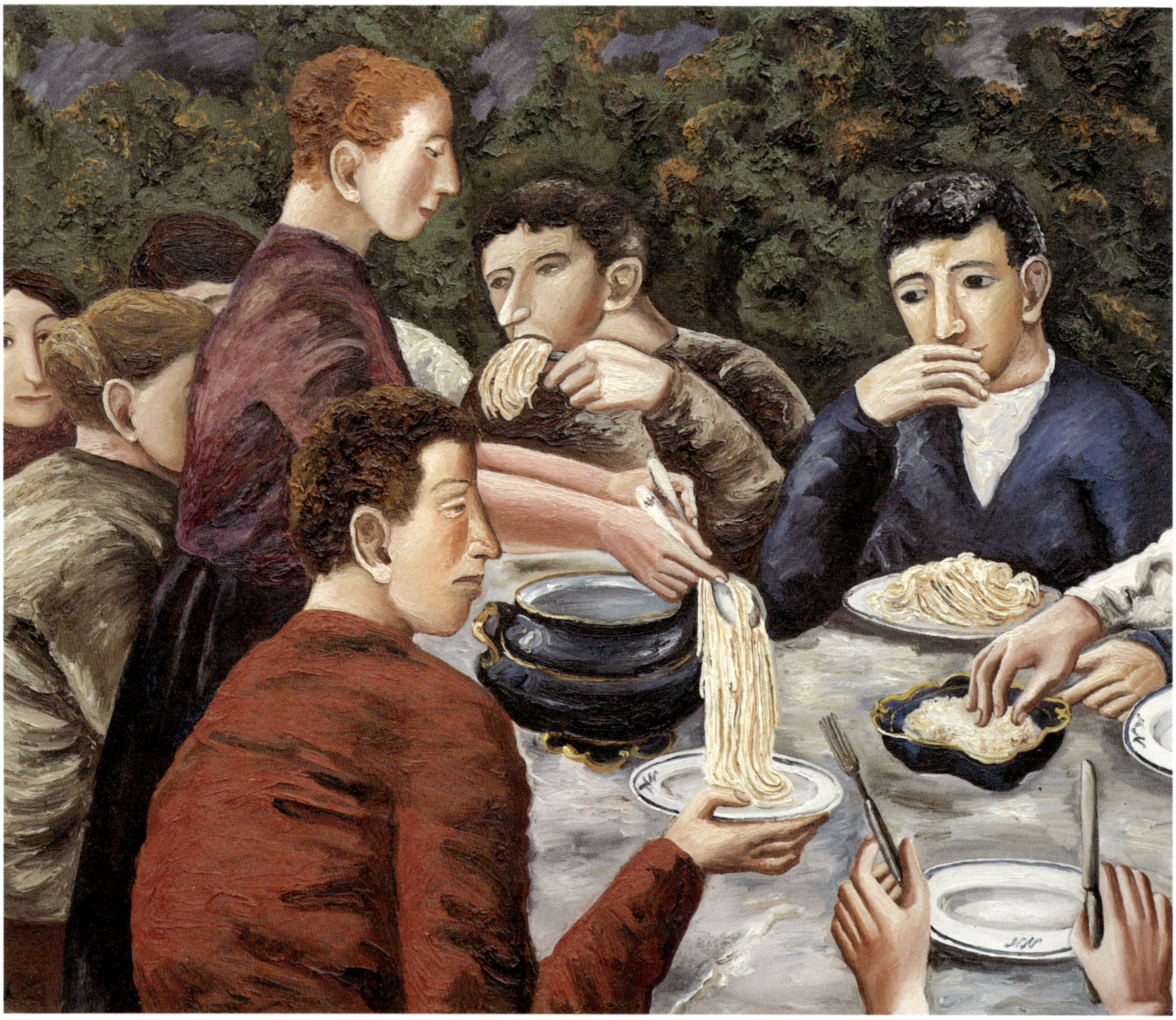

Pl. 49 *Spaghetti*, 1985
Oil on canvas, 39 3/8 × 47 1/4 inches (100 × 120 cm)
Collection of Nancy and Norton Dodge

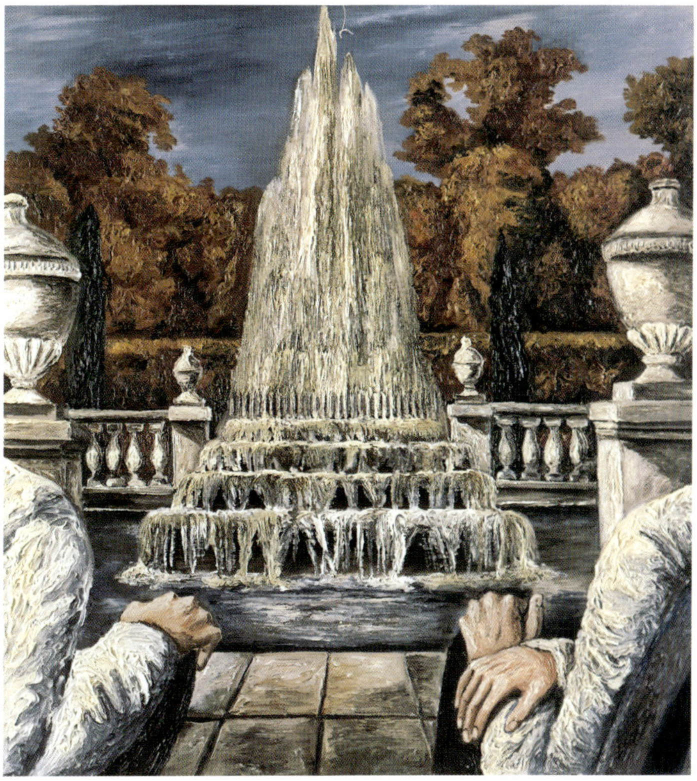

Pl. 50 *Petrodvorets*, 1984
Oil on canvas, $38^{1}/_{4} \times 35$ inches (97×89 cm)
Montreal Museum of Fine Arts, purchase, bequest of Harold Lawson, bequest of Miss Marjorie Caverhill, bequest of Harry W. Thorpe, and Mona Prentice Funds

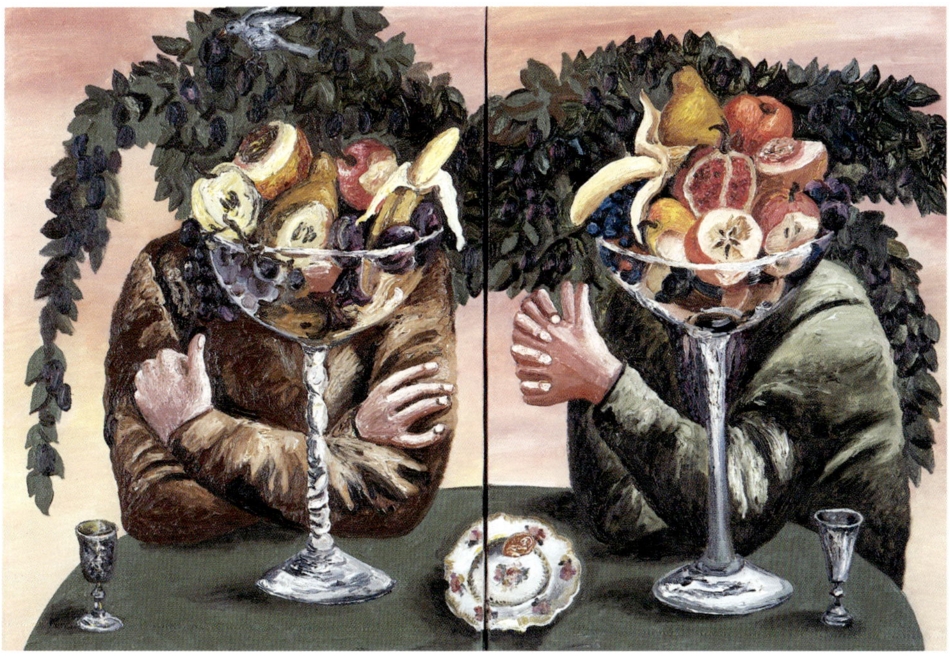

Pl. 51 *Bird on Plum*, 1988
Oil on canvas, $31^{1}/_{2} \times 47^{1}/_{2}$ inches (78.8×118.8 cm)
Collection of Hal Bromm, New York

ANATOLI NIKICH

BORN 1918

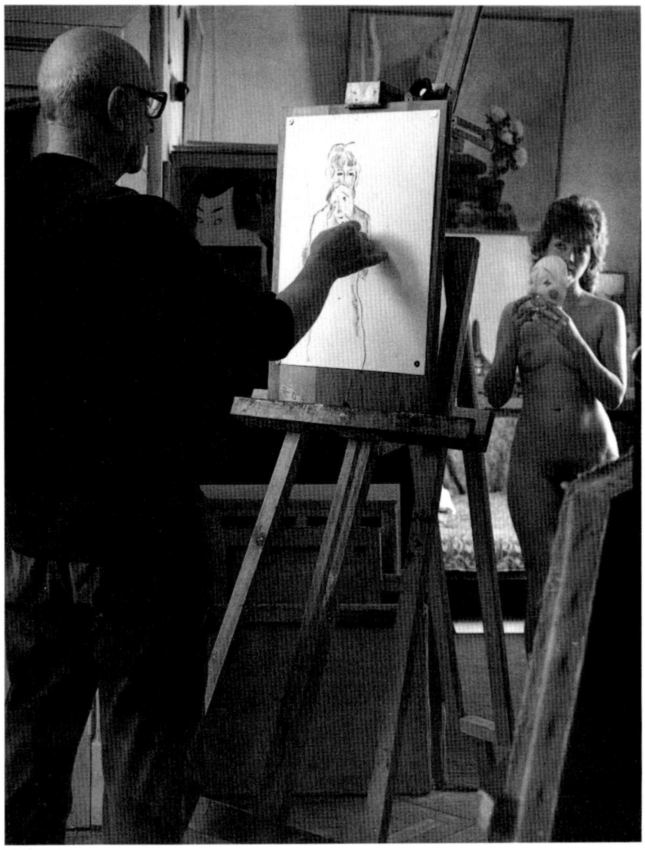

Is it possible at all to tell in words how a fresh cucumber or a watermelon smells? I think not. The same is true for painting: it is impossible to put in words, to explain. Everyone sees what he can. I would like people to be able to look at my pictures for a long time without getting irritated, simply looking.

The world of my studio, its solemn silence meets me every day when I enter it. How I love these canvases, stretchers, frames, flowers.

My work is my happiness, everyday, with brushes and paints, a gift of fate. I bless it.

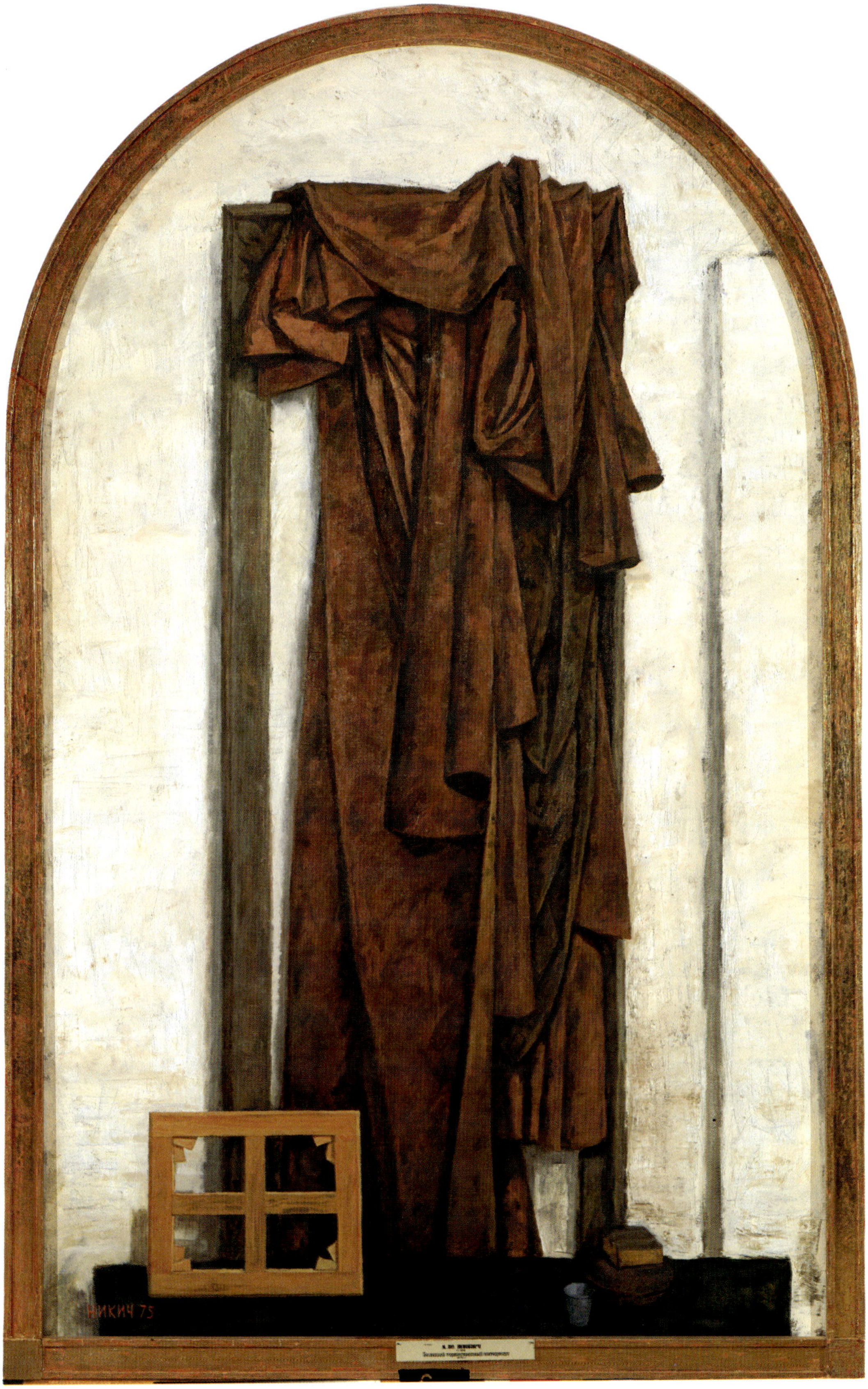

Pl. 52 *Ceremonial Still Life*, 1975
Oil on canvas, 79 × 49 inches (201 × 125 cm)
Russian Museum, Leningrad

Vladimir Ovchinnikov

Born 1941

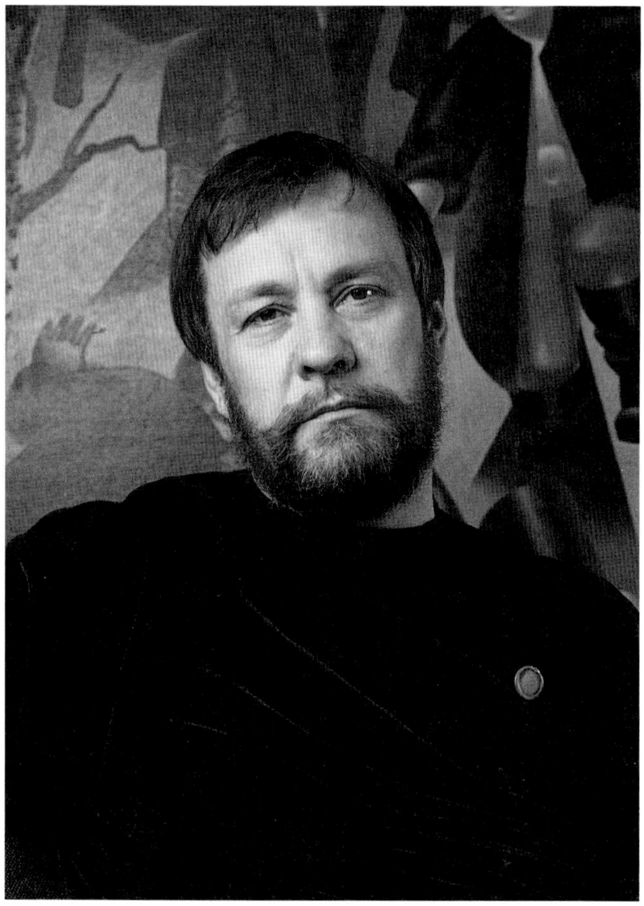

The verbal "scientific" posturing or emotional packaging in which empty picturesque or plastic ideas are presented very often turns out to be the same pretentious nonsense as the "universal" formulations of an ideology so fortunately suffering collapse.

If consciousness capable of resisting the heinousness of existence is preserved in the artist, if the word is given to him for a prayer and not for carrying out a verdict, he will be understood and accepted, no matter what language he uses.

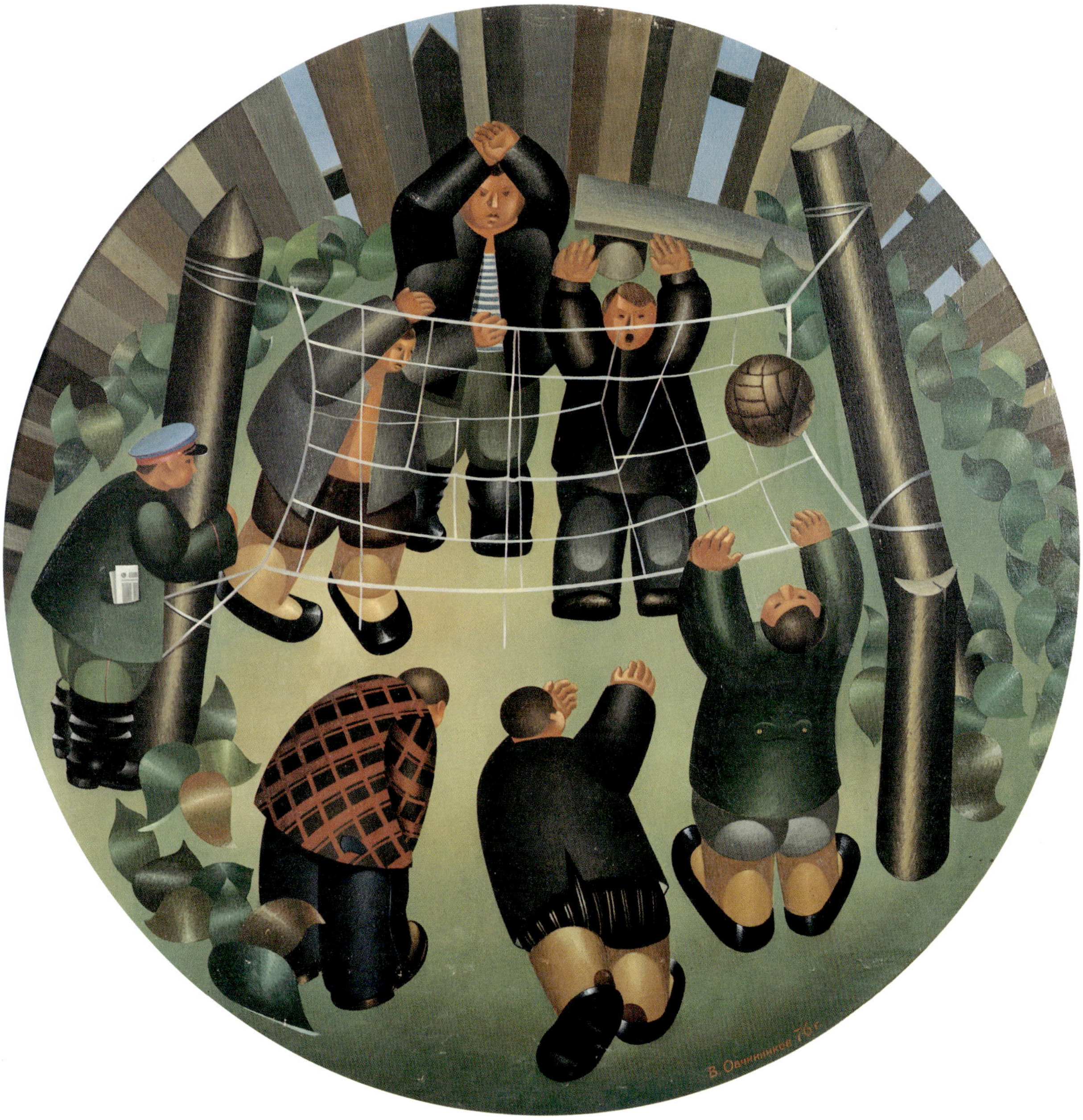

Pl. 53 *Volleyball*, 1976
Oil on canvas, Diam. 32 1/2 inches (83 cm)
Collection of Nancy and Norton Dodge

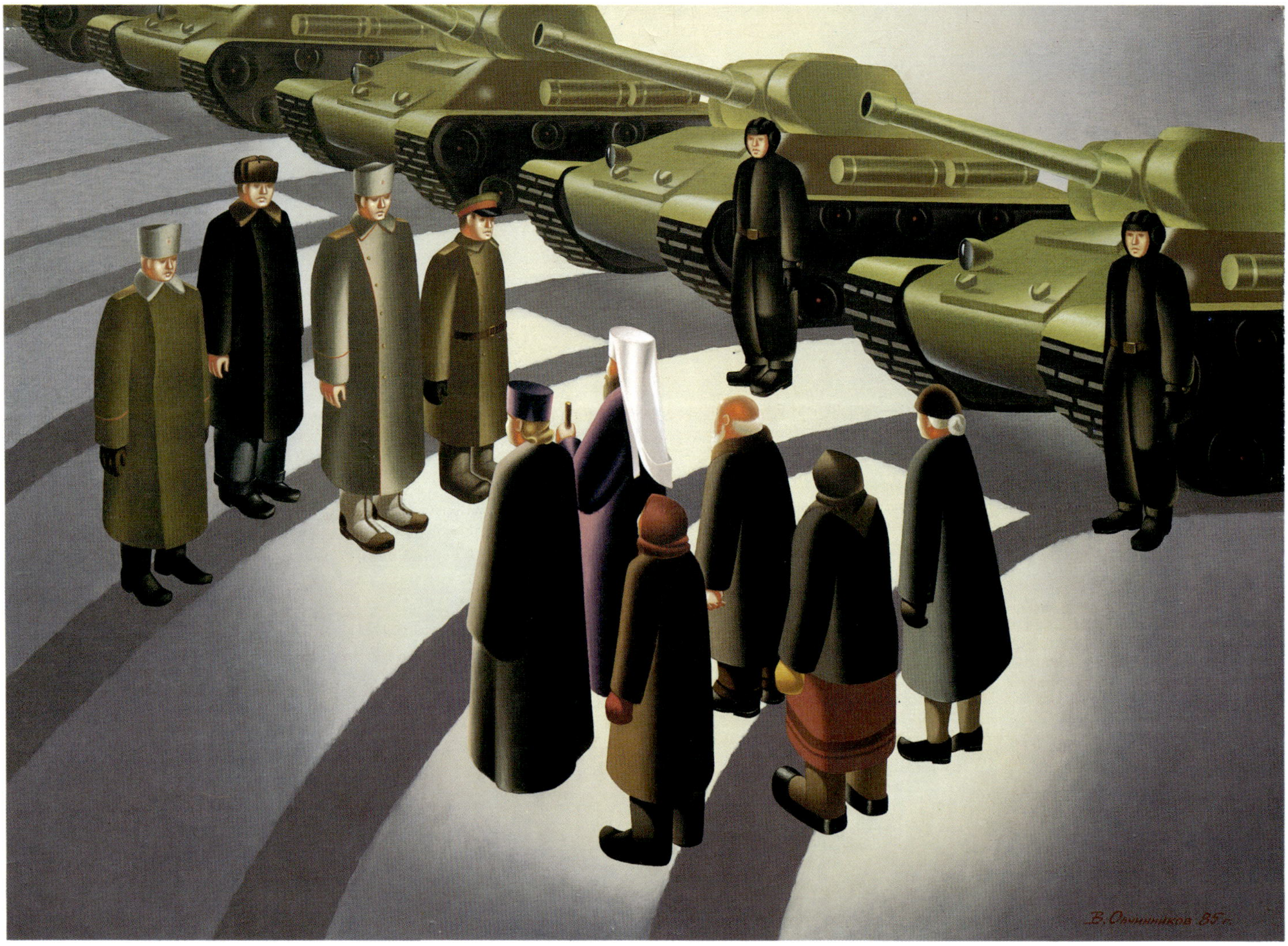

Pl. 54 *Handing Over the Command of the Dmitri Donskoi Tank Column, Which Was Established with Contributions from Believers, March 7, 1944*, 1985
Oil on canvas, 39 1/2 × 58 1/2 inches (100 × 149 cm)
Collection of Nancy and Norton Dodge

ALEXANDER PETROV

BORN 1951

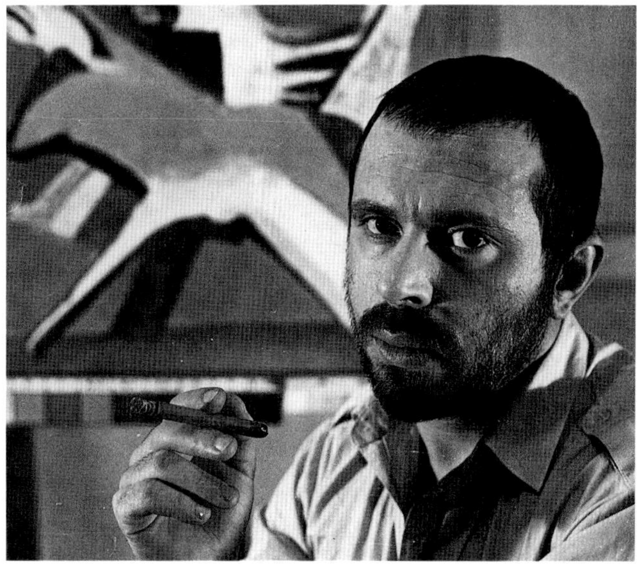

Yes. Yes. Yes. Yes. Yes. Yes. Yes. Yes. Yes. Yes. Yes. Yes. Yes. Yes. Yes. Yes. But maybe not.

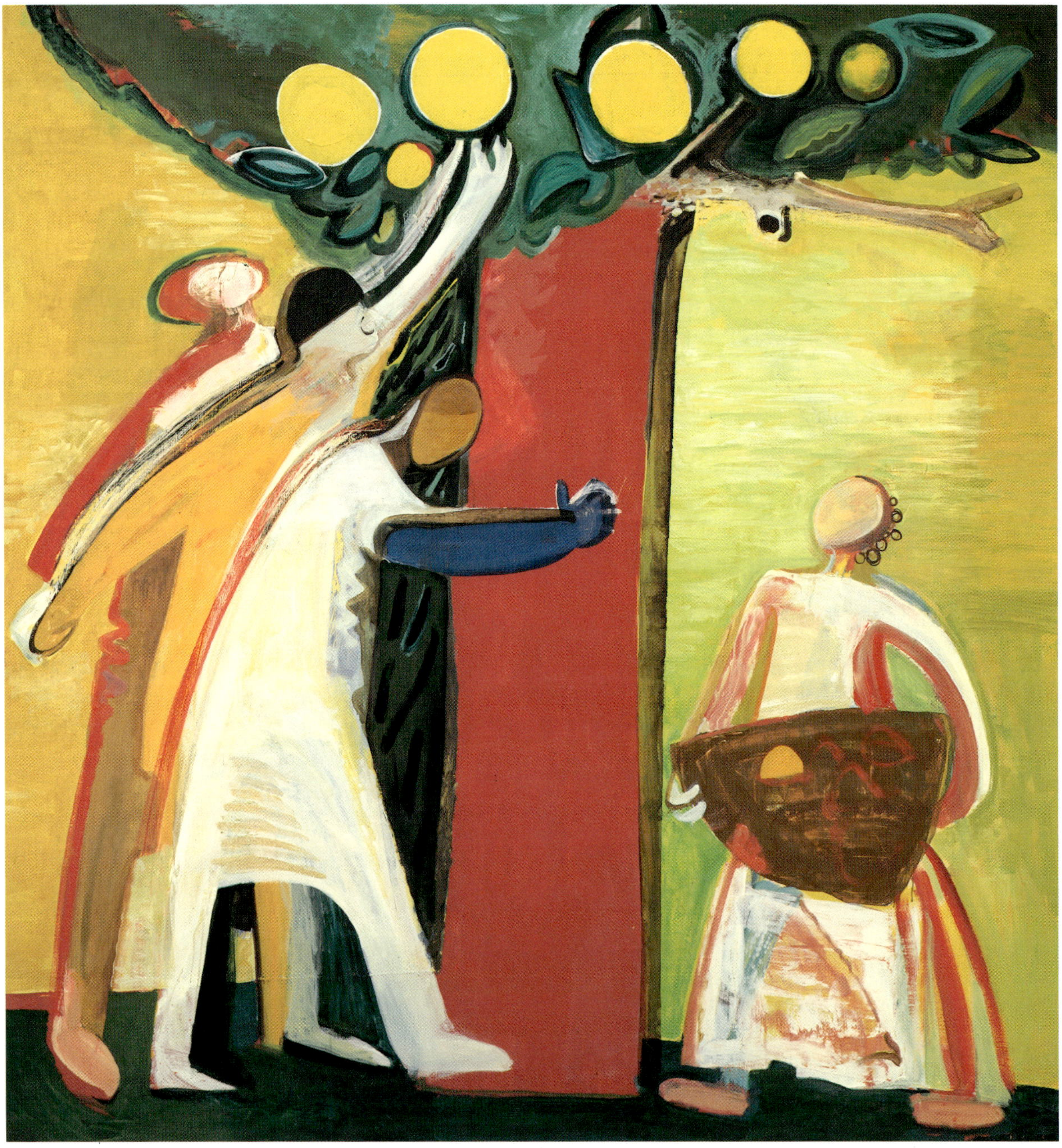

Pl. 55 *By the Tree* (half of diptych), 1989
Oil on canvas, $78^{3}/_{4} \times 74^{3}/_{4}$ inches (200×190 cm)
Courtesy of the Artist

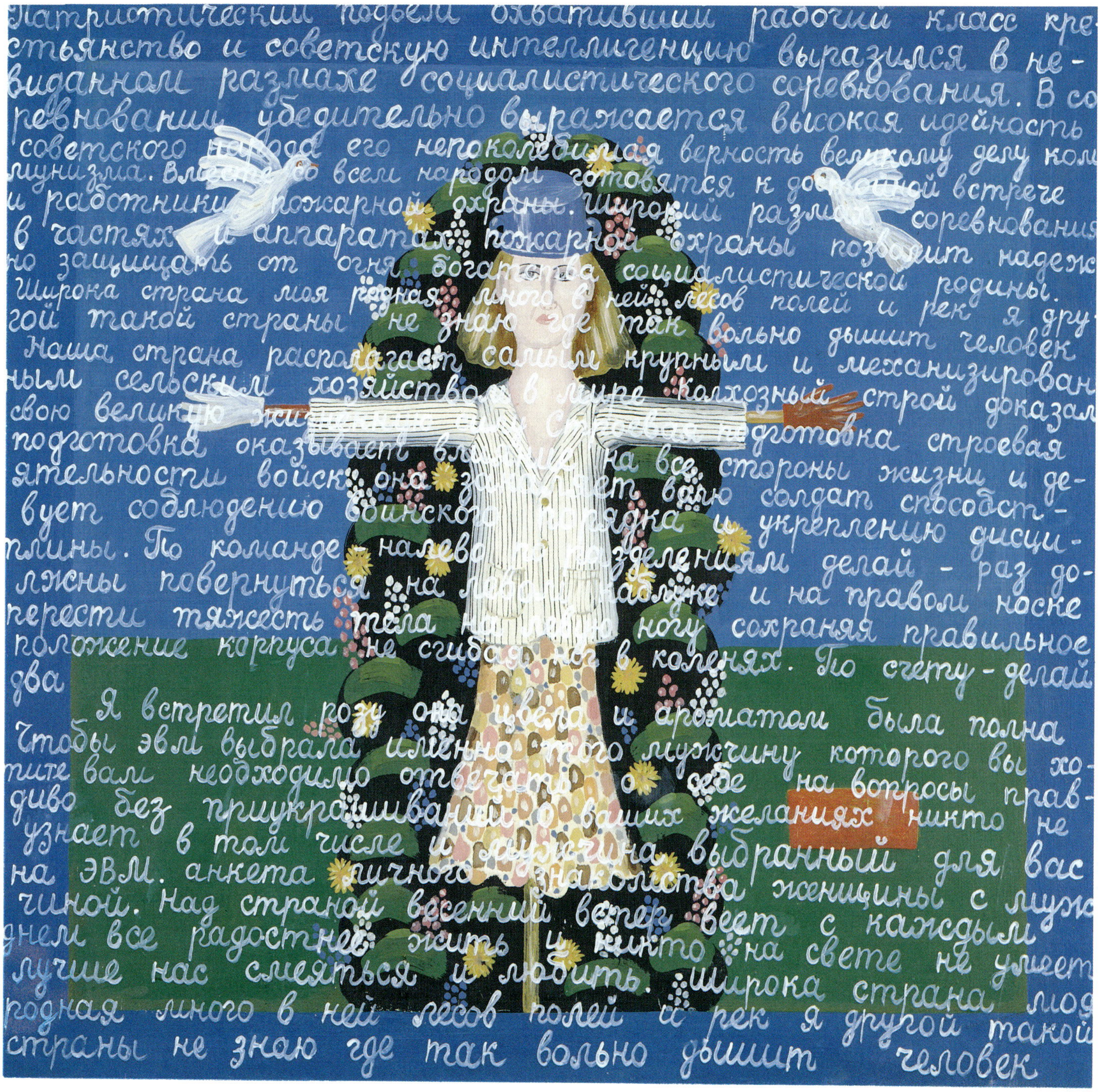

Pl. 57 *Scarecrow*, 1980
Oil on masonite, $40^{3}/_{4} \times 40$ inches (102×100 cm)
Courtesy of the Artist

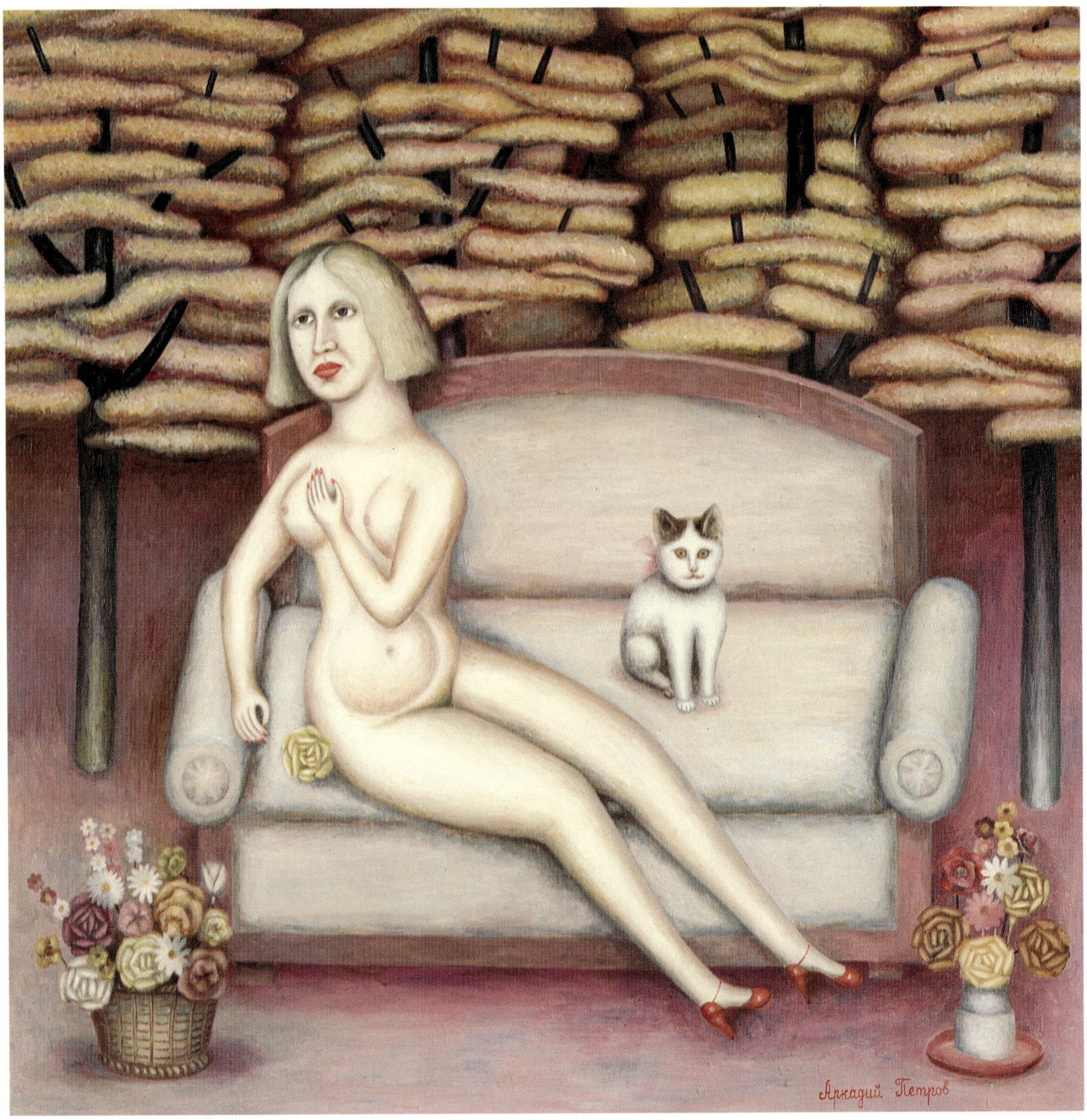

Pl. 58 *Beauty with Cat,* 1981
Oil on canvas, $46\frac{3}{4} \times 46\frac{3}{4}$ inches (117×117 cm)
Courtesy of the Artist

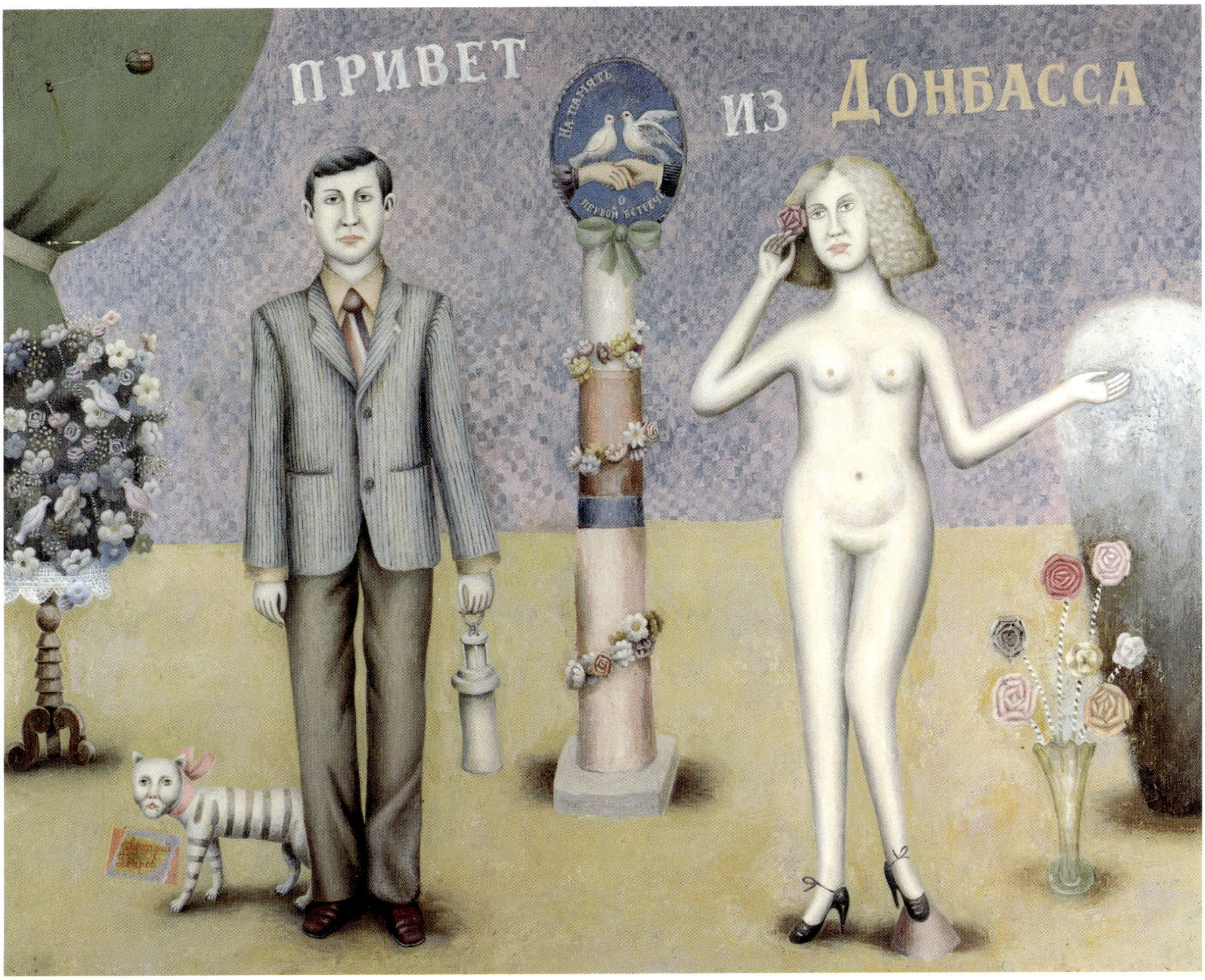

Pl. 59 *Greetings from Donbass,* 1983
Oil on canvas, 55 × 72¾ inches (140 × 185 cm)
Courtesy of the Artist

VIKTOR POPKOV

1932–1974

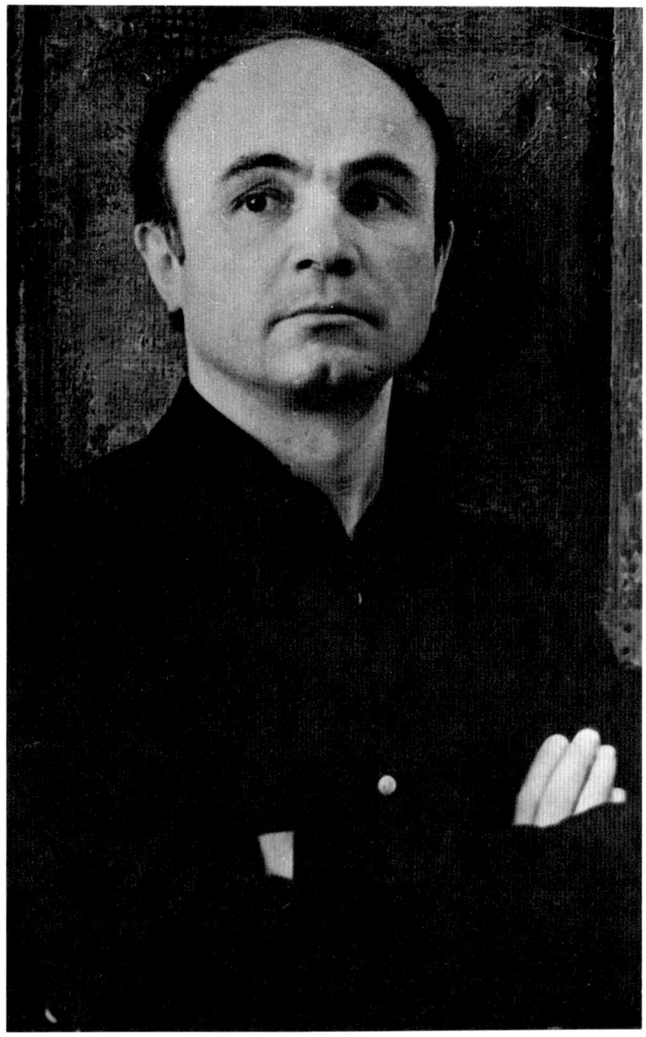

I now understand that in order to be remembered with gratitude after your death, you should have the courage to live in torment, to love joy, laughter, health, all that is beautiful, strong, alive, and everything that moves, the body, thought, the soul. And also, each age possesses its own beauty of body and soul. But the most beautiful body is—in youth and spirit—in old age.

The most important thing is what you want to express, what idea motivates you. Regardless of where you are, what you see, with whom you are, your subconscious will choose what you need to fulfill this idea.

The sincerity of feelings and their sincere expression on canvas—this is and will be innovation.

Statement courtesy USSR Union of Artists

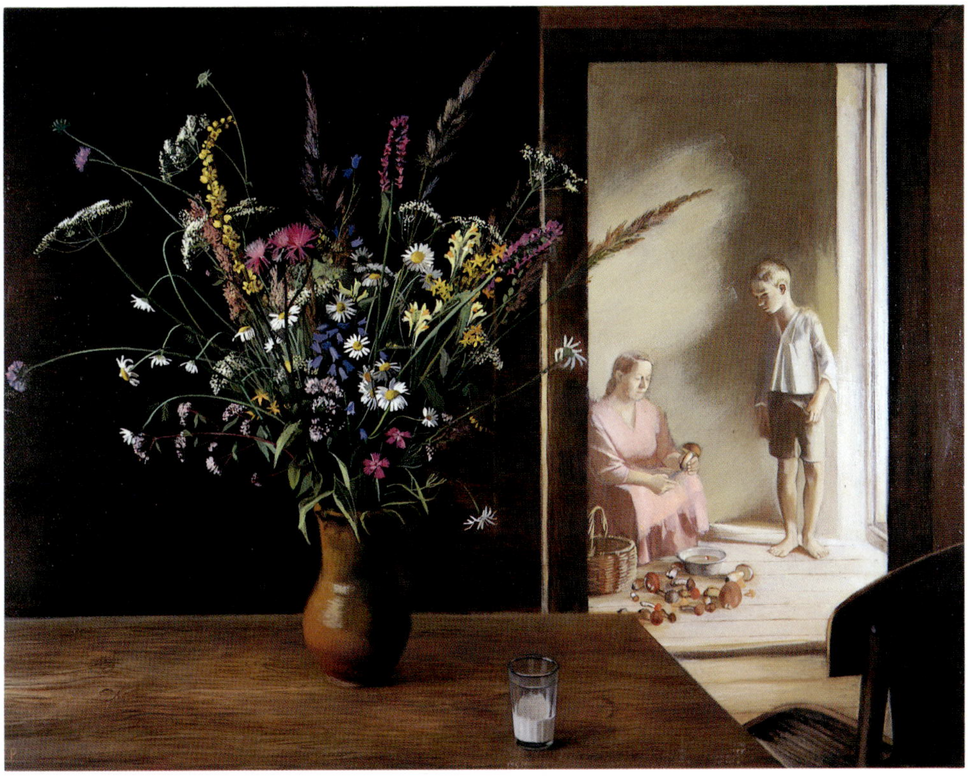

Pl. 66 *Midday, Summer*, 1987
Oil on canvas, 49 1/4 × 53 inches (125 × 135 cm)
Collection of Val and Majid Arbab

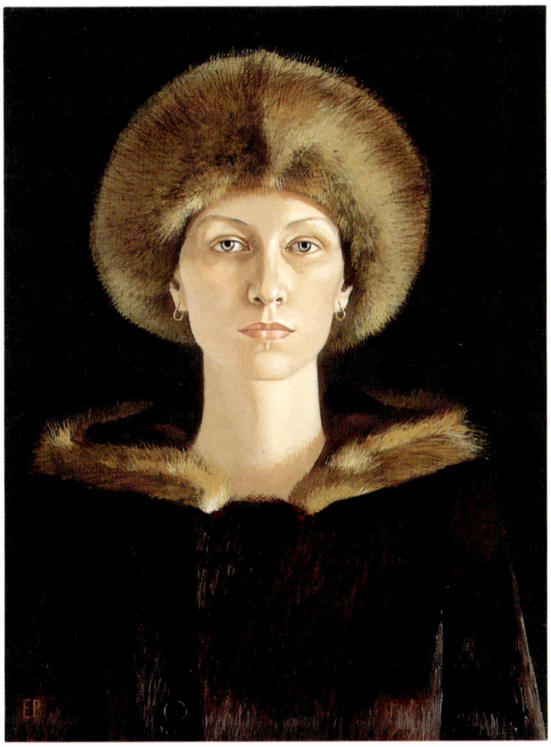

Pl. 67 *Self-Portrait in a Fur Hat*, 1988
Oil on canvas, 25 1/2 × 19 5/8 inches (65 × 50 cm)
John G. Pickard Collection

Evgeni Rukhin

1943–1976

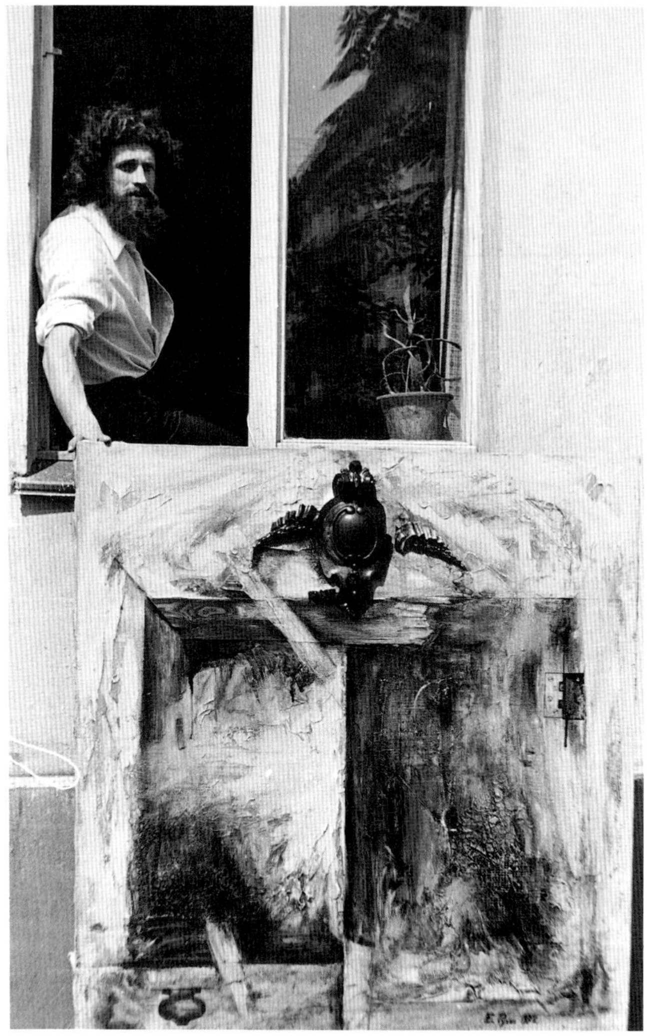

I, Evgeni Rukhin, was born in Saratov, July 2, 1943, into a family of scientists. In 1963, to the great surprise of those who knew me, I began to paint. My acquaintances found these paintings bizarre. My first canvases were symbolic in their motifs and had forms which were far from traditional. Frequently they were completely abstract, non-objective. I was most interested in relief and color. At the same time I wanted to find out about classic graphic arts, but nonetheless was ignorant of schools of contemporary painting.

In my new series of works I use pieces of furniture: old broken chairs, tables, boxes, and other objects which civilization has discarded as useless. They lose their concrete or even schematic reality and are reborn into abstract shapes and patterns. For example, the tables, in which the rectangular form predominates, become in my works suddenly spread out and combined with the painted image.

The shapes of my canvases are almost square, because this shape is most independent of the proportions of a portrait (vertical) or of a landscape (horizontal). Yet I almost never use a perfect square for my canvases because that seems to me dull and devoid of internal dynamism. I spend a lot of time thinking about the ultimate effect of the surface of my work, because a painting has to radiate new experiences every day.

In many respects I owe a great deal to the examples of my colleagues, Vladimir Nemukhin and Oskar Rabin. Since I am an optimist by nature, I am sure that one day our works will be widely exhibited in my country.

Excerpts reprinted from *Rukhin* (Los Angeles: Gallery 1912, 1989), p. 17.

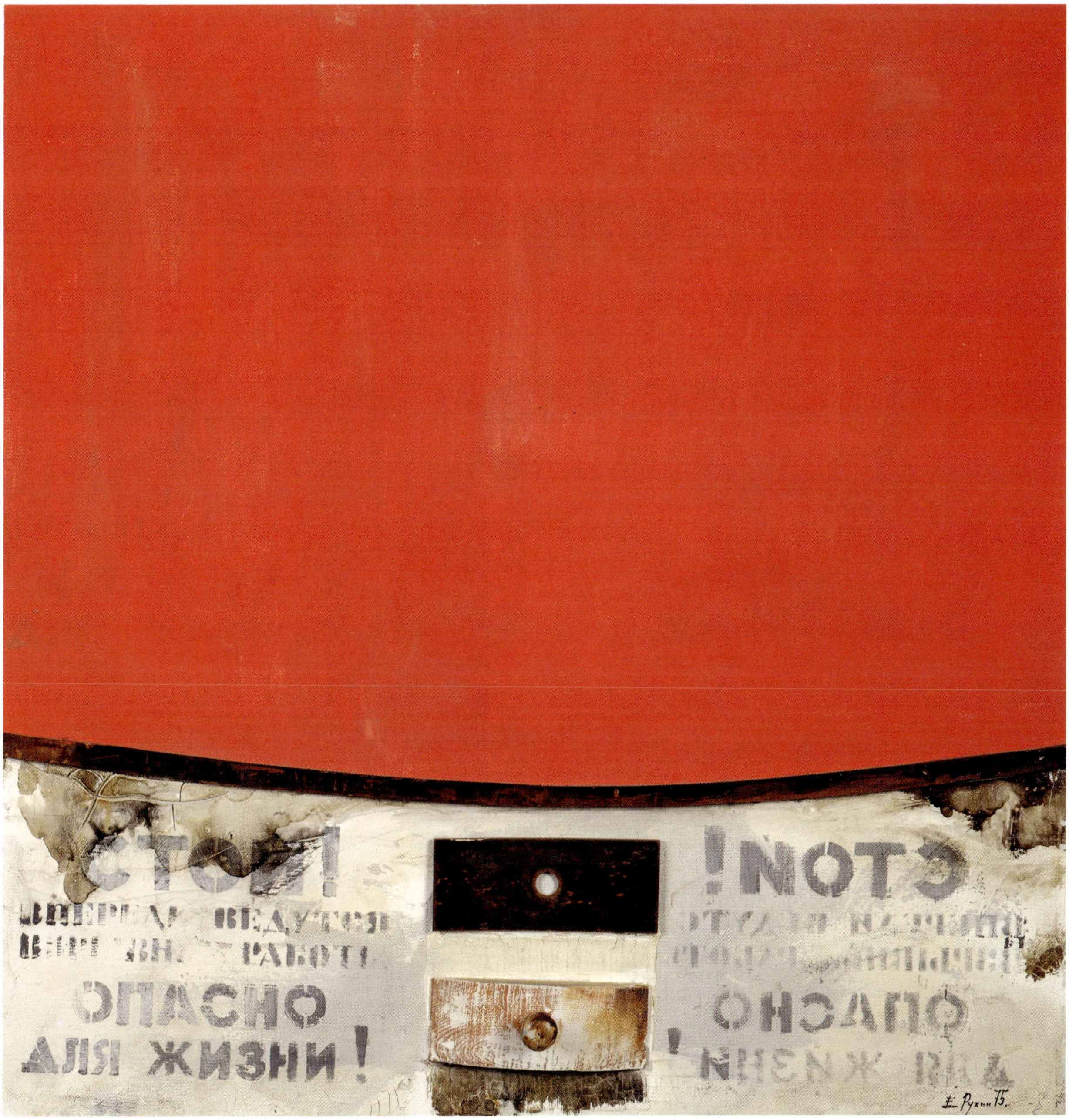

Pl. 68 *Untitled*, 1975
Mixed media on canvas, 39½ × 39½ inches
(100 × 100 cm)
Collection of Nancy and Norton Dodge

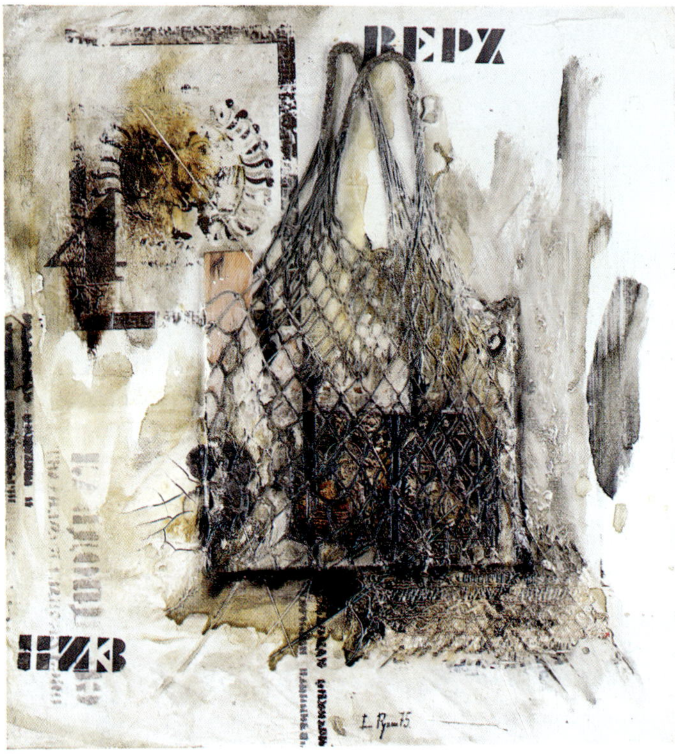

Pl. 69 *Untitled*, 1975
Oil, synthetic polymer assemblage on canvas, $27^{1}/_{2} \times 25^{3}/_{4}$ inches (70×65.5 cm)
George Mayers, Gallery 1912, Los Angeles, California

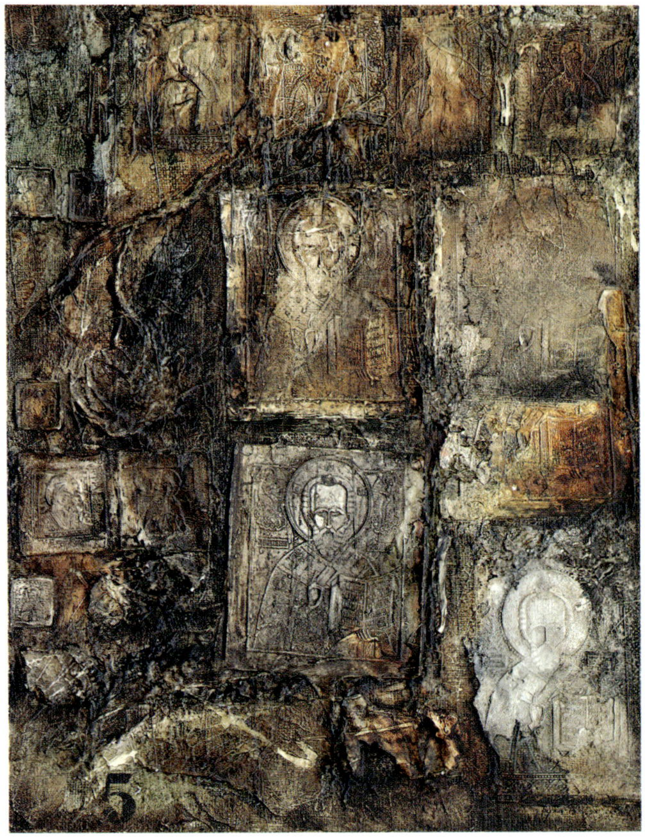

Pl. 70 *Untitled*, n.d.
Mixed media on burlap, $37 \times 29^{1}/_{8}$ inches (94×74 cm)
Collection of Nancy and Norton Dodge

Sergei Sherstiuk

BORN 1951

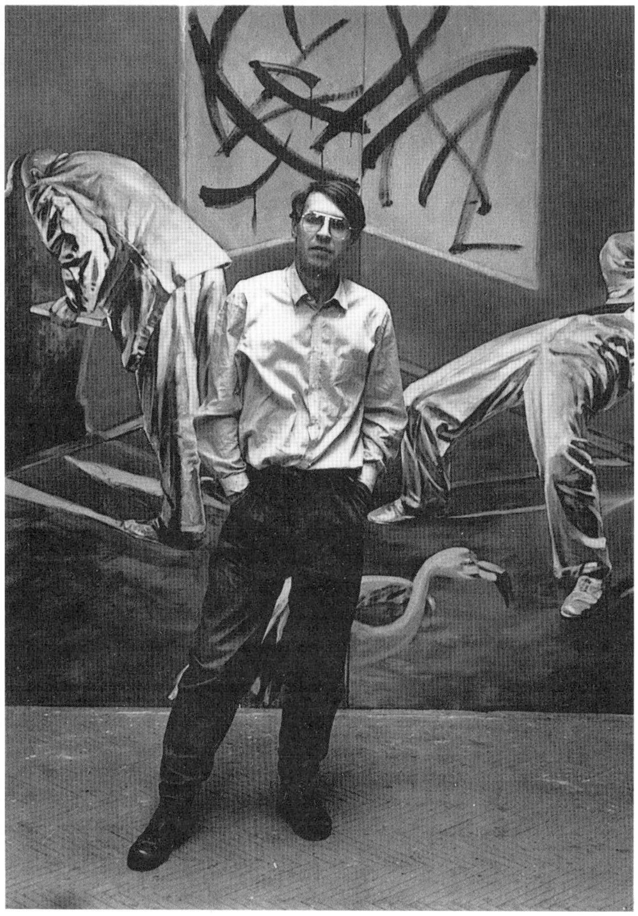

Culture is a book and art is its page. I do not know what the book means because its pages are infinite. No artist is given the opportunity to see to the end. At times I think of myself as a man who is given a book printed on a Xerox machine. The book drops to the floor, and I crawl along the floor assembling the book, page by page, not reading it. Sometimes I read the top few lines of a page. It seems to be the truth. And that is the subject of my paintings.

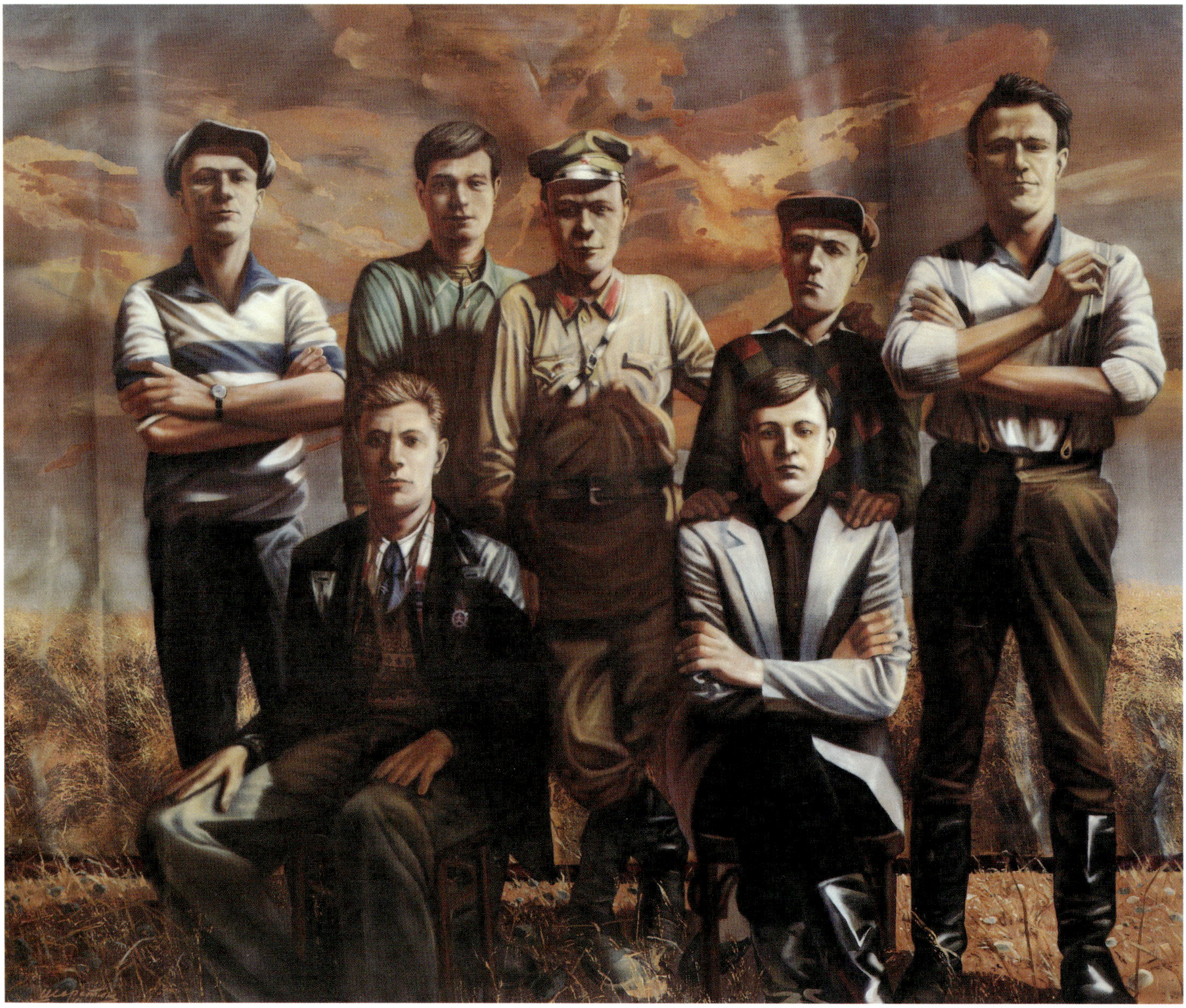

Pl. 71 *Men of One Family: 1941 and 1945* (diptych), 1985
Oil on canvas, each 71 × $86^{1}/_{2}$ inches (180 × 220 cm)
Collection of Nancy and Norton Dodge

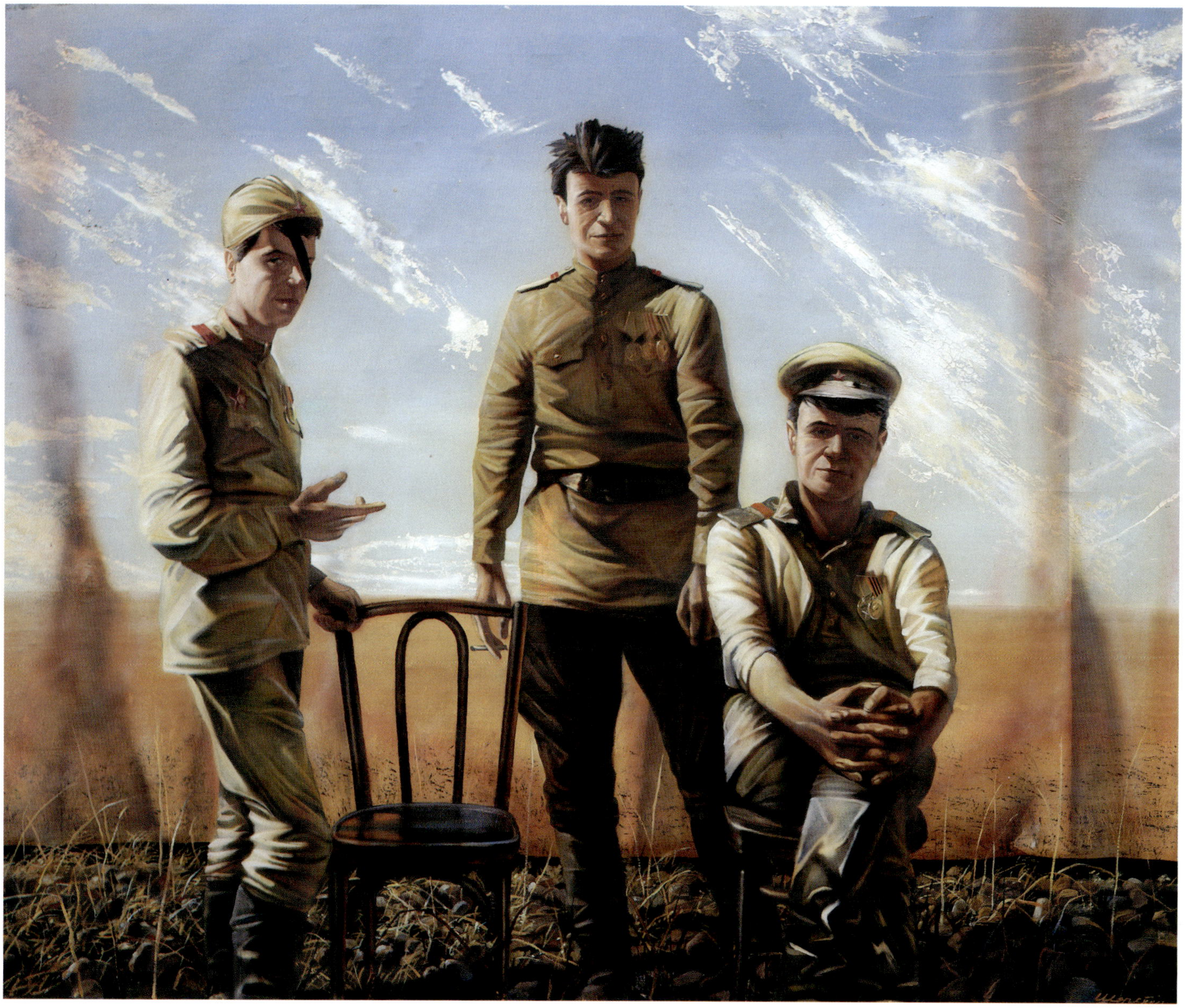

Sergei Sherstiuk

Edik Shteinberg

BORN 1937

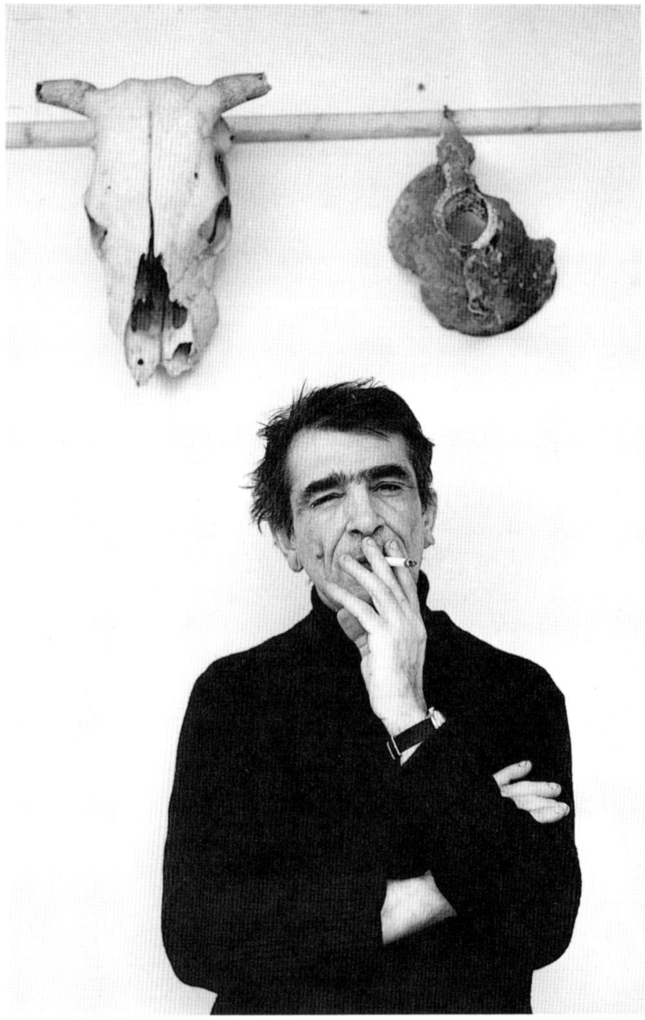

Leaving the viewer free, the language of geometry forces the artist to repudiate the "I." The attempt to make it either ideological or utilitarian is coercion.

The language of geometry became, for me, the means of existence during nights which You (K. Malevich) gave the name "Black Square." I believe that the memory of mankind will always return to it in the moments of mystical experience of the tragedy of God's abandonment of mankind.

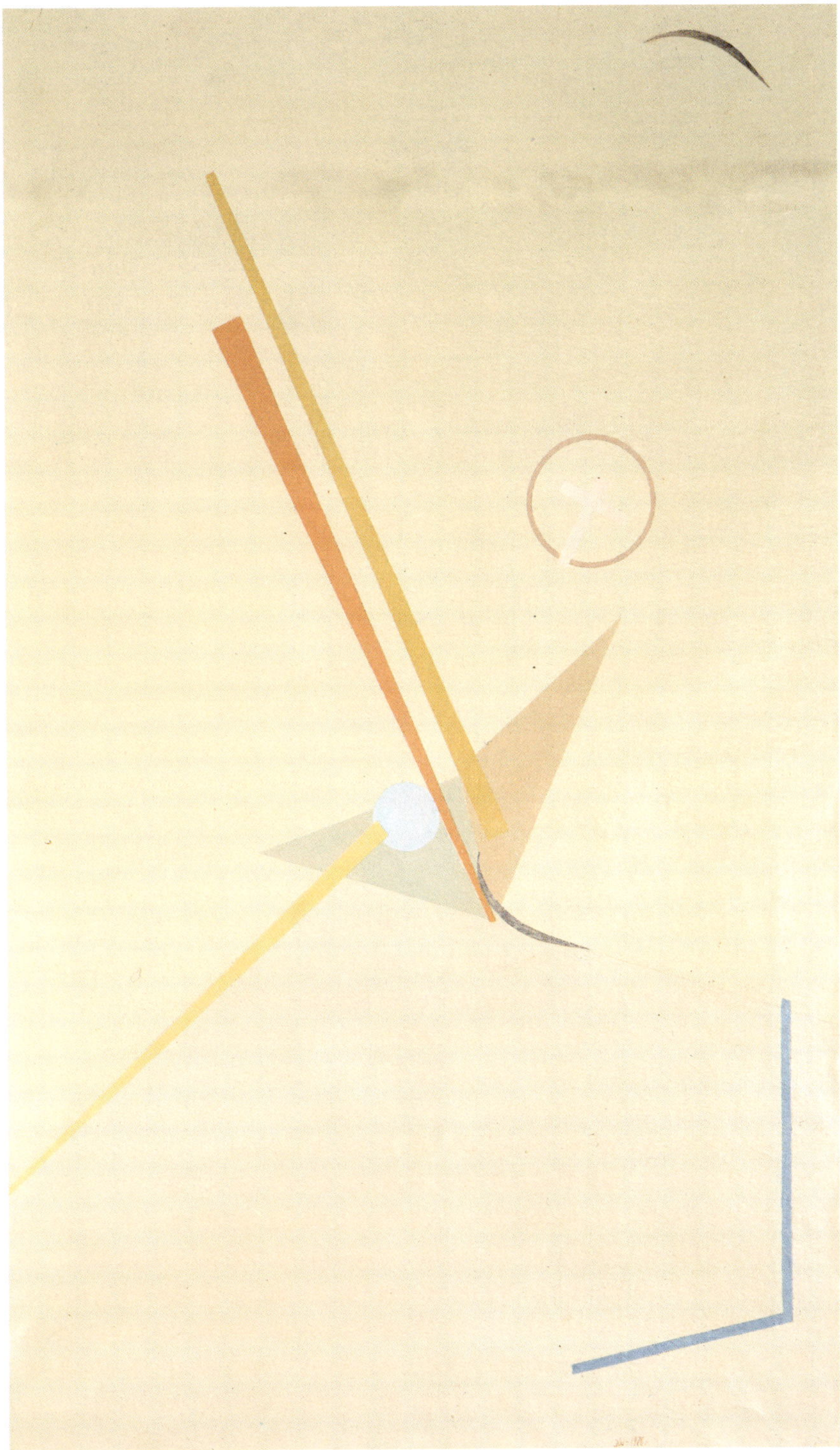

Pl. 72 *Composition December 1976*, 1976
Oil on canvas, 45 1/2 × 27 3/8 inches (115.6 × 69.9 cm)
Collection of Nancy and Norton Dodge

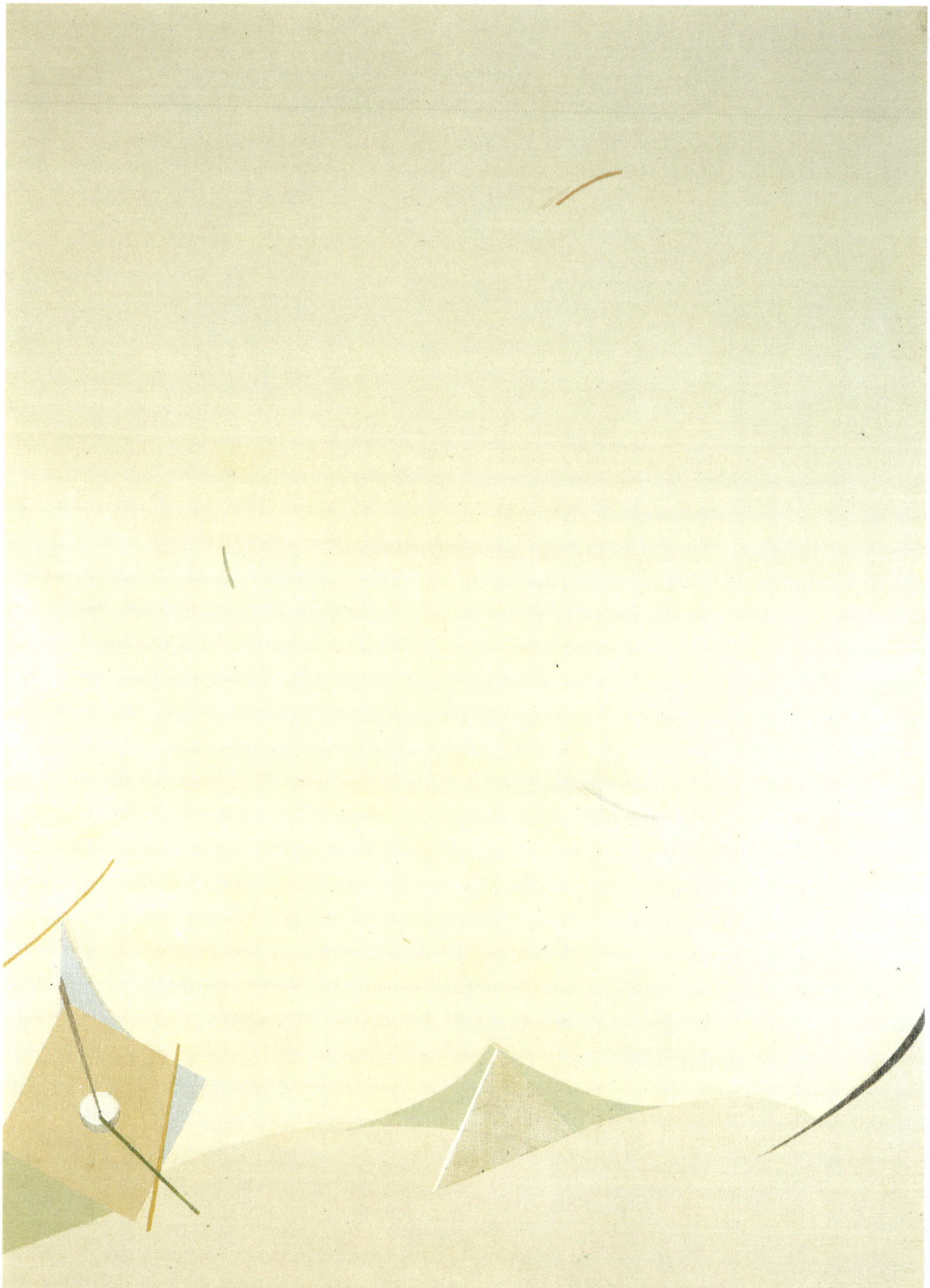

Pl. 73 *Composition March 1979*, 1979
Oil on canvas, $47^{1}/_{4} \times 38^{1}/_{2}$ inches (120 × 97 cm)
Collection of Nancy and Norton Dodge

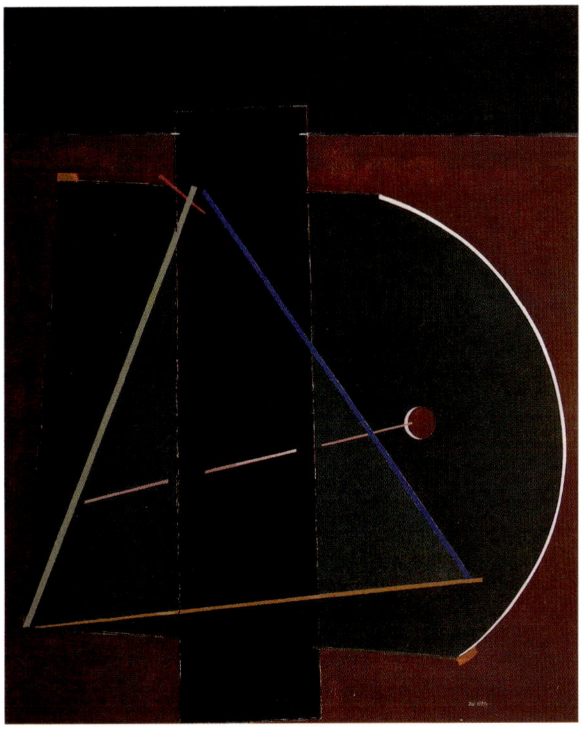

Pl. 74 *Composition January–February 1989*, 1989
Oil on canvas, $43^1/_4 \times 35^3/_{16}$ inches (110×89.5 cm)
Courtesy of Claude Bernard Gallery, New York

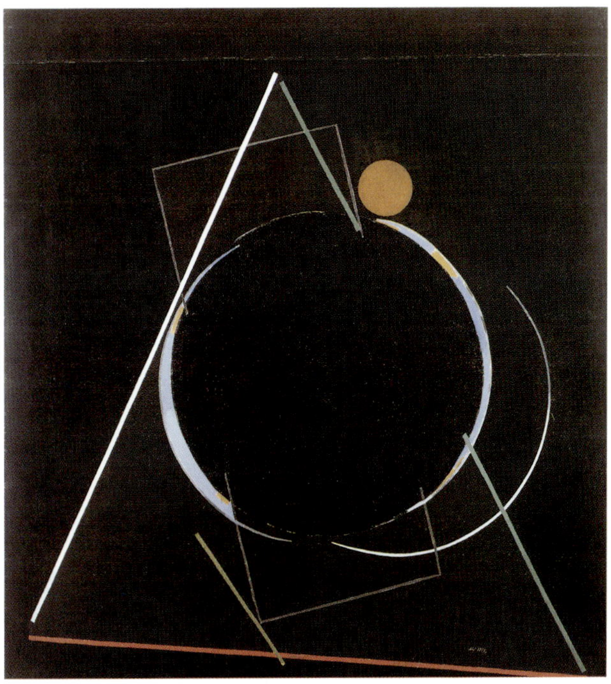

Pl. 75 *Composition March 1989*, 1989
Oil on canvas, $47^1/_2 \times 43^1/_4$ inches (118.5×110 cm)
Courtesy of Claude Bernard Gallery, New York

ALEXANDER SITNIKOV

BORN 1945

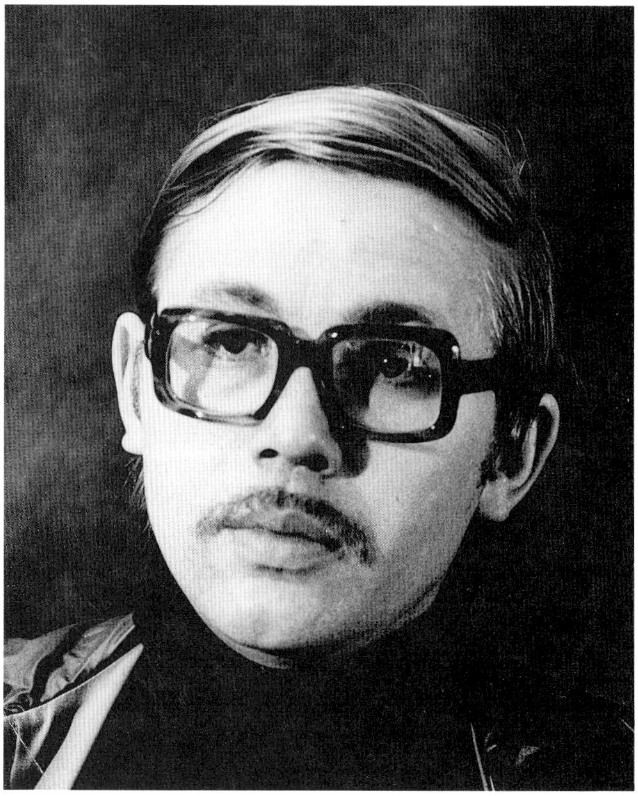

The white square of memory
Reverse sequence of numbers
While the bitter drops of eternity
Flow into the heart of the poet

The conductor of the carnival of time
The flapping of black wings
Chance celebrates hope
History celebrates fear.

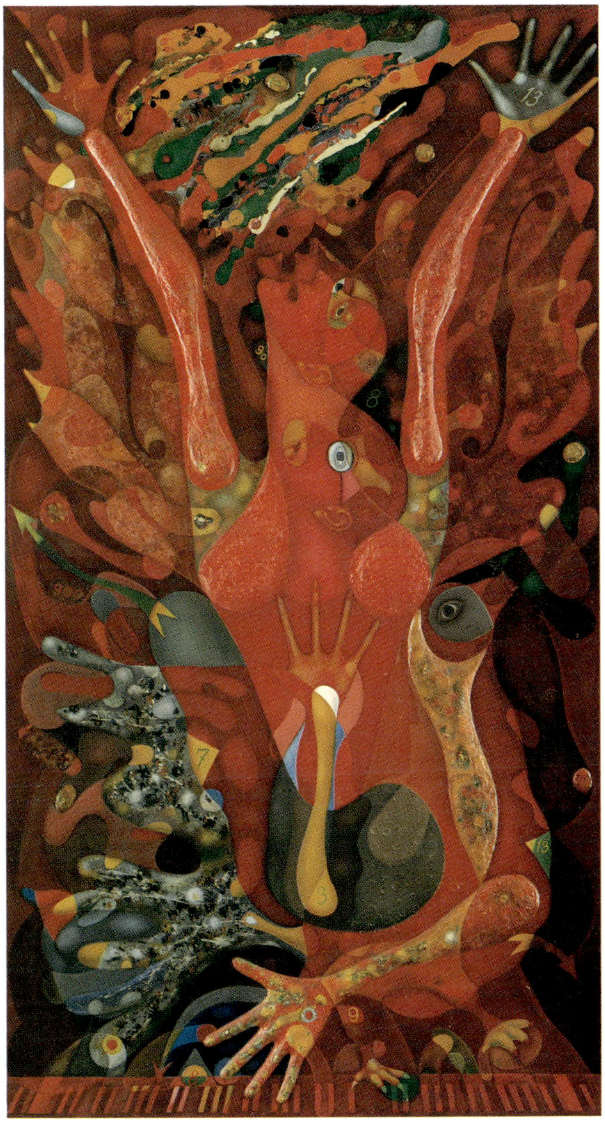

Pl. 76 *Shostakovich*, 1986
Oil on canvas, 63 × 35 3/8 inches (160 × 90 cm)
Courtesy of the Artist

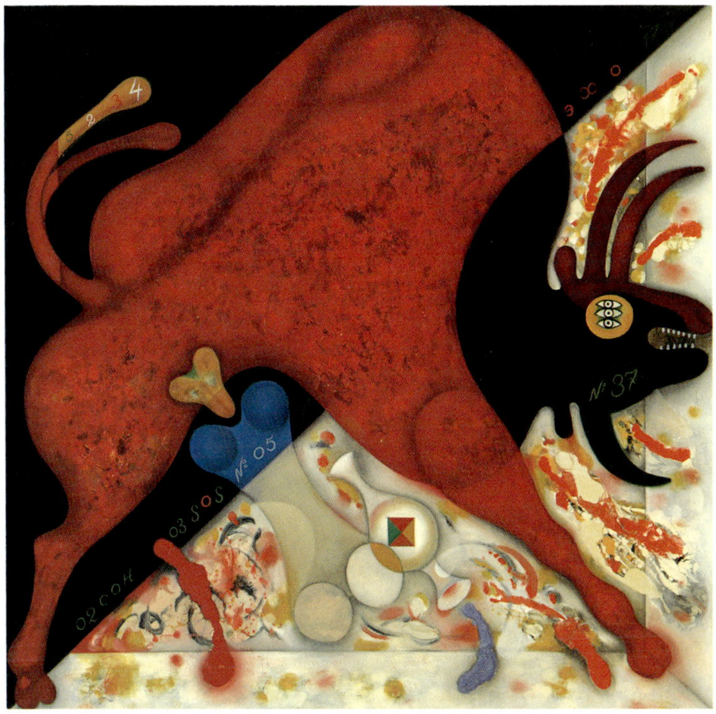

Pl. 77 *The Red Echo*, 1986
Oil on canvas, 50 3/8 × 50 3/8 inches (128 × 128 cm)
Courtesy of the Artist

Andrei Tutunov

Born 1928

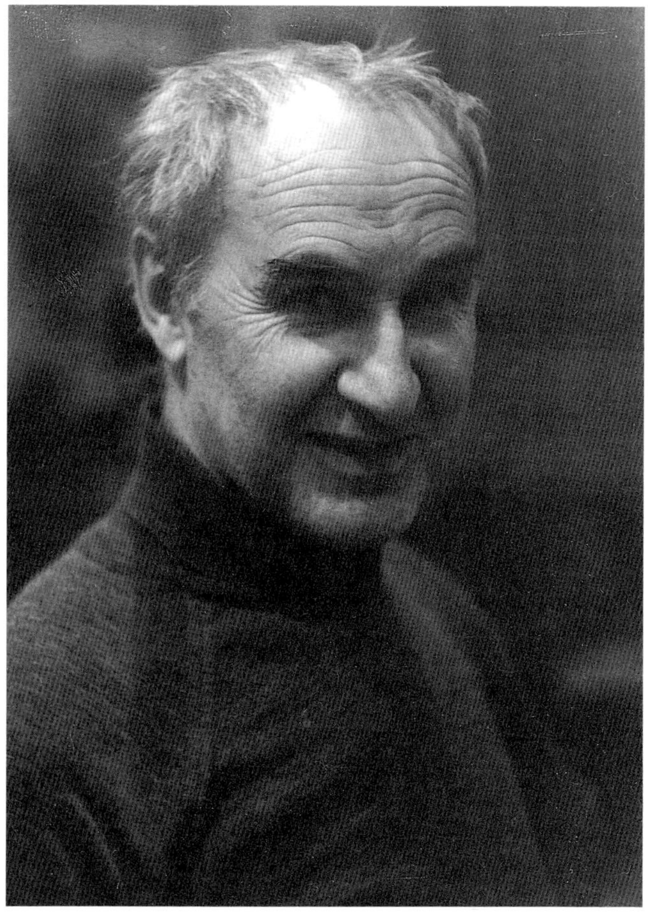

My views of art have changed. Like a person who matures, reaches adulthood, gains life experience and presumably becomes wiser, so the artist is in a state of development. As a man is guided by his conscience, so the artist is guided by his intuition. Intuition in many respects saves the artist. It is like a guiding star. But sometimes in creative work a crisis strikes, and then intuition no longer suffices. That is how I came to a conclusion about the necessity for a precise, positive ideal. Because in essence only this ideal stimulates creation, and in our tragic times people feel a need and a thirst for it. The positive ideal is not directly depicted in the picture. Like a flower, it exudes fragrance, but it is invisible. To attain in a painting a similar atmosphere—invisible, with the presence of spirit is my dream and my goal today.

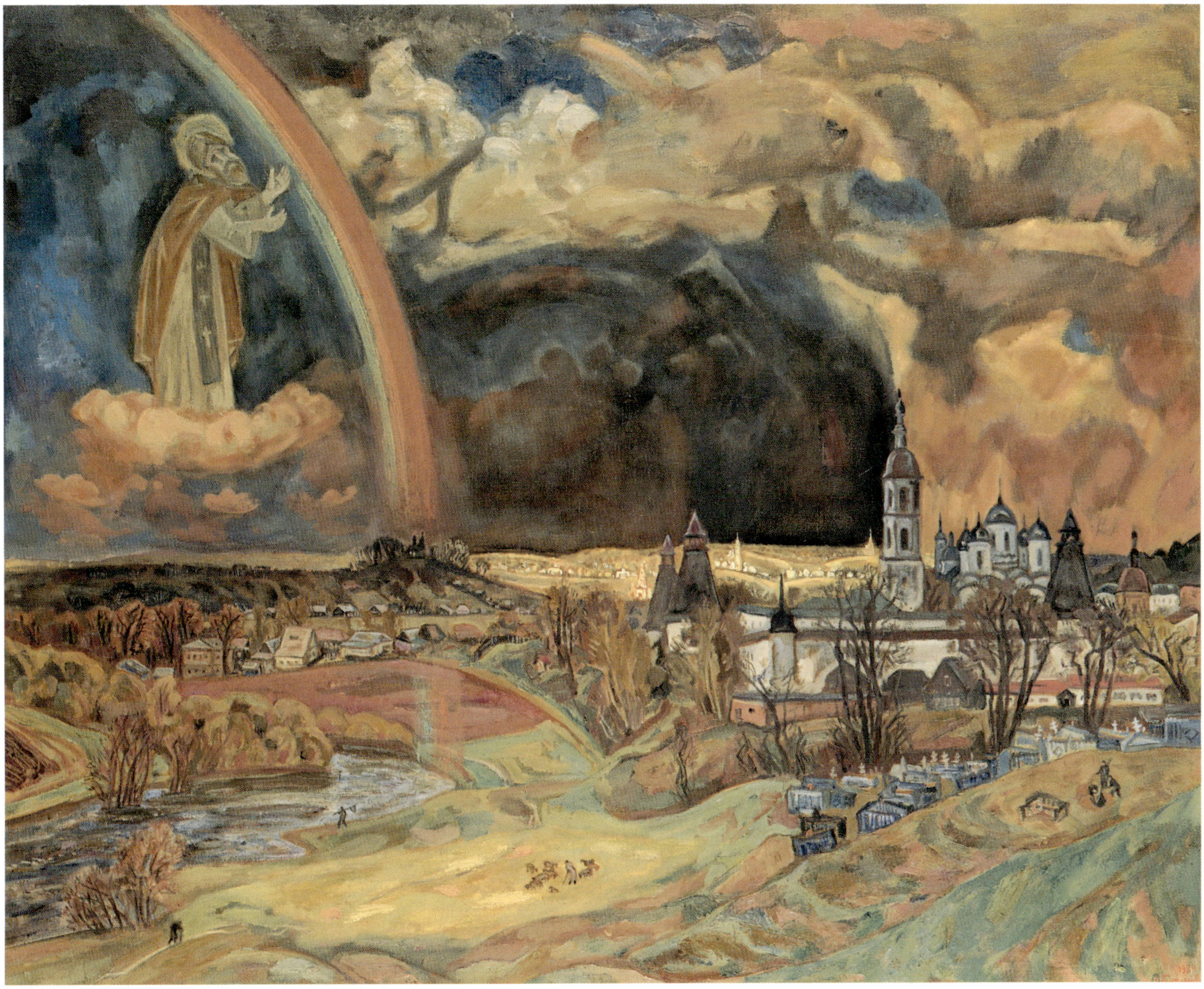

Pl. 78 *View of Pafnutiev Monastery*, n.d.
Oil on canvas, 48 × 60½ inches (120 × 151 cm)
Courtesy of the Artist

Alexander Tyshler

1898–1980

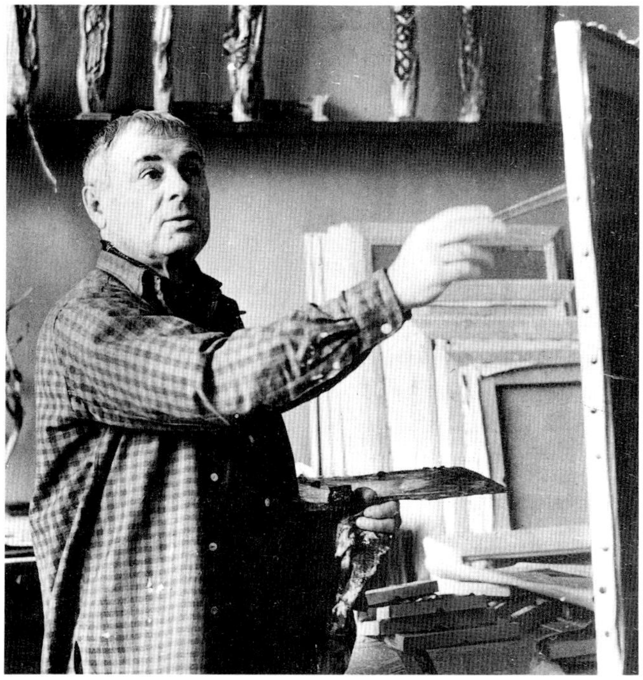

Alexander Tyshler was a poet. He thought in metaphors, allegories, and symbols of fine art. He had his own image-bearing vision of the world—at times ironic, sometimes romantic. He appreciated the grotesque as well. He usually worked in cycles in order to completely develop his theme. His imagination was unpredictable. He evolved from abstractionism to figurative painting, from spectral coloring to pale tones, and then to new, local colors. Having possessed irrepressible imagination and unbending willpower, he did not believe in the canons of official art. For many years he was labeled a formalist and suffered discrimination from the authorities.

Prepared by Flora Syrkina (Tyshler), widow of the artist

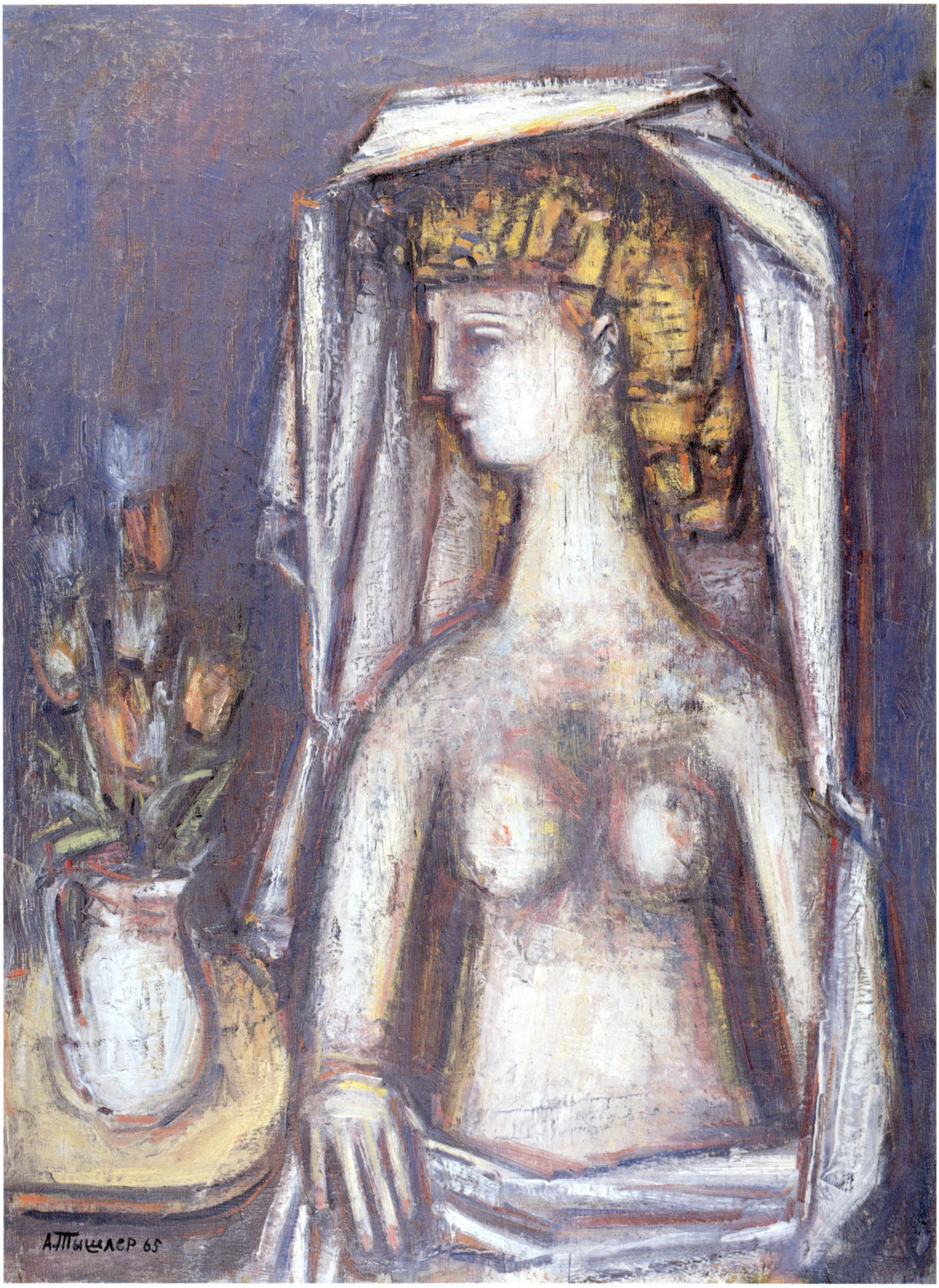

Pl. 79 *Girl and Flowers*, 1965
Oil on canvas, 32 1/2 × 24 1/2 inches (81.9 × 62.2 cm)
Private Collection

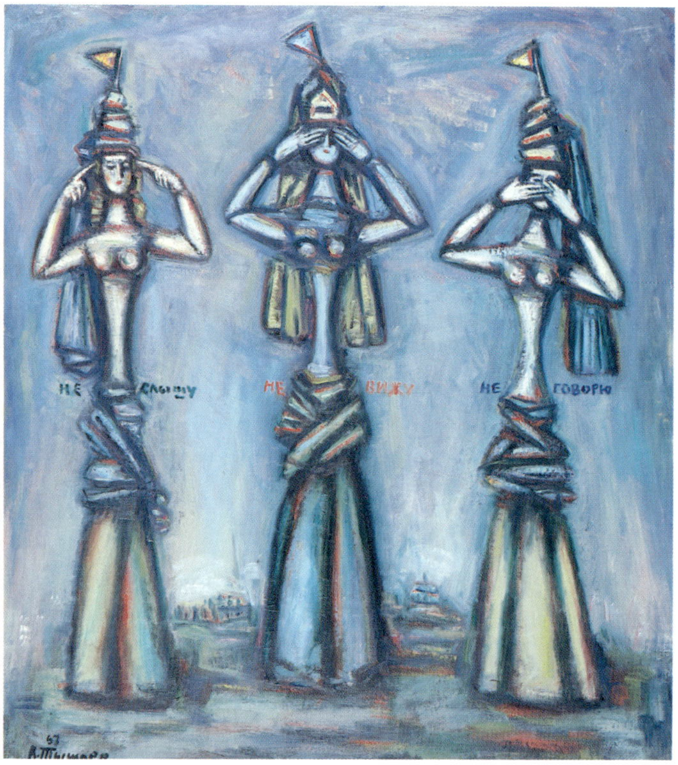

Pl. 80 *I Don't Hear, I Don't See, I Don't Speak,* 1967
Oil on canvas, 25 1/2 × 23 inches (64 × 58 cm)
Private Collection

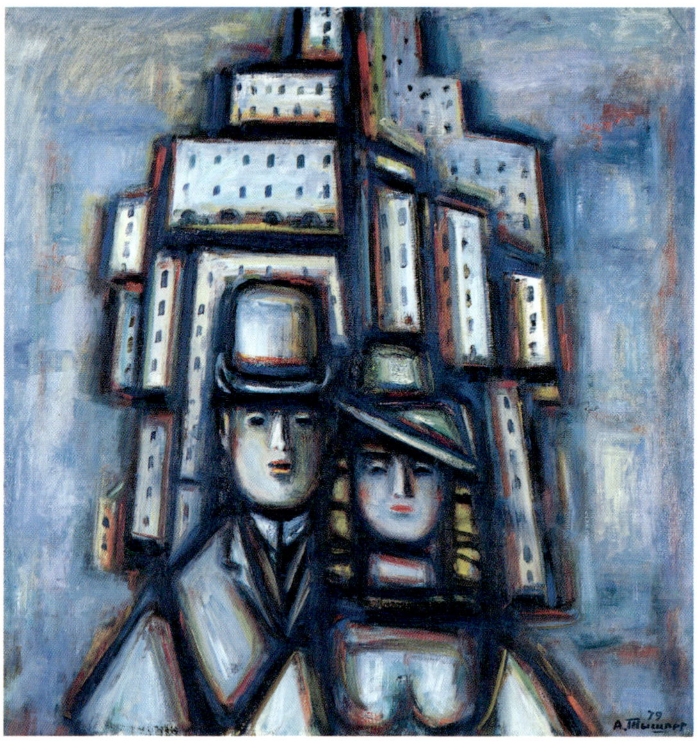

Pl. 81 *Family Portrait,* 1979
Oil on canvas, 24 × 24 inches (61 × 61 cm)
Private Collection

Valeri Vatenin

1933–1977

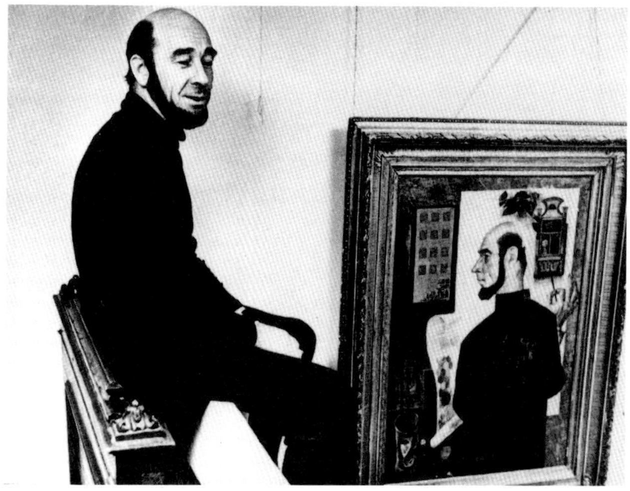

The creation of a picture is an everyday act of will, and not an accidental, whimsical event.

In the twentieth century, side by side with objective realism, in which the main task for the artist is to convey real forms with visual integrity, there is also subjective realism, or rather synthetic realism. In the new realism, nature is not an object to be portrayed, but rather a means for the artist to develop ideas and style; in this way forms which have not previously been portrayed become the material of fine art. From the vocabulary of natural forms the artist takes not so much nature as it appears, but rather an inner perception of objects in nature. In spite of its great abstractness, this kind of realism is more flexible and more expressive. Nevertheless, this realism is indeed realism, because the real world is its source.

From the artist's notebooks

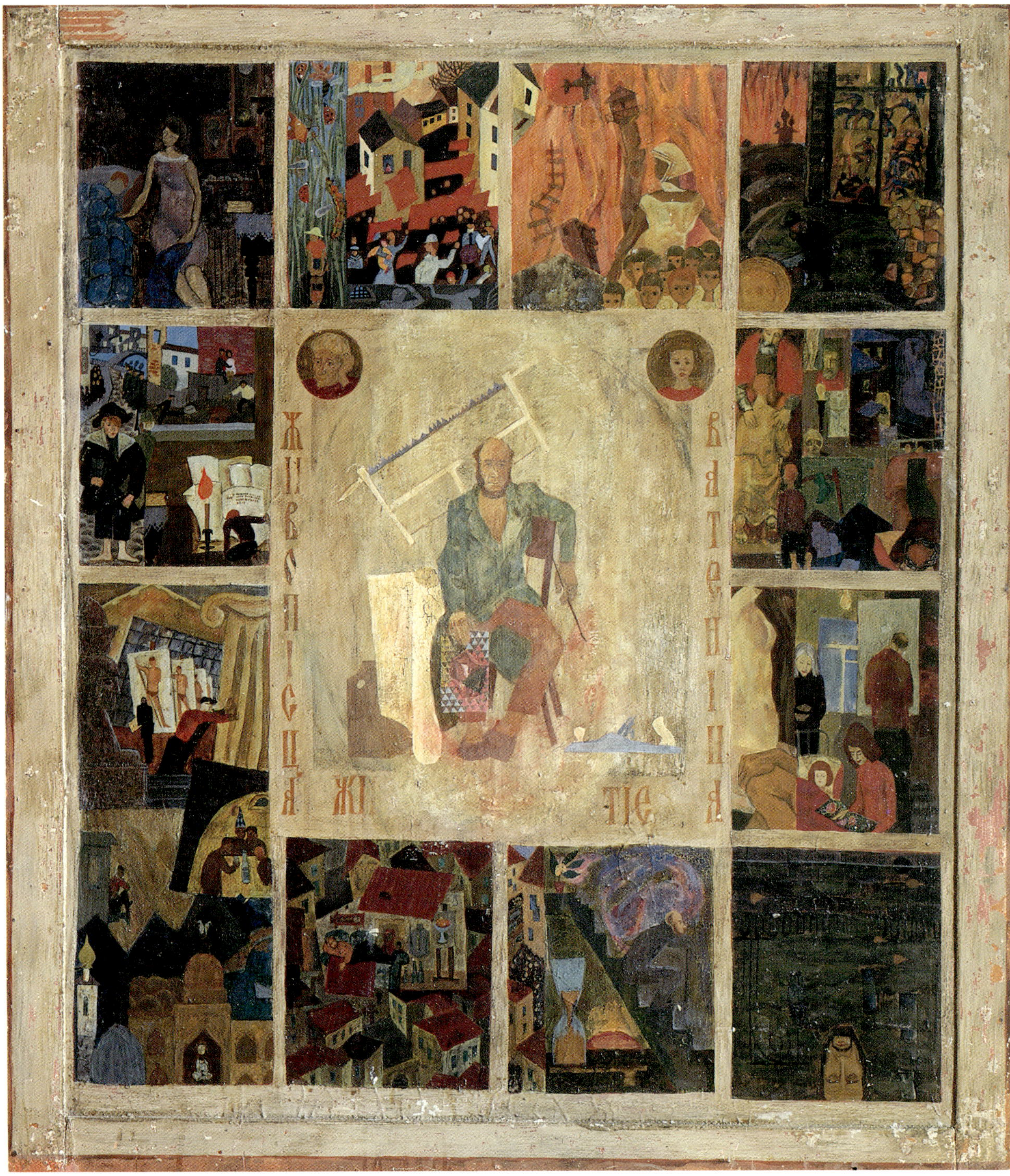

Pl. 82 *The Painter Vatenin's Life Story*, 1968 and 1973
Egg tempera on canvas pasted on cardboard, $39^{1}/_{2} \times 35$ inches (100.5 × 89 cm)
Collection of the Artist's Family, Leningrad

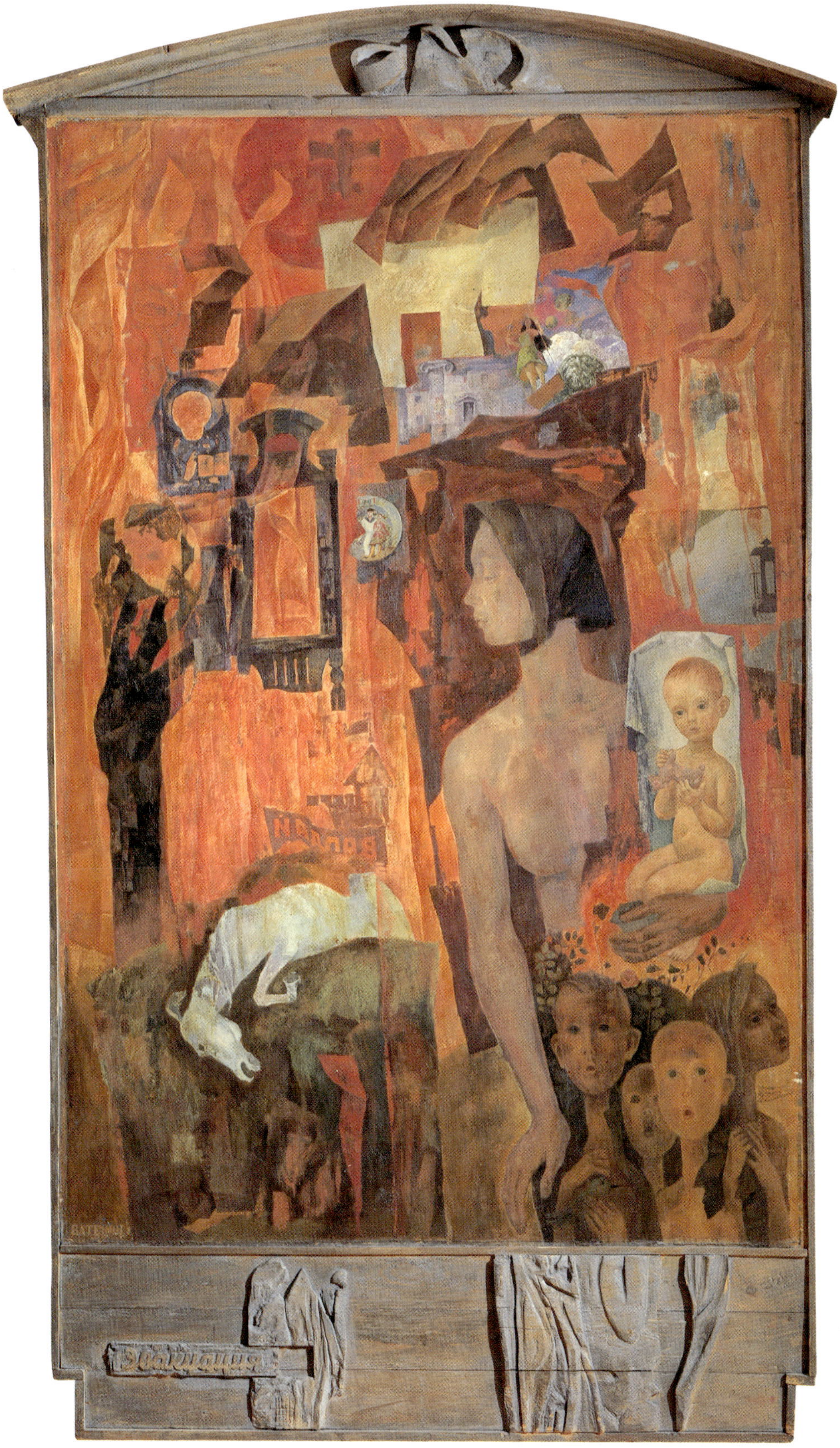

Pl. 83 *The Evacuation*, 1975
Egg tempera on canvas pasted on cardboard, 69 5/8 × 47 3/4 inches (177 × 121.5 cm)
Collection of the Artist's Family, Leningrad

Vladimir Weisberg

1924–1985

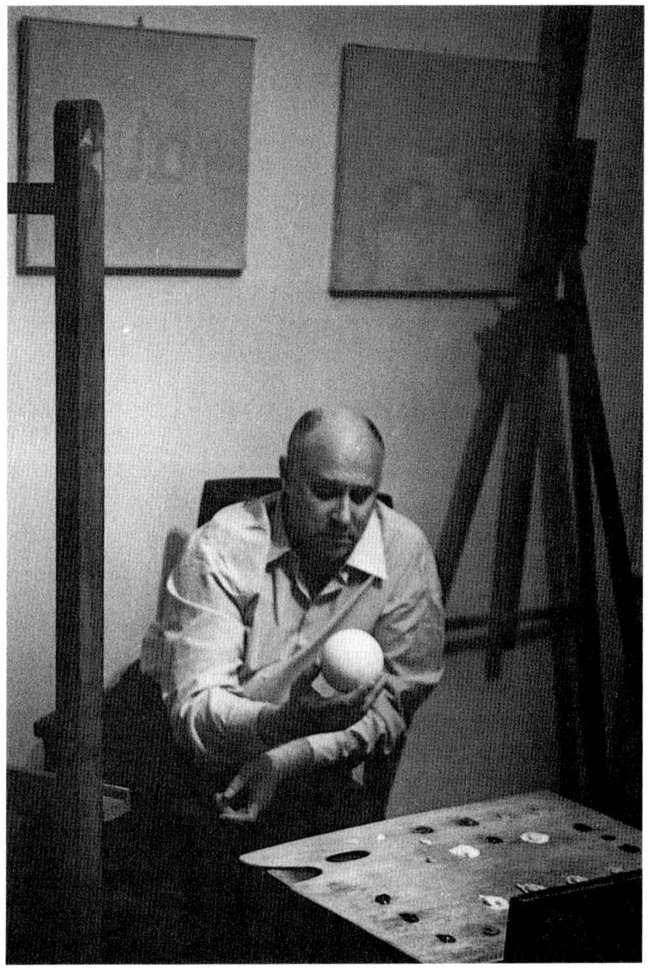

My experience in painting is based on both the study of European masters and an intuitive knowledge of the creative process.

The study of European masters of colorism led me to the conclusion that before Cézanne colorism was just an attribute of the talent of certain artists, such as El Greco, or the Venetians: Titian, Veronese, Tintoretto. Only after Delacroix did colorism begin to be considered from a scientific standpoint, and after Cézanne colorism finally became, in absolute terms, a formal study of the composition of color structures.

From a paper presented by the artist at the symposium on the "Study of Sign Systems," Moscow, 1962.

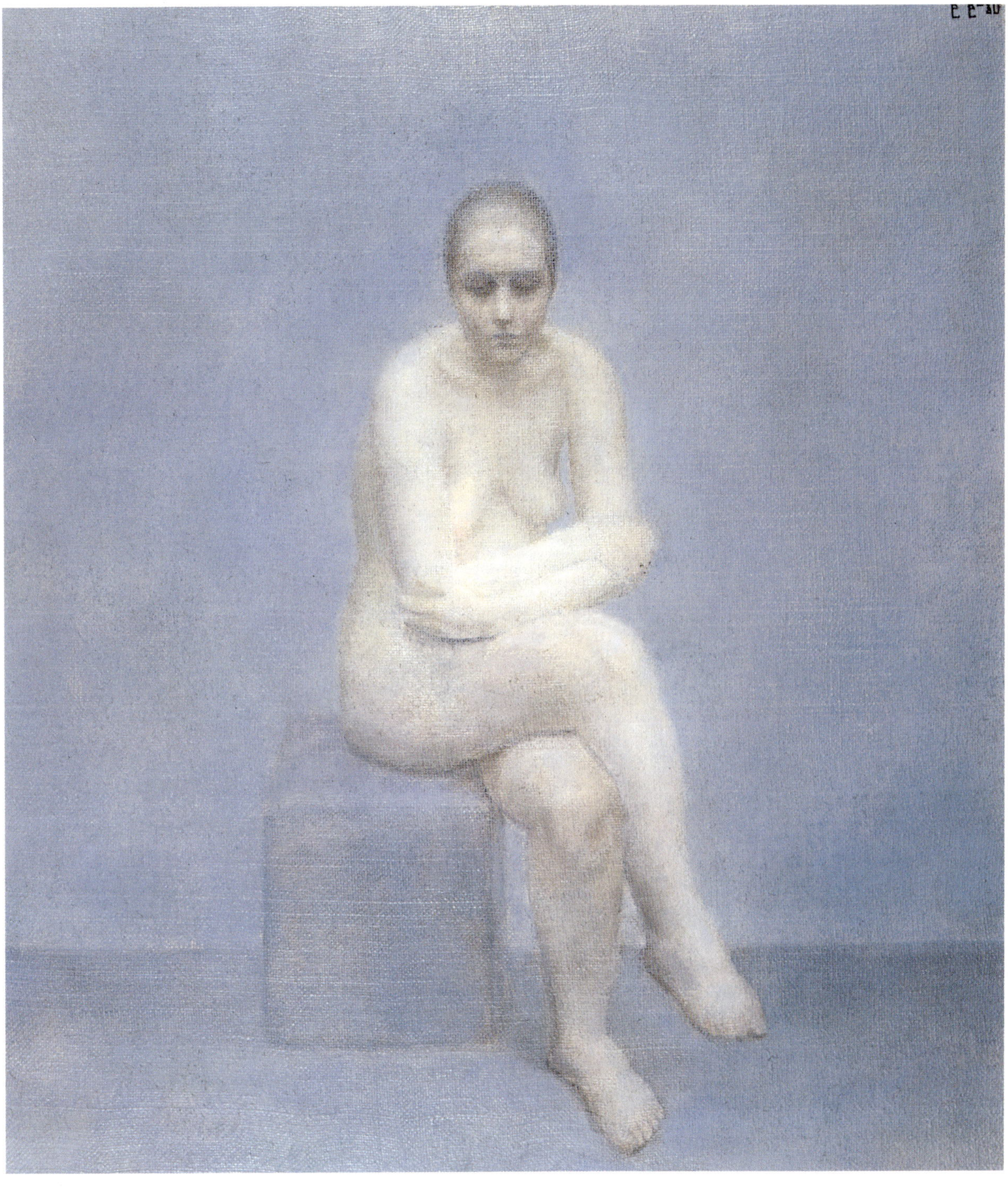

Pl. 84 *Nude*, 1980
Oil on canvas, 23 3/4 × 20 1/2 inches (59 × 52 cm)
Private Collection

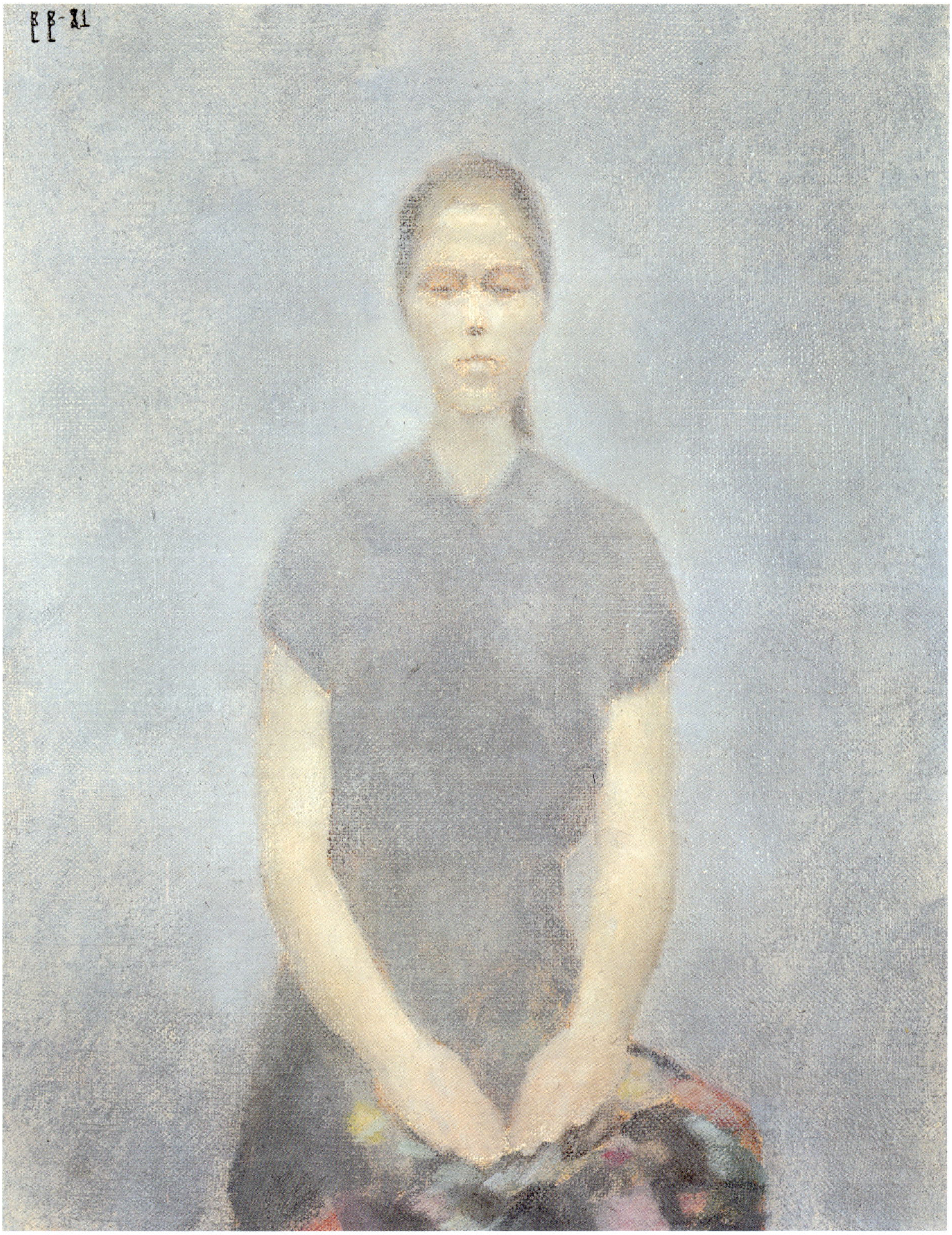

Pl. 85 *Portrait of Marina*, 1981
Oil on canvas, 19⅝ × 15¾ inches (50 × 40 cm)
Collection of Nancy and Norton Dodge

Pl. 86 *Untitled,* 1980
Oil on canvas, $18^{1}/_{2} \times 25$ inches (46×62 cm)
Collection of Nancy and Norton Dodge

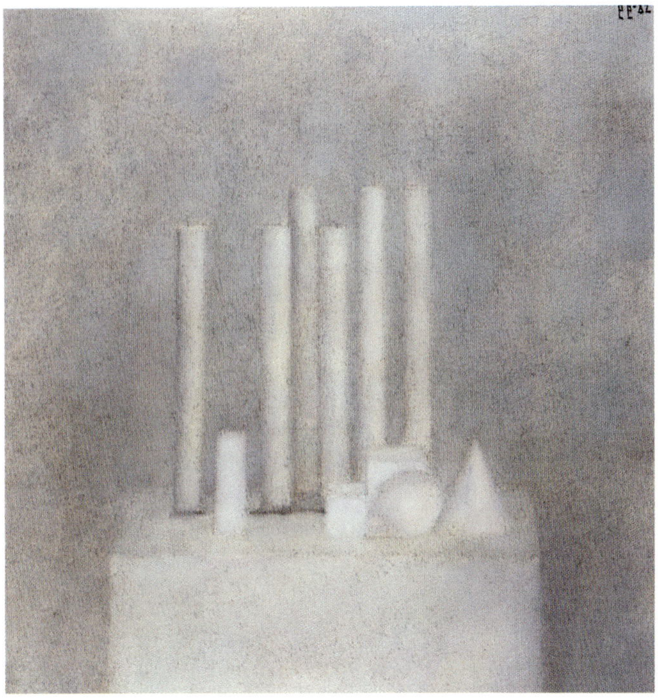

Pl. 87 *Composition in Columns and Other Shapes,* 1982
Oil on canvas, 23×22 inches (58×56 cm)
Private Collection

Andrei Yakhnin

BORN 1966

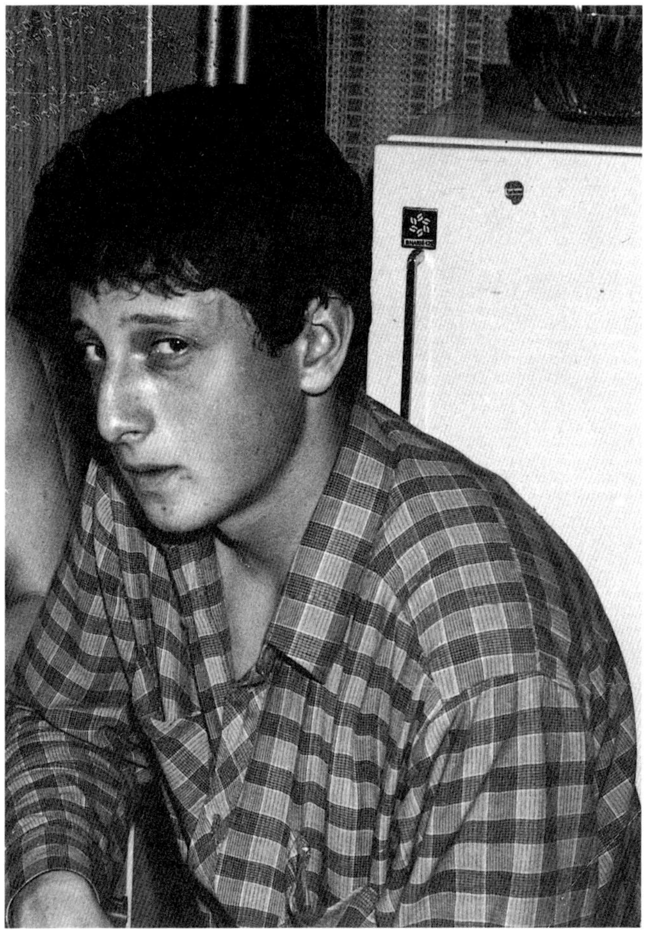

My painting entitled *The Philosophy of Dr. Schnitke* relates to a period of self-examination and self-description under the general title "My Home Is My Fortress." Photographing myself and those close to me on color film; drawing self-portraits, my favorite foods, parts of my body; taping myself on videotape and then reviewing it afterwards, I distance myself with regard to myself. In this manner the artist removes from himself all responsibility not only for the pictures but also for the actions and the further life of his hero, who is himself.

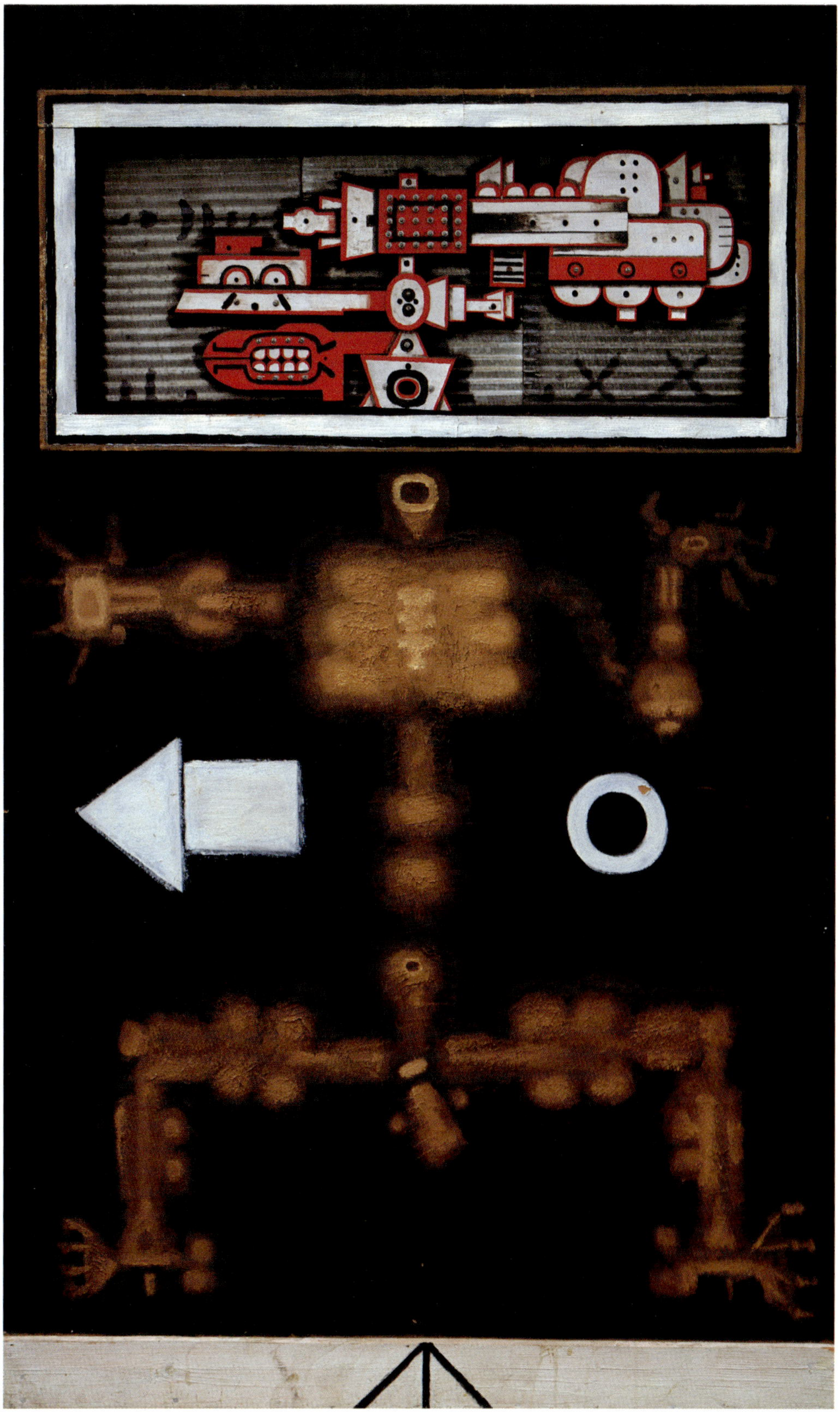

Pl. 89 *The Prophet*, mid-1970s
Mixed media, 66 1/2 × 40 × 3 1/2 inches (166 × 100 × 9 cm)
Collection of Nancy and Norton Dodge

Dmitri Zhilinsky

Born 1928

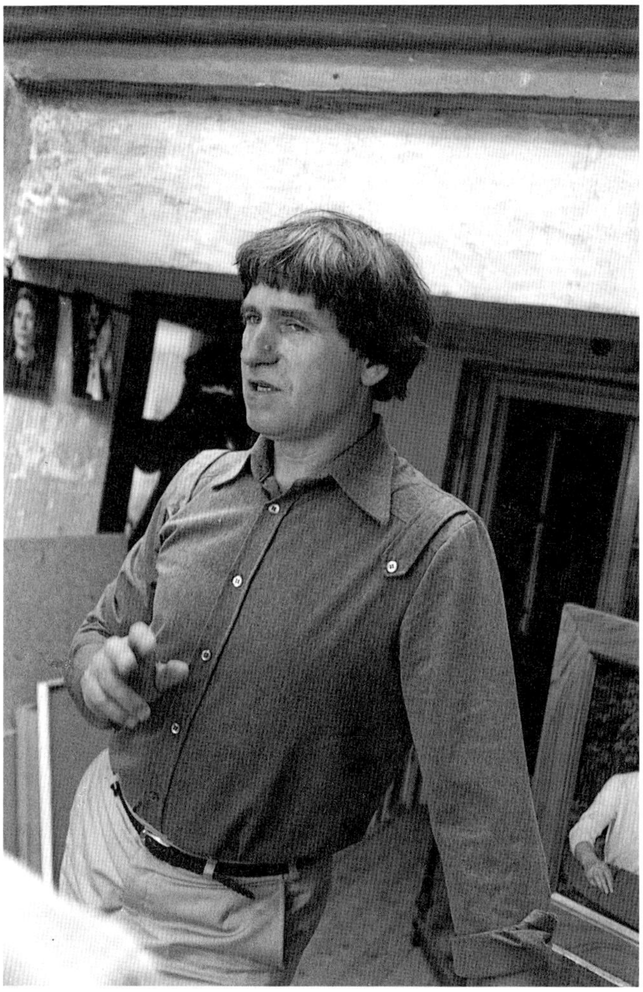

In an era of mindless striving for the new, I want with even more passion to work in the traditional manner, and to even more deeply immerse myself in the inimitable Divine Beauty of natural forms with their spiritual essence.

Many of the artists in their pride turned away from the Creator, disregarding a thousand-year-old culture, imagining themselves to be unique, while in fact resembling one another.

I believe that the day is not far away when mankind finally awakens from the nightmare of cultural decay, just as [we] have come to a realization of the necessity to save nature.

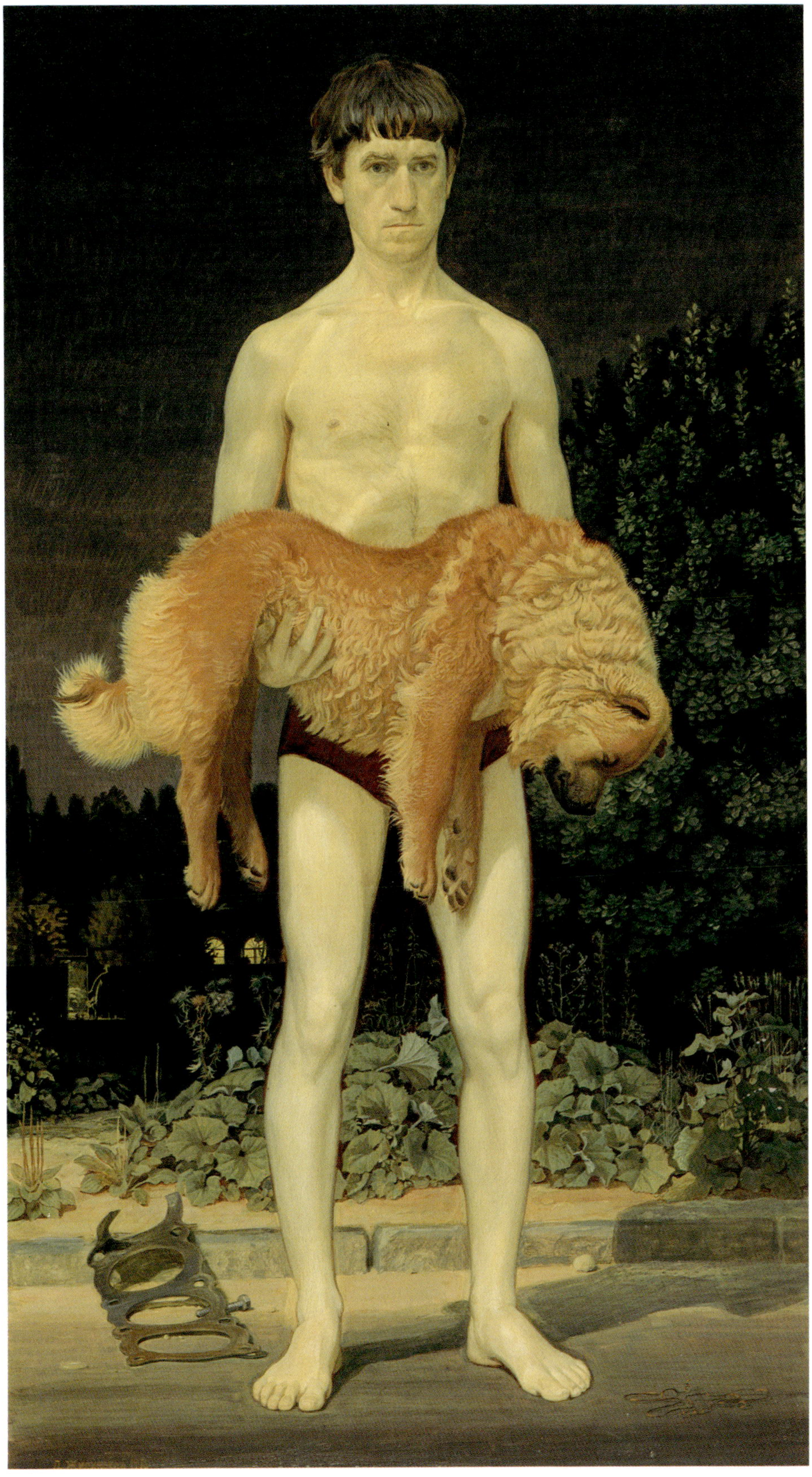

Pl. 90 *Man with Slain Dog*, 1976
Tempera on board, $46^{1}/_{2} \times 26^{1}/_{2}$ inches (117.5×67.5 cm)
Courtesy of the Artist

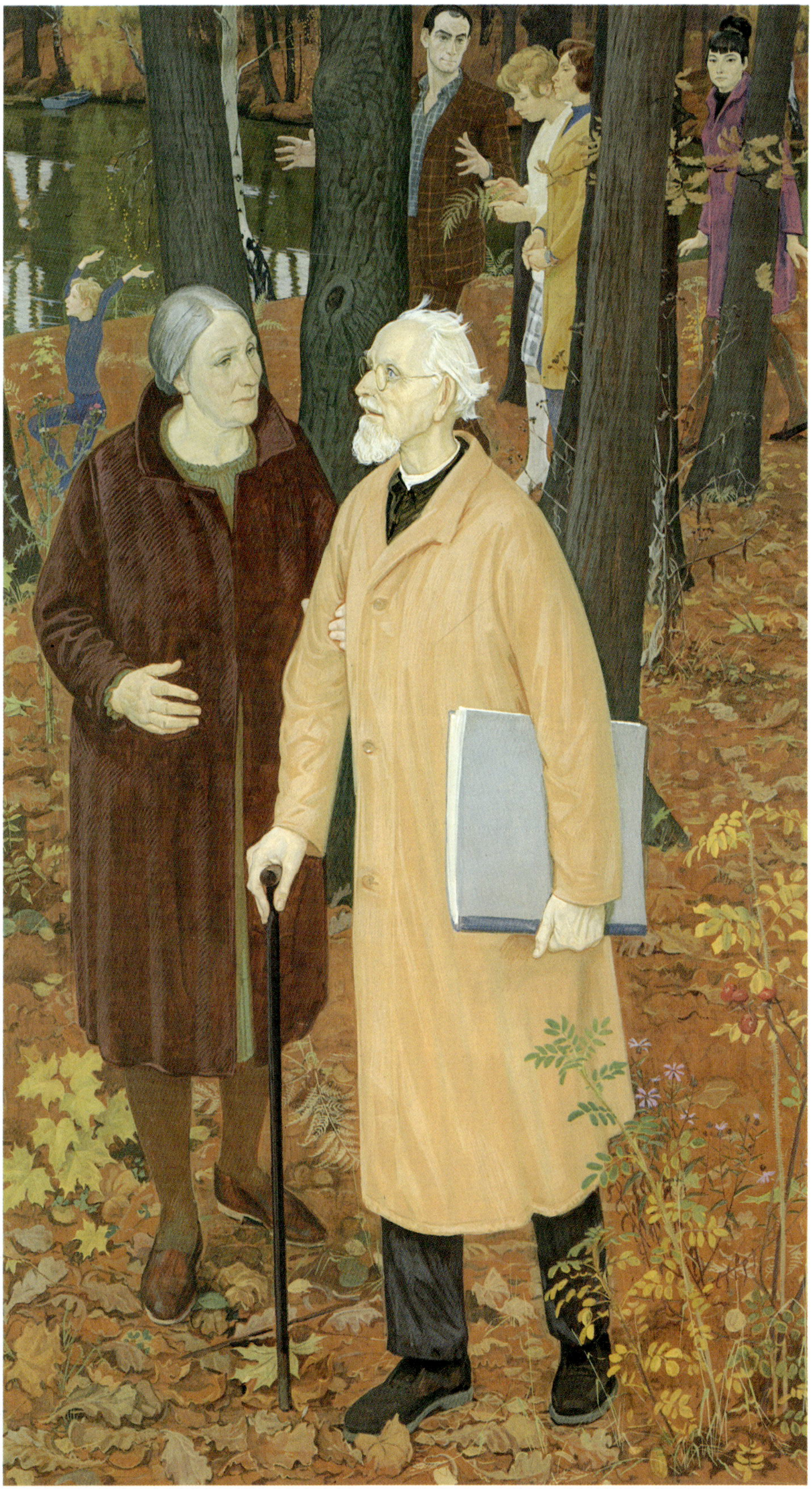

Pl. 91 *Portrait of the Artist Chernyshev with His Wife,* 1985
Tempera on board, 56 1/2 × 34 inches (141 × 85 cm)
Courtesy of the Artist

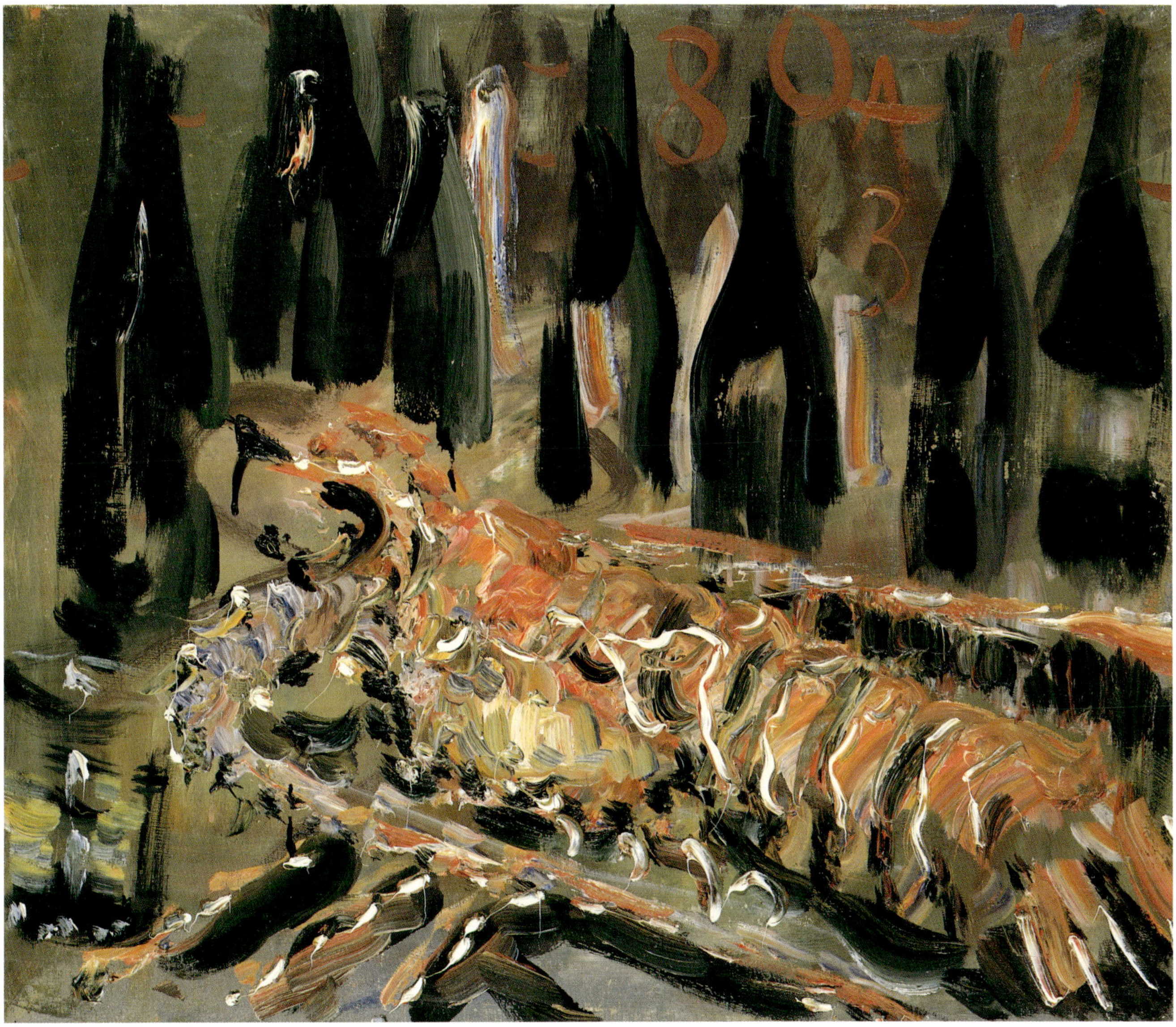

Pl. 93 *Still Life with Lobster*, 1980
Oil on canvas, 20 3/4 × 24 5/8 inches (52.5 × 62.5 cm)
Collection of Vladimir Nemukhin

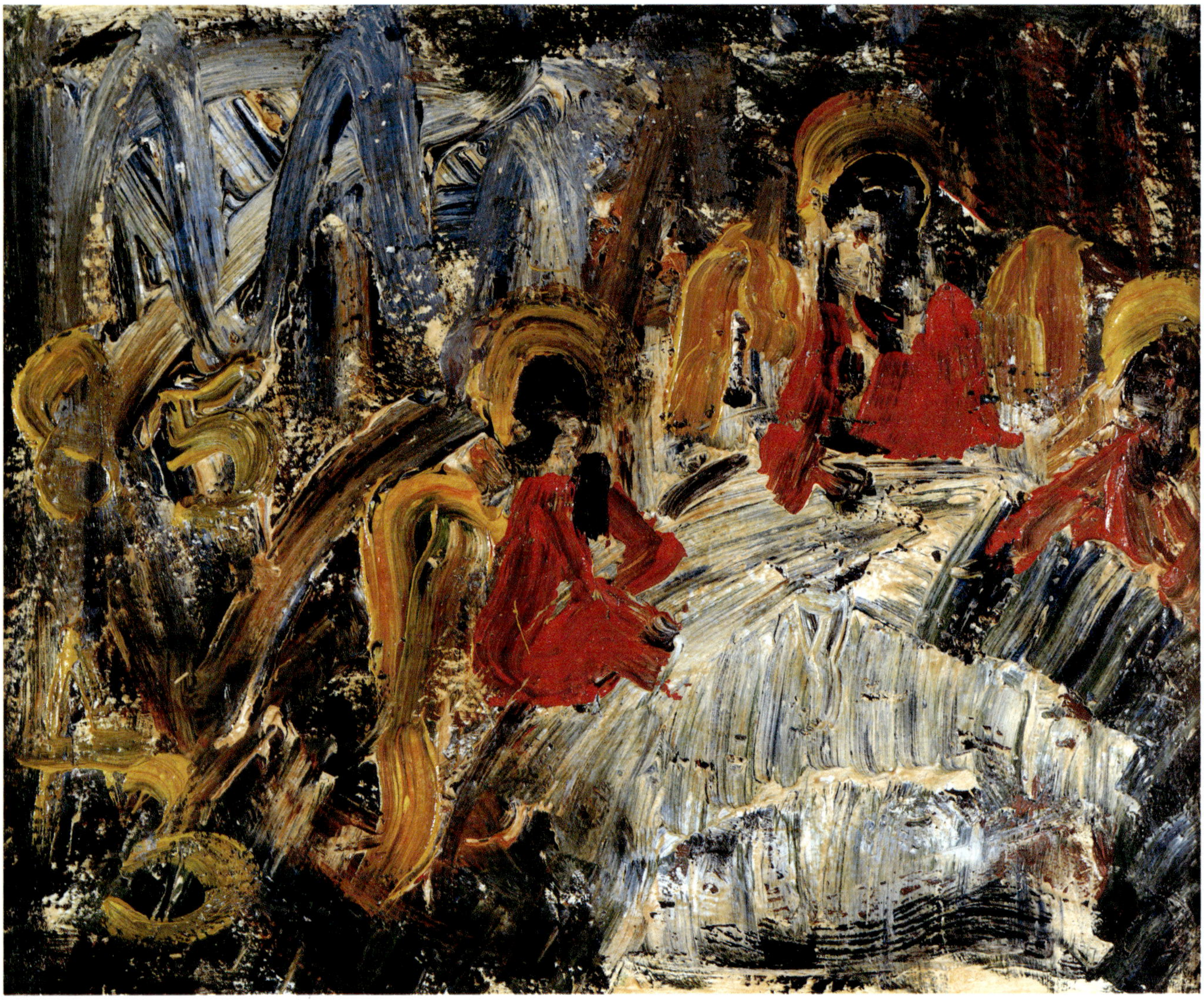

Pl. 94 *Trinity*, 1985
Oil on board, 15 × 20 inches (38 × 50.8 cm)
Private Collection

ARTISTS' BIOGRAPHIES

Guram Abramishvili

Abramishvili was born in 1966 in Moscow. Since 1988 he has resided in abandoned apartment buildings of Old Moscow, on Furmanny Lane, near the Sretensky Boulevard studios of Kabakov, Bulatov, and other unofficial artists of the sixties generation. Since 1986 he has participated in city exhibitions, including the 1988 *Labyrinth* show at the Palace of Youth, Moscow, and in exhibitions in Poland, West Germany, Italy, Portugal, France, and the United States. In 1986 he became a member of the group Champions of the World, which includes Bogdalov, Yakhnin, and others. In 1989 he joined the Graphics Union. In 1990 he exhibited at the Venice Biennale.

Until 1988, members of the Champions of the World worked in groups as anonymous painters. Initially their works were not created for sale but were often destroyed or incorporated in part into new works. Conceptualism and performance art have been part of these artists' creative processes. Abramishvili participated in the performances of the *Sandunovsky Baths* of 1988, organized by the Avant-Gardists Club. Since 1989, artists like Abramishvili have been working more independently and with the art market in mind. Currently, Abramishvili is interested in the subject of social stereotypes. In his works he often incorporates photography and texts, sometimes in English, perhaps responding to an international clientele.

Nikolai Andronov

A prominent artist of the sixties generation, Andronov was born in 1926 in Moscow, where he presently lives. He studied at the Repin Art Institute in Leningrad from 1948 to 1952, and at the Surikov Art Institute in Moscow from 1952 to 1954. Since 1951 he has participated in many exhibitions at home and abroad. He became a member of the USSR Union of Artists in 1958. He is an Honored Artist of the Russian Republic and a USSR State Prize winner. In 1962, he was one of the young experimental artists of the Moscow Union of Artists who exhibited in *Thirty Years of Moscow Art* at the Manezh exhibition hall. His works are in museums such as the Tretyakov Art Gallery, Moscow; the Russian Museum, Leningrad; the Museum of Russian Art, Kiev; and the Ludwig Museum, Cologne.

Andronov was one of the initiators of the Severe Style, which, in contrast to the grandiose optimism of Stalin-era Socialist Realism, shows peasants, workers, and soldiers responding to the realities of everyday life with grim determination. His genre, landscape, and figure paintings impart an unvarnished austerity in their muted tonalities and compositional logic.

Zaven Arshakuni

Arshakuni was born in 1932 in Leningrad, where he continues to live and work. From 1954 to 1962, he studied at the Repin Art Institute in Leningrad. In 1962 he joined the USSR Union of Artists. Since 1960 he has participated in youth, city, republic, and all-union exhibitions in the USSR and in exhibitions in Poland, Hungary, Bulgaria, Denmark, elsewhere in Europe, and in Japan. In 1966, he became acknowledged for his set designs. His works are in the collections of many museums, including the Russian Museum, Leningrad; the Tretyakov Art Gallery and the Pushkin Museum, Moscow; the Picture Gallery of Armenia, Yerevan; and the Ludwig Museum, Cologne.

A member of the Group of Eleven, which constituted the left wing of the Leningrad Union of Artists, Arshakuni was one of the prominent artists of the sixties generation. He is a painter, graphic artist, book illustrator, set and costume designer, stained-glass artist, ceramicist, furniture maker, wood carver, and musician. Easel painting and printmaking are his favored media. His pictures are festive and joyous, with figures, architecture, and decorative objects broadly and spontaneously sketched in bold combinations of vivid, primary colors. The theatrical quality of his works is enhanced by his use of narrative elements, often superimposed or enlarged for dramatic impact.

Pyotr Belenok

Belenok was born in Korogod in the Chernobyl Region of the Ukraine in 1938. A sculptor by profession, he graduated from the Kiev Art Institute in 1963. In 1967 he became a member of the USSR Union of Artists and moved to Moscow, where he became acquainted with many unofficial artists. He exhibited in the *Second Autumn Open-Air Exhibition* in Moscow in 1974. He has continued to exhibit in Moscow and in West Berlin, Paris, Helsinki, Tokyo, the United States, and elsewhere. His works are in collections in Europe and the United States, including the Cremona Foundation; and, since 1989, are included in the collections of the Russian Museum in Leningrad.

Belenok's theme of alienation is expressed through images of human figures, miniaturized in an endless space, often gesturing in horrified response to unexplained yet cataclysmic forces.

Eli Belyutin

Belyutin was born in 1924 in Moscow, where he now lives. He graduated from the Department of Art at the Moscow Pedagogical Institute in 1949 and studied at the Repin Art Institute, Leningrad in 1952. He taught at the Polygraphic Institute in Moscow until 1959, when he was released because of his modernist approach to art. Subsequently, he founded the Studio of Experimental Painting and Graphic Arts in Moscow and was well known for his innovative teaching of abstract art. In 1962, Belyutin and his followers were participants in the famous exhibition *Thirty Years of Moscow Art*; their works, installed on the second floor of the Manezh Hall, so enraged Khrushchev that he ordered the entire level to be permanently closed to the public. Since the early 1960s, Belyutin has exhibited at home and in Warsaw, Paris, London, and Rome. His work was first shown in the United States in 1976. His works are in museums in France, Italy, and Poland, and in European and American collections, including the Cremona Foundation, Maryland.

Belyutin's paintings of figures are characterized by bright contrasting colors applied with energetic brushstrokes, aggressively forcing the forms to the limits of the canvas.

Farid Bogdalov

One of the artists of the eighties generation, Bogdalov was born in 1963 at Lukhovitsy; he lives and works in Moscow. From 1980 to 1984 he studied at the Kalinin Secondary Art School, specializing in tapestry and kilim. He also attended classes in the painting department of the Surikov Art Institute, Moscow, in 1984 and 1985. In 1986 he was one of the first artists to settle in Furmanny Lane; like other artists residing there, he considers himself an heir of Conceptual artists Kabakov, Bulatov, and others of their circle. He participated with the group Flybanes (named after a type of colorful, poisonous mushroom) in their Apt-Art exhibitions and is also associated with the Champions of the World. Bogdalov became a member of the Graphics Union in 1989. He has participated in city, republic, and all-union exhibitions. His works are in private collections in the USSR and abroad.

Bogdalov's current work is characterized by large canvases with a heavy impasto of dark colors depicting a single everyday object such as a pool table, a sink, or a typewriter in grand scale.

Gleb Bogomolov

A self-taught artist, Bogomolov was born in 1933 in Leningrad, where he continues to live and work. Since 1947, he has participated in exhibitions at home, in unofficial apartment exhibits, and abroad in Norway, Sweden, West Germany, and the United States. In 1975, Bogomolov became a member of an unofficial group of independent Leningrad artists called the Fellowship for Experimental Art. His works are in the Russian Museum, Leningrad; the Tretyakov Art Gallery, Moscow; the Russian Museum in Exile, Montgeron, France; the Khabarovsk Picture Gallery; the Museum of Modern Art, Seoul; and the Cremona Foundation, Maryland.

Bogomolov's works are complex, with exquisite layerings of paint, fragments of gold foil, printed texts, and playing cards. His compositions reflect the Russian icon tradition as well as the aesthetic and philosophical inquiries of the early avant-garde.

Erik Bulatov

Along with Kabakov, Chuikov, and other conceptual artists, Bulatov is a significant member of the older generation of unofficial artists. He was born in Sverdlovsk in 1933 and presently lives and works in Moscow. Bulatov studied at the Moscow Secondary Art School from 1946 to 1952 and graduated from the Surikov Art Institute, Moscow, in 1958. In the early 1960s he was a member of the Sretensky Boulevard group of unofficial artists, which included Ilya Kabakov, Viktor Pivovarov, Vladimir Yankilevsky, and Edik Shteinberg. He is considered to be one of the spiritual forebears of the Champions of the World, a group of young eighties generation artists working in nearby Furmanny Lane. Bulatov has exhibited in the USSR and in France, Switzerland, West Germany, Great Britain, and the United States. His works are in private collections in Europe and the United States. Many of Bulatov's canvases incorporate slogans in large Cyrillic or English block letters ("Stop-Go," "Danger," "Revolution-Perestroika"), either filling the entire surface or superimposed over realistically rendered landscapes or figure groups. To him the flat, opaque letters create a boundary between the actual space of the viewer and the pictorial space "behind" the picture plane, wherein lies real substance.

Olga Bulgakova

Bulgakova is one of the important seventies artists whose reputations were firmly established in the landmark *Exhibition of 23*, held in 1981 at the Central House of Artists of the USSR Union of Artists in Moscow. Bulgakova was born in Moscow in 1951 and lives there today with her husband Alexander Sitnikov, also an artist. In 1969 Bulgakova graduated from the Moscow Secondary Art School and in 1975 from the Surikov Art Institute, Moscow. Since 1972 she has participated in youth, city, republic, and all-union art exhibitions. She became a member of the USSR Union of Artists in 1976 and that year began to exhibit throughout Europe and the United States. Her works are in several museums, including the Tretyakov Art Gallery, Moscow; the Russian Museum, Leningrad; the Ludwig Museum, Cologne; and the Cremona Foundation, Maryland.

Bulgakova's exquisitely rendered surrealist pictures reflect a highly intellectual and formal approach to subject matter. Her themes include the complex world of good and evil, especially as these forces are revealed in the world of the theater and circus.

Evgeni Dybsky

Dybsky was born in 1955 in Konstanza, Rumania, and he presently resides in Moscow. Dybsky attended the Moscow Secondary Art School from 1973 to 1978 and graduated from the Surikov Art Institute, Moscow, in 1984. He is a member of the Youth Section of the USSR Union of Artists. Since 1975 he has participated in youth, city, republic, and all-union exhibitions in Moscow, and since 1987 has exhibited in Greece, France, Poland, Italy, West Germany, Finland, Great Britain, Sweden, and the United States. His works are in private collections in the USSR, Europe, and the United States, and in public collections including the Novosibirsk Art Museum; the Ludwig Museum, Cologne; and the Kunsthalle Stiftung Henri Nannen, Emden, West Germany.

Dybsky uses rich color and textural contrasts as his principal means of expression. A favored theme of his abstract paintings is figures in a landscape, with features overlapping a painted, frame-like border. Such works express the artist's conviction that art is a journey toward discovery; the unknown is revealed as the complex spatial relationships emerge and take shape.

Simon Faibisovich

Faibisovich was born in Moscow in 1949. He studied at the Moscow Secondary Art School from 1959 to 1964 and graduated from the Moscow Architectural Institute in 1972. In 1979, he joined the Graphics Union and began to participate in city and all-union exhibitions. Since the mid-1980s he has exhibited in Western Europe and the United States, and his works are included in several private and public collections in the United States and abroad, including the Museum of Modern Art, Lodz, Poland; the Ludwig Museum, Cologne; and the Cremona Foundation, Maryland.

Faibisovich is best known for his Hyperrealist paintings of people riding on trains, buses, and subways, seen through or reflected in windows in such a way that the works take on an unreal, almost surreal, dimension.

Elena Figurina

Figurina was born in Ventspils, Latvia, in 1955 and now lives in Leningrad. She began painting in 1976, had her first exhibition in 1978, and graduated from the Leningrad Institute of Aircraft Construction in 1979. She is a member of the Fellowship for Experimental Art, an alliance of independent artists in Leningrad. She has participated in exhibitions in Finland, France, West Germany, Poland, and the United States. Works by the artist are in the Russian Museum, Leningrad; the University of Oregon, Eugene; and in private collections in Europe, the United States, and the Soviet Union.

Figurina's gentle, childlike creatures evoke sorrow and sympathy as they awkwardly attempt to escape an alien world portrayed in intense, often dissonant colors.

Andrei Gennadiev

Gennadiev was born in 1947 in Leningrad, where he continues to live and work today. He studied at the Leningrad Graphic Arts Institute from 1964 to 1968 and then undertook his own art education by immersing himself in the study of treasures at the Hermitage Museum—in particular, Russian icons and the art of Bosch, Brueghel, Dürer, Titian, El Greco, Velázquez, Cézanne, Van Gogh, and Matisse. He also became preoccupied with astrology, palmistry, Eastern culture, and Christianity. Other influences include the metaphysical concepts of the St. Petersburg Group, who viewed the icon as the most perfect form for the revelation of beauty. Gennadiev became a member of the USSR Union of Artists in 1978. He is an accomplished painter, a printmaker who excels in hand-colored etching techniques, and a master of the *ex libris*, or bookplate design. He has participated in many exhibitions at home and abroad; his works were first introduced in the United States in 1984. He is represented in numerous public and private collections including the Pushkin Museum, Moscow; the Dostoevsky Museum, Leningrad; the Metropolitan Museum of Art, New York; and the Cremona Foundation, Maryland.

Gennadiev's works combine a variety of symbols from different cultures and eras, creating unique, almost supernatural, images.

Ilya Glazunov

Glazunov was born in Leningrad in 1930 and was the only member of his family to survive the siege of that city in World War II. He graduated in 1957 from the Repin Art Institute, Leningrad. He has painted genre scenes showing the loneliness and alienation of Soviet life, and his illustrations of characters from Dostoevsky have been highly praised. In 1964, soon after the landmark Manezh exhibition, Glazunov held a one-artist show at the Manezh that was attended by thousands of people and supported by the Ministry of Culture, while the Union of Artists unsuccessfully bid for the closing of the exhibition. Glazunov was refused entry into the union until 1967 because of his "decadent and bourgeois" pictures with mystical and religious connotations, yet in 1973 he was awarded the title of People's Artist of the USSR. He has also been named an Honorary Academician of the Royal Academies of Fine Arts in Barcelona and Madrid. The Ministry of Culture continues to sponsor exhibitions of his work abroad. His works are in European and American private collections and in public collections such as the Tretyakov Art Gallery, Moscow; the Russian Museum, Leningrad; and UNESCO, Paris.

Glazunov is perhaps best known for his illustrative pictures of czars, saints, heroes, and the faith and culture of old Russia. He has also created exceptional canvases of socio-political and religious commentary, such as *Return of the Prodigal Son*, which depicts a jeans-clad youth kneeling before a Christ-like figure, great Russian heroes from the past, guzzling pigs, destroyed churches, and concentration camps. His twenty-foot-long canvas, *Mystery of the Twentieth Century*, portraying many famous people—from Nicholas II, Lenin, Mao, and Sartre to the Beatles and Solzhenitsyn—was at one time banned from exhibition.

Olga Grechina

Grechina was born in Kovrov in the Vladimir Region of Russia in 1947; she presently lives in Moscow. A graduate of the Surikov Art Institute, Moscow, in 1972, she has been a member of the USSR Union of Artists since 1974. One of the prominent young seventies artists, she was represented in the landmark *Exhibition of 23*, held in 1981 in Moscow at the Central House of Artists of the USSR Union of Artists. Grechina is a painter and printmaker. She has exhibited extensively in the Soviet Union, Europe, and the United States.

Grechina's works are in collections such as the Tretyakov Art Gallery, Moscow; the Ludwig Collection, Cologne; and the Cremona Foundation, Maryland. Her brightly painted scenes from contemporary life combine crisp Photorealist imagery with feathery out-of-focus forms, creating a nearly hallucinatory world of blurred movement and tension.

Francisco Infante

Infante was born in 1943 in Vassilyevka, a suburb of Moscow. He studied at the Surikov Art Institute from 1957 to 1962, at the Moscow College of Decorative and Applied Arts from 1962 to 1966, and at the Moscow Art School from 1966 to 1968. From 1962 to 1968 he was a member of the *Dvizhenie*, or "Movement," group, organized by self-taught artist Lev Nusberg. From 1963 to 1988, Infante participated in more than thirty unofficial exhibitions in the Soviet Union. He has also exhibited in more than fifty exhibitions in West Germany, Italy, The Netherlands, the United States, and elsewhere. Works by Infante are in private collections in Europe and the United States and in public collections such as the Russian

Museum in Exile, Montgeron, France, and the Cremona Foundation, Maryland.

Infante, an unofficial artist who produces nonobjective, kinetic sculptures, is concerned with upholding the traditions of the Russian Constructivists of the 1920s. Understanding "kinetic" to mean that which is alive, he has designed abstract systems and artificial environments in which moving and revolving forms, color, light, and sound play an important role. Ironically, these constructions have been admired by the government's Ministry of Building and Ministry of Radiotechnological Industry, and some of his kinetic works have been exhibited through such organizations as the Leningrad Architects Club (1965) and Moscow's Kurchatov Institute of Atomic Energy (1966). In 1970 Infante organized a group of artists and engineers called ARGO with the idea of creating artificial systems analagous to natural phenomena. Since 1975, he has focused on the creation of ARTEFACTS, which, presented through photographs, document open-air installations, juxtaposing artificial (art) objects with nature. In works such as his *Spiral* series of 1965, Infante represents in gouache his theories about the phenomenon of the spiral. The alternation of an infinite tendency toward an ideal horizontal and vertical line creates a line turning in space, which in its momentum has associations with other opposing aspects of the cosmos such as good and bad, living and dead.

Ilya Kabakov

Kabakov is one of the premiere Conceptual artists of the unofficial art movement of the sixties. He is highly regarded by many of the young eighties generation artists such as those working in Furmanny Lane, who consider themselves to be the heirs of early Conceptualism and Pop Art. Kabakov was born in the Ukrainian city of Dniepropetrovsk in 1933; he presently lives and works in Moscow. He graduated in 1951 from the Moscow Secondary Art School and in 1957 from the Surikov Art Institute, Moscow. Since 1957 he has been a successful illustrator of children's books. In 1965 he became a member of the USSR Union of Artists. He also belongs to the Sretensky Boulevard group, along with Erik Bulatov, Edik Shteinberg, Vladimir Yankilevsky, and Viktor Pivovarov. He has exhibited in city and republic exhibitions in the USSR, including *Twenty Moscow Artists*, the first officially sanctioned unofficial art show, in 1975. He has also exhibited in France, West Germany, Italy, Great Britain, Switzerland, the United States, and elsewhere. Works by the artist are in private collections in France, West Germany, and the United States, and in public collections such as the Centre Georges Pompidou, Paris, and the Museum für Gegenwartskunst, Basel.

Kabakov's earlier text-and-image and found-object paintings combine elements of literature, art, and Soviet postwar mass culture. His gentle humor and irony and his contemplative intellect are reflected in these works. To the artist, meaning lies behind or beyond the fictitious painted surface. Therefore, a dialogue must be created between the viewer and the content of the picture, evoking philosophical consideration of life's contradictions. Since 1981 Kabakov has been concentrating on a series of installations.

Viktor Kalinin

Kalinin was born in 1946 in the village of Zalesovo in the Altai Territory of Russia. One of the young seventies artists, he lives and works in Moscow. From 1960 to 1962, he studied at the Surikov Secondary Art School in Krasnoyarsk, at the Gorky Secondary Art School from 1962 to 1965, and at the Moscow Higher College of Industrial Art from 1965 to 1971. He joined the USSR Union of Artists in 1974 and since 1966 has exhibited in city, republic, and all-union exhibitions, including the landmark *Exhibition of 23* in Moscow; he has also participated in exhibitions abroad. Works by Kalinin are in the collections of several museums: among others, the Tretyakov Art Gallery, Moscow; the Russian Museum, Leningrad; and the Ludwig Museum, Cologne.

Kalinin's simple themes of man's restless search for a harmonious life are portrayed with monumental feeling in an expressive, painterly manner influenced by Russian icon painting, Russian Impressionism, early avant-garde Expressionism, and the works of Mikhail Vrubel.

Anatoli Kaplan

Kaplan was born in 1902 in the provincial town of Rogachev in Belorussia, and he lived in Leningrad until his death in 1980. He studied at the Leningrad Academy of Arts from 1921 to 1926, and became a member of the Union of Artists when it was established in 1939. Beginning in the 1960s, he participated in group exhibitions at home and abroad and had several one-artist shows in the West. No solo exhibition of his work was organized in his homeland during his lifetime, and to this day Soviet officialdom resists honoring the artist with a one-man show, despite his worldwide acclaim.

Kaplan was a painter and ceramicist and one of the greatest contemporary Soviet graphic artists. He is also well known for his pastels and gouaches. His themes are from Jewish folklore and the life of the provincial Russian Jewish community. Through his preservation of the colorful details of Jewish life, recalled from childhood, Kaplan became the recorder of a bygone era. The profound simplicity of his works speaks to everyone's life and traditions and preserves an irretrievable link with the past.

Igor Kopystiansky

Kopystiansky was born in the Ukrainian city of Lvov in 1954; he currently divides his time between Lvov and Moscow. A graduate of the Lvov Institute of Applied and Decorative Arts in 1977, he is a member of the Youth Section of the Russian Artists' Union. From 1980 to 1985, he was a member of the Group of Six, an organization of Hyperrealist artists headed by Alexander Tegin and including Sergei Sherstiuk, Sergei Geta, Sergei Basilev, and Nikolai Filatov. He has exhibited in Lithuania, France, Spain, West Germany, and the United States.

Kopystiansky creates what he calls "destroyed paintings," images derived from European old masters, photographs, or tombstone memorials, scarred by time with cracks, paint losses, and patches. He also creates installations of painted canvases—again frequently quoting old master pictures—which are rolled up to form columns, draped over tables, or shaped into chairs in ironic reference to the Socialist Realist credo that art must be socially useful.

Valeri Lukka

Lukka was born in 1945 in the Yaroslavl region, in the village of Porokhovo; today he lives and works in Leningrad. In 1977, he graduated from the Repin Art Institute, Leningrad. Since 1978 he has participated in city, republic, and all-union art exhibitions. In 1984, 1987, and 1989 he also participated in group exhibitions with the artists Volosenkov and Mikhailov of Leningrad. Lukka paints portraits, genre scenes, architectural views of Leningrad, and intriguing variants on old master pictures. These combine traditional methods of paint application with dripped paint additions for texture and form. The works, especially the portraits and genre pictures, reflect the artist's wry sense of humor about everyday people and events, and often contain a note of sarcasm.

Tatiana Nazarenko

Born in Moscow in 1944, Nazarenko is one of the best-known artists of the seventies generation. She studied at the Moscow Secondary Art School from 1955 to 1962, and from 1962 to 1968 at the Surikov Art Institute, Moscow, where she was a pupil of Dmitri Zhilinsky. From 1967 to 1972 she completed postgraduate work at the USSR Academy of Arts, and in 1969 joined the liberal ranks of the USSR Union of Artists. Since 1966, she has participated in city, republic, and all-union exhibitions, including the 1981 *Exhibition of 23*; she has also participated in exhibitions in Bulgaria, Austria, Hungary, West Germany, the United States, and elsewhere abroad. Nazarenko's work is in many public and private collections in the USSR, Europe, and the United States, including the Tretyakov Art Gallery, Moscow; the Russian Museum, Leningrad; the Museum of Russian Art in Kiev; the Ludwig Museum, Cologne; and the Cremona Foundation, Maryland. She is a winner of the Lenin Komsomol Prize and the Moscow Komsomol Prize.

Nazarenko's subjects are her country's revolutionary history and scenes from everyday life, in which her self-portrait often appears. The symbolic and stylistic foundations upon which she builds her work are those of Renaissance masters such as Piero della Francesca, Jan van Eyck, and Pieter Brueghel. Through her personal symbolism Nazarenko creates a dialogue between contemporary life and a cultural and historic past, and thereby expresses the individual's search for identity in today's world.

Vladimir Nemukhin

Nemukhin is one of the premiere artists of the unofficial art movement of the 1960s. He was born in Moscow in 1925 and continues to live and work there today. In 1942 he entered the studio of P. E. Sokolov, a student of Malevich, and Pavel Kuznetsov. He worked in a factory for many years and painted in his spare time. In 1957 he entered the Surikov Art Institute, Moscow, but was soon expelled for his unorthodox ideas. Since 1959 he has been a member of the Graphics Union. In the late 1950s and through the 1960s he was a member of the Lianozovo Group, whose members were some of the most uncompromising advocates for freedom of self-expression. Nemukhin participated in many private apartment exhibitions. He also exhibited in several controversial shows: the 1967 Druzhba Workers Club exhibition, shut down by the Moscow Party Committee and the KGB; the 1969 exhibition in Moscow at the Institute of World Economics and International Relations which closed after forty-five minutes; the *First Autumn Open-Air Exhibition* and the *Second Autumn Open-Air Exhibition* in 1974; and *Twenty Moscow Artists* in 1975. In 1977 his works were included in exhibitions at the Metropolitan Museum of Art, New York; the Institute of Contemporary Arts, London; and the Venice Biennale. Throughout the 1970s and 1980s he has exhibited in Poland, Italy, West Germany, Denmark, Switzerland, France, and the United States. Works by the artist are in the Centre Georges Pompidou, Paris; the Museum of Modern Art, New York; and private collections in France and the United States.

Nemukhin has been strongly influenced by the art of Cézanne, the Cubists, Malevich, Rauschenberg, and Johns. Since 1963, he has concentrated on the subject of playing cards, incorporating the real object and its painted counterpart in still lifes in which he seeks to resolve aesthetic problems of geometric form, color, texture, and plane. For him, the cards evoke universal associations with mystery, riddles, chance, and fate—the elements of the game of life. Nemukhin is also a sculptor; he creates bronzes dedicated to other nonconformist artists, such as Weisberg, Infante, Kabakov, and Yankilevsky.

Natalia Nesterova

Nesterova was born in Moscow in 1944. One of the best-known artists of the seventies generation, she lives and works in Moscow today. From 1955 to 1962 she studied at the Moscow Secondary Art School, and from 1962 to 1968 at the Surikov Art Institute, Moscow, where she was a pupil of Dmitri Zhilinsky. Since 1968, she has participated in city, republic, and all-union exhibitions, including the *Exhibition of 23* in Moscow. In 1969, she joined the USSR Union of Artists, and along with Nazarenko and others was part of the left movement led by Zhilinsky. Nesterova has exhibited in more than twenty countries, including Bulgaria, Rumania, Norway, France, Germany, Japan, and the United States. Works by Nesterova are in the Tretyakov Art Gallery, Moscow; the Russian Museum, Leningrad; the Arkhangelsk Museum of Fine Arts; the Ludwig Museum, Cologne; and the Cremona Foundation, Maryland.

Nesterova's often drastically cropped images of daily life in Moscow and the resorts of the Crimea and the Caucasus are characterized by poetic lyricism and psychological complexity. In stagelike narratives, figures are juxtaposed or fused grotesquely with the world of nature, sculpture, or architecture, evoking irony, ambiguity, and contradiction to express the dilemma of man in the modern world.

Anatoli Nikich

Nikich has been named an Honored Artist of the Russian Republic. Born in Petrograd (now Leningrad) in 1918, he currently lives in Moscow. He graduated from the Surikov Art Institute, Moscow, in 1942 and became a member of the USSR Union of Artists in 1944. Since 1948, he has participated in city, republic, and all-union art exhibitions. Beginning in 1955, his works have been exhibited in Bulgaria, Hungary, Great Britain, France, Japan, India, the United States, and elsewhere in Europe and Asia. Many of his works are in public collections, including the Tretyakov Art Gallery, Moscow; the Russian Museum, Leningrad; and the Ludwig Museum, Cologne.

Influenced by such artists as Cézanne and Bonnard, Nikich's still lifes and figure paintings are inspired by the classic order and monumentality of frames, canvases, books, postcards, and drapery as well as the lyrical beauty of fruits, flowers, and the artist's model.

Vladimir Ovchinnikov

Ovchinnikov is one of the prominent unofficial artists of Leningrad. He was born in 1941 in the Ural Mountains, and in 1945 he moved with his family to Leningrad, where he later graduated from the Leningrad Art School. Since the early 1960s he has been a part of the nonconformist movement and has participated in landmark exhibitions of unofficial art, including the 1964 Hermitage Museum exhibition that was shut down by the KGB and resulted in the dismissal of the museum's director. More recently, Ovchinnikov has displayed works in exhibitions organized by the Leningrad Fellowship for Experimental Art, which includes artists Gleb Bogomolov and Elena Figurina, among others. He has exhibited frequently in France, West Germany, Italy, Austria, Japan, and the United States. His works are included in major collections such as the Russian Museum, Leningrad; the Metropolitan Museum of Art, New York; and the Cremona Foundation, Maryland.

Ovchinnikov's scenes are drawn from life around the Leningrad suburb of Shuvalovo. His figures and objects are depicted as wooden and doll-like, as if turned on a lathe. Angels appear in some works, bathing the scene in a mysterious, otherworldly light, but the miracle is unnoticed by the characters in the drama. Ovchinnikov's primary theme is the search for religious faith in a spiritually bankrupt modern Russia, and that has been the principal reason for the censorship of his paintings.

Alexander Petrov

Petrov was born in 1951 in Leningrad, where he continues to live and work. In 1975 he graduated from the Repin Art Institute, Leningrad, and became a member of the USSR Union of Artists. Since 1975 he has participated in city, republic, and all-union art exhibitions in the USSR and in exhibitions abroad. Works by Petrov are in the collections of the Russian Museum in Leningrad; the Vereshchagin Art Museum in Nikolaev; and in private collections in France, Finland, Italy, West Germany, and the United States.

Continuing in the tradition of Abstract Expressionism, Petrov paints mainly figurative works characterized by simple forms with broad areas of local color and bold outlines.

Arkadi Petrov

Petrov was born in 1940 in Gorlovka, in the Don region; he lives and works in Moscow. Petrov graduated from the Moscow Pedagogical Institute in 1963 and from the Surikov Art Institute, Moscow, in 1969. In 1971 he joined the USSR Union of Artists. Since 1965 he has exhibited in city, republic, and all-union exhibitions and has participated in exhibitions in Greece, Poland, Spain, and West Germany. Works by the artist are in the Russian Museum, Leningrad; the Ludwig Museum, Cologne; the Museum of Modern Art, Seoul; and the Cremona Foundation, Maryland. His works are also in private collections in the USSR, France, West Germany, Switzerland, Greece, and the United States.

In Petrov's paintings slightly primitive or naive figures are staged in landscape or interior settings inspired by objects of provincial Russian material culture (photos, postcards, valentines, souvenirs, and plastic bouquets fill his studio). More recent works are experiments in *Sots* Art, a Soviet form of Pop Art.

Viktor Popkov

One of the prominent artists of the 1960s who influenced artists of the seventies generation, Popkov was born in Moscow in 1931; he died in Moscow in 1974, the victim of an accidental shooting. From 1948 to 1952 he studied at the Moscow Secondary Graphic Arts School and from 1952 to 1958 at the Surikov Art Institute, Moscow. In 1959 he became a member of the USSR Union of Artists. Beginning in 1958, he participated in city, republic, and all-union exhibitions in the USSR and in exhibitions abroad. He was awarded the State Prize of the USSR posthumously in 1975 for his series of pictures entitled Reflections on Life. Paintings by Popkov are found in many museums, including the Tretyakov Art Gallery, Moscow; the Russian Museum, Leningrad; and the Picture Gallery of Armenia, Yerevan.

Popkov's personal symbolism, his portrayals of suffering, his references to peasant Russia, Russian religious and cultural traditions, and the land were significant breaks from Socialist Realism. The introspective quality of his pictures has inspired artists such as Nazarenko and others of the seventies generation.

Evgeni Rastorguev

Rastorguev was born in 1920 in the village of Nikola-Pogost near the historic town of Gorodets on the Volga River. In 1940, he graduated from the Gorky Secondary Art School and had his first exhibition at the Gorky Art Museum in 1941. Following his service in World War II, he graduated from the Moscow Art Institute in 1952 and in 1953 became a member of the USSR Union of Artists. Since 1951 he has participated in city, republic, and all-union exhibitions; in addition, he has exhibited in West Berlin, Tokyo, Warsaw, and Paris, among other cities. In 1969, 1975, and 1985, he exhibited as a member of the Moscow Group of Sixteen at Kuznetsky Bridge Exhibition Hall. His works are in many Soviet public collections, including the Tretyakov Art Gallery and the Decorative Arts Museum of the USSR in Moscow and the Russian Museum in Leningrad.

Rastorguev lives in Moscow. His paintings, book illustrations, and sculptures are inspired by memories of life in Gorodets—for centuries famed for its folk art. Rastorguev paints enchanting vignettes which recall the merry fairs of Gorodets, the colorful clothing of townsfolk, the carved decorations of wooden houses, and the spirit and gentle humor of provincial Russia.

Elena Romanova

Romanova is one of the prominent seventies artists of Moscow. Born in 1944, she attended the Moscow Secondary Art School from 1956 to 1963 and the Surikov Art Institute, Moscow, from 1963 to 1969. Since 1965, she has participated in youth, republic, and all-union exhibitions in the USSR and in more than twenty countries, including France, Great Britain, Finland, Japan, and the United States. She also participated in the Venice Biennales of 1974–1982. Her works are in several Soviet public collections, including the Tretyakov Art Gallery, Moscow; the Kiev Museum of Russian Art; and the Russian Museum, Leningrad; as well as private collections in Europe and the United States. A member of the USSR Union of Artists, she is an Honored Artist of the Russian Republic and has received several prestigious awards: the Moscow Komsomol Prize, the Lenin Komsomol Prize, and others.

Romanova's portraits and still lifes are based on the theme of harmony with nature. They are characterized by classical smoothness, logical clarity of design, and the meticulous accuracy that reflects the influence of Early Renaissance painting, the Russian icon tradition, and the art of Andrew Wyeth (who, along with Rockwell Kent, was for many years the most universally known American artist in the Soviet Union).

Evgeni Rukhin

Rukhin, one of the great leaders of the unofficial art movement, died in 1976 at the age of thirty-two in a mysterious fire at his Leningrad studio. He was born in Saratov in 1943 and studied geology at the University of Leningrad. He began to paint in 1963, after attending lectures at the Mukhin Art Institute in Leningrad. An active dissident, he divided his time between Leningrad and Moscow, joining these two ranks of independent artists. He was one of the organizers of the landmark *First Autumn Open-Air Exhibition* in Moscow in 1974 and was one of four artists arrested. That same year he participated in the *Second Autumn Open-Air Exhibition* in Moscow and in *Fifty Leningrad Artists* at the Gaza House of Culture in Leningrad, relentlessly exerting pressure on authorities to allow peaceful exhibits by unofficial artists. When it was nearly impossible to export unofficial art, Rukhin managed to have one-artist shows at the Betty Parsons Gallery in New York in 1966, the North Carolina Museum of Art (Raleigh) in 1975, and the Phillips Collection (Washington, D.C.) in 1976. His works have been in many exhibitions in Western Europe, South America, and the United States and are in major collections such as the Museo de Ciudad Bolivar, Caracas, Venezuela; the Russian Museum in Exile, Montgeron, France; the North Carolina Museum of Art, Raleigh; the Phillips Collection, Washington, D.C.; and the Cremona Foundation, Maryland.

Rukhin's art comments on the disappearance of objects rather than their abundance; he worked in a style that is reminiscent of Jasper Johns, an artist whom he greatly admired. In his canvases he has preserved impressions of icons, fragments of antique furniture and frames, which civilization has discarded as useless; juxtaposed with these are net shopping bags, commercial stencils (especially the warning "Dangerous to Life"), and other symbols of contemporary life, evoking nostalgia for a cultural past.

Sergei Sherstiuk

Sherstiuk was born in Moscow in 1951. He received training in graphics at the Shevchenko Art Institute in Kiev from 1964 to 1970, and in the theory of art and art history at the Moscow State University from 1974 to 1979. He became a member of the USSR Union of Artists in 1980 and began to exhibit in city, republic, and all-union exhibitions. From 1980 to 1985, he belonged to the Group of Six, organized by Alexander Tegin, whose members (Sergei Geta, Sergei Basilev, Nikolai Filatov, and Igor Kopystiansky) concentrated on Hyperrealism. Sherstiuk's paintings were first exhibited abroad in Paris in 1982 and in the United States in 1984. His works are in the collections of the USSR Union of Artists; the USSR Ministry of Culture; and the Cremona Foundation, Maryland. He often works in series, and his pictures have a surreal quality.

Edik Shteinberg

Shteinberg was born in 1937 in Moscow, where he presently lives. He had no academic art training, but he studied under his father, Arcadi Shteinberg, and worked with artists Boris Sveshnikov and Oskar Rabin. He joined the Graphics Union in 1967, but not until 1988 did he become a member of the USSR Union of Artists. In the early 1960s, he was a member of the Sretensky Boulevard group of unofficial artists, which included Ilya Kabakov, Viktor Pivovarov, Vladimir Yankilevsky, and Erik Bulatov. Since 1961, he has participated in city and republic exhibitions, the 1967 Druzhba Club show, and the 1975 *Twenty Moscow Artists* exhibit at the Bee-Keeping Pavilion of the Exhibition of Economic Achievements. He has exhibited in Austria, West Germany, France, Sweden, and the United States. Works by Shteinberg are in private collections in Austria, Brazil, France, Italy, Sweden, West Germany, and the United States.

In the early 1970s, Shteinberg developed a severe geometric style that is indebted to Malevich and other Russian Suprematists and Constructivists of the early avant-garde. His compositions of squares, circles, triangles, crosses, and arcs—the early works of opaque pastels, the more recent ones darkly painted—create a lively tension between figure and ground. These works are contemplative and philosophical, gentle and subtle manifestations of the artist's metaphysical sensibility.

Alexander Sitnikov

Sitnikov was born in 1945 in the village of Iva in the Penza Region of Russia. He graduated from the Surikov Art Institute, Moscow, in 1972. One of the seventies artists, Sitnikov joined the USSR Union of Artists in 1975. Since 1966 he has participated in city, republic, and all-union exhibitions, including the 1981 *Exhibition of 23*; he has also exhibited abroad in the Venice Biennale (1982) and in more than twenty countries, including Bulgaria, Italy, France, Great Britain, and the United States. His works are in private collections in Europe and the United States and in museums such as the Tretyakov Art Gallery, Moscow; the Russian Museum, Leningrad; the Ludwig

Museum, Cologne; and the Cremona Foundation, Maryland.

Sitnikov's brilliantly colored and highly varnished paintings reflect the Russian icon tradition, Egyptian art, and Surrealism. As with other artists of the seventies generation, Sitnikov uses recurring subjects—self-portraits, his family (Olga Bulgakova is his wife), or the composer Shostakovich—and often includes allegorical motifs of numbers, birds, and animals, especially bulls. All intertwine to express the moral battle to uphold beauty and good in a complicated world.

Andrei Tutunov

An Honored Artist of the Russian Republic, Tutunov was born in Moscow in 1928 and continues to live and work there. He studied at the Moscow Secondary Art School from 1940 to 1947, and at the Surikov Art Institute, Moscow, from 1948 to 1954. In 1954, he became a member of the USSR Union of Artists and began to participate in city, republic, and all-union exhibitions as well as exhibitions in France, Italy, Japan, Bulgaria, and elsewhere in Europe. His works are in many museums, including the Tretyakov Art Gallery, Moscow; the Russian Museum, Leningrad; and the Ludwig Museum, Cologne.

Tutunov was inspired by the Russian landscape tradition. His poetic landscapes portray scenes of midland Russia, and in a peaceful, contemplative way express close bonds with his native land.

Alexander Tyshler

An avant-garde artist, Tyshler is a vital link between pre-Stalinist traditions and contemporary Soviet art. He is considered the mentor of many of the artists of the sixties and seventies generations. Tyshler was born in Melitopol in the Ukraine in 1898; he died in 1980 in Moscow. A painter, draftsman, graphic artist, sculptor, stage designer, and book illustrator, he studied at the Kiev Art Academy from 1912 to 1917. In 1924, he was a founding member of the Moscow avant-garde group OST (Society of Easel Painters), with whom he exhibited through 1928. He produced much work for the theater in the 1930s through 1961. The 1960s and 1970s were periods of intensive work in easel painting. Tyshler was considered a "moderate" avant-garde artist of the 1920s (compared to Malevich or Tatlin), yet his art was condemned by officials at the 1962 Manezh exhibition and elsewhere. He continued to participate in exhibitions in the USSR and abroad in countries such as East and West Germany, France, Italy, Norway, Sweden, Switzerland, Japan, and the United States. His works are represented in the Tretyakov Art Gallery and Pushkin Museum, Moscow; the Russian Museum, Leningrad; the Ludwig Museum, Cologne; and the Cremona Foundation, Maryland.

Tyshler merges reality, invention, poetic charm, and gentle irony in his images of women, landscapes, and still lifes. Especially characteristic of his work are the figures crowned with fantastic headdresses of architecture or candles who become personifications of cities, birthdays, or other places or events from everyday life.

Valeri Vatenin

Vatenin was born in 1933 in Leningrad; he lived and worked in Leningrad until his untimely death in a motorcycle accident in 1977. As a child during World War II, he was evacuated with his school to the Kirov Province during the Leningrad Blockade of September 8, 1941–June 18, 1943; scenes of the evacuation appear frequently in his paintings. He studied at the Leningrad Secondary Art School from 1947 to 1952 and at the Repin Art Institute, Leningrad, from 1953 to 1959. Vatenin joined the USSR Union of Artists in 1965 and was a member of the Leningrad Group of Eleven, which included Arshakuni and other left-wing artists. He participated in city and republic exhibitions in the USSR and in exhibitions in China, Finland, and elsewhere abroad. His works are in the Tretyakov Art Gallery, Moscow, and the Russian Museum, Leningrad.

Vatenin's portraits, genre scenes, and still lifes, painted in tempera on canvas or board, have stylistic affinities with Russian icons, early Renaissance painting, and Cubism. Drawing from childhood memories of war as well as everyday life, he created multifaceted images that combine reality with a parallel world of hopes and dreams in a vital, poetic manner.

Vladimir Weisberg

Weisberg was one of the most influential artists of the sixties generation. He was born in 1924 in Moscow, where he lived and worked until his death in 1985. He attended lectures at the Surikov Art Institute, Moscow, around 1946, but he was not a student there. He began to participate in city, republic, and all-union exhibitions in 1955. In 1961 he joined the USSR Union of Artists and became a member of the Group of Eight, whose works were the most extreme departures from Socialist Realism at the time. He participated in the celebrated 1962 Manezh exhibition, in which one of his works—a painting of a nude—was deemed pornographic. Following the Manezh exhibition, Weisberg's works were banned from official exhibits, although he remained a member of the union and later taught drawing at the Moscow Secondary Architectural School. In 1967, he participated in various unofficial exhibitions and thereafter exhibited in many Western countries, including France, West Germany, and Austria. His works are in the Tretyakov Art Gallery and the Pushkin Museum, Moscow; the Russian Museum, Leningrad; and the Cremona Foundation, Maryland.

Weisberg's still lifes, portraits, and nudes are based upon his analytical notions of recognition and non-recognition in artistic perception. In his still lifes especially, the complex variations of white geometric shapes arranged against a white ground elicit long contemplation in which recognition of forms in space must be reconciled with perceptions of the laws of color and composition.

Andrei Yakhnin

Yakhnin was born in 1966 in Moscow; he works with the Furmanny Lane group in Old Moscow. Yakhnin graduated from the Moscow Institute of Architecture in 1989 and the same year became a member of the Graphics Union. In 1986 he joined the Champions of the World. Since 1987 he has participated in exhibitions and performance art in Moscow, including the 1988 *Labyrinth* exhibition held at the Palace of Youth in Moscow, and the *Sandunovsky Baths* show of 1988, organized by the Avant-Gardists Club. In 1990 he exhibited at the Venice Biennale. He has also exhibited in France, Poland, West Germany, and the United States.

Yakhnin's works are abstract and expressive in manner. He incorporates primitivist and grotesque forms as well as verbal-visual juxtapositions.

Vladimir Yankilevsky

Yankilevsky was born in Moscow in 1938. A leader of the Moscow Conceptual art movement and one of the Belyutintsy, he attended the Moscow Secondary Art School from 1949 to 1956, and the Moscow Polygraphic Institute from 1957 to 1962. From 1957 to 1958 he studied painting under Belyutin and continued thereafter to work with the Belyutin group. In 1962 he participated in the Belyutin Studio exhibition in Moscow, and that same year exhibited with the Belyutintsy at the ill-fated Manezh exhibition. Yankilevsky is a member of the Sretensky Boulevard group of Conceptual artists, which includes Ilya Kabakov, Erik Bulatov, Viktor Pivovarov, and Edik Shteinberg. He has participated in many exhibitions in Moscow, including the 1975 *Twenty Moscow Artists* exhibition of unofficial art. He has also exhibited in Czechoslovakia, France, Great Britain, West Germany, Japan, and the United States. To the artist, the most important exhibitions have been the first personal show with Edik Shteinberg in Moscow in 1978 and his second one-artist exhibition in Moscow in 1987, entitled *Retrospective 1957–87*.

In his 1987 retrospective show Yankilevsky exhibited for the first time his unique triptychs, some of which he had produced twenty-six years earlier. The triptychs are combinations of painting and relief, typically depicting a robot-like male on one wing and his female counterpart on the other, with the central panel devoted to a complex composition of primitive, biological, and cybernetic forms. The artist is interested in existential concepts, including the destruction of male and female individuality through the mechanisms of social convention. Thus his triptychs, and smaller, single-panel versions, are dominated by mutant and machine forms that recall the early work of Duchamp and Malevich.

Dmitri Zhilinsky

A leader of the left wing of the Moscow Union of Artists, Zhilinsky was one of the first artists of the sixties generation to reject Socialist Realism. He was born in 1928 in Sochi in the Crimea; he presently lives and works in Moscow. From 1945 to 1951, he studied at the Surikov Art Institute, Moscow, under Nikolai Chernyshev and Alexei Gritsai. He has been participating in city, republic, and all-union exhibitions since 1953. Zhilinsky taught for over thirty years at the Surikov Art Institute; Nazarenko and Nesterova were among his students. In the late 1970s, he was elected to the Board of the USSR Union of Artists and nominated as Associate Member of the USSR Academy of Arts. He became a full member of the Academy in 1990. Zhilinsky serves on the editorial board of one of the leading Soviet art magazines, *Tvorchestvo*. He is an Honored Artist of the Russian Republic and a winner of the Repin Prize of the Russian Republic. His exhibitions include the Venice Biennale of 1982 and others in Italy, Austria, Greece, West Germany, France, and elsewhere abroad. His works are in many Soviet, European, and American private collections and in public collections such as the Tretyakov Art Gallery, Moscow; the Russian Museum, Leningrad; the Museum of Modern Art, Sofia; and the Ludwig Museum, Cologne.

Zhilinsky paints portraits and thematic pictures of family, friends, mentors, and cultural figures in a meticulous, hard-edged style in tempera on board. His unique contribution to Soviet art is his fusion of the precision and symbolic metaphor of early Renaissance art with the collapsed space and reverse perspective of icon painting. His very personal and self-conscious focus became a hallmark of the seventies generation of artists.

Anatoli Zverev

Zverev was born in 1931 in Moscow, where he worked until his death in 1986. From 1946 to 1950, he attended a secondary art school in the Preobrazhenskaya region. He entered the 1905 Art Institute but was soon expelled for his experimentations in formalism. Zverev was one of the most prolific and imaginative of the unofficial artists. The exhibition of more than one hundred of his paintings, gouaches, and watercolors at the Motte Gallery in Geneva, Switzerland, in May 1965 was at the time the largest one-artist show by an unofficial Soviet artist in the West. He continued to exhibit works in West Germany, France, and the United States and was also included in nonconformist and highly controversial exhibitions in Moscow, such as the Druzhba Club exhibition of 1967 and *Twenty Moscow Artists* of 1974. His works are in the collections of the Cremona Foundation, Maryland; and the Museum of Modern Art, New York.

Zverev was an important part of the Russian Expressionist movement of the 1960s. His portraits, still lifes, and figurative works are characterized by an agitated technique of emotional abandon which was inspired by the action painting methods of American artists such as Harry Coleman. Zverev saw Coleman's works at the seminal *International Art Exhibition* at the VI International Youth Festival in Moscow in 1957.

SUGGESTIONS FOR FURTHER READING

Austrian Museum of Applied Arts. *Kunst und Revolution: Russische und Sowjetische Kunst 1910–1932*. Vienna, 1988.

Becker, Wolfgang, and Gerhard Kolberg, eds., *Aspekte Sowjetische Kunst der Gegenwart*. Cologne: Greven & Bechtold GmbH, 1982.

Bowlt, John E. *The Silver Age: Russian Art of the Early Twentieth Century and the "World of Art" Group*. Newtonville, Massachusetts: Oriental Research Partners, 1979.

————. ed. *Russian Art of the Avant-Garde: Theory and Criticism 1902–1934*. New York: Thames and Hudson, reprint 1988.

————. "Rehabilitating the Russian Avant-Garde." *ARTnews* (February 1989): 117–119.

Bown, Matthew Cullerne. *Contemporary Russian Art*. New York: Philosophical Library, 1989.

Bulletin of the Archives and Documentation Centers for Modern and Contemporary Art 1, 2 (1989). Double issue, on New Realities in Soviet Art and Research. Eds. Hans-Jorg Heusser, Karin Rosenberg, Alexander Yakimovich.

Centre Georges Pompidou and the USSR Ministry of Culture. *Paris-Moscow: 1900–1930*. Exhibition catalogue. Paris, 1979.

Christie's. *A Selection of Russian Avant-Garde Works, formerly the property of Kurt Benedikt*. Auction catalogue. London: April 5, 1990.

Dekhtiar, Anna. *Molodye Zhivopistsy 70th godov* (*Young Painters of the Seventies*). Sovetskii Khudozhnik, 1979.

Deutsche Bank et al. *Russische und Sowjetische Kunst: Tradition und Gegenwart*. Ed. M. N. Sokolov. Exhibition catalogue. USSR Ministry of Culture, 1984–1985.

Dodge, Norton T., Alison Hilton, et al. *New Art from the Soviet Union: The Known and the Unknown*. Washington, D.C.: Acropolis Books, 1977.

Douglas, Charlotte. "Report from Moscow: Return of the Suppressed." *Art in America* (June 1988): 35–41.

————. "Russians on the Road." *Art in America* (October 1988): 49–57.

————. "Behind the Suprematist Mirror." *Art in America* (September 1989): 164–177, 227.

Elliott, David, and Valery Dudakov, eds. *100 Years of Russian Art 1889–1989: From Private Collections in the USSR*. London: Lund Humphries, 1989.

Fateyev, Valery, ed. *Fantastic and Imaginative Works by Russian Artists*. Leningrad: Aurora Art Publishers, 1989.

Filipovsky, Nikolai I. "Emblems of Perestroika." *Apollo* (January 1990): 12–13.

Galerie der Stadt Esslingen am Neckar. *Russische Kunst des 20. Jahrhunderts: Sammlung Semjonov*. Stuttgart: Klett-Cotta, 1984.

Gambrell, Jamey. "Soviet Art Today." *Art in America* (November 1985): 31–43.

————. "Notes on the Underground." *Art in America* (November 1988): 127–134.

————. "Perestroika Shock." *Art in America* (February 1989): 124–134, 179.

————. "The Perils of Perestroika." *Art in America* (March 1990): 47–59.

Golomshtok, Igor, and Alexander Glezer. *Unofficial Art from the Soviet Union*. London: Martin, Secker and Warburg, 1977. Also published as *Soviet Art in Exile*. New York: Random House, 1977.

Gray, Camilla. *The Russian Experiment in Art: 1863–1922*. Revised by Marian Burleigh-Motley. London: Thames and Hudson, 1986.

Guernsey's. *Artwork of the Soviet Union*. Auction catalogue. New York: October 22–23, 1988.

Habsburg-Feldman. *Soviet Contemporary Art: The Property of the Kniga Collection, Paris*. Auction catalogue. New York: May 5, 1990.

Hirshhorn Museum and Sculpture Garden. *Russian and Soviet Paintings 1900–1930*. Exhibition catalogue. Washington, D.C.: Smithsonian Institution, 1988.

Hochfield, Sylvia. "Soviet Art: New Freedom, New Directions." *ARTnews* (October 1987): 102–107.

————. "Soviet Union: Up from the Underground." *ARTnews* (May 1990): 152–159.

Kamenskii, Aleksandr. *Romanticheskii Montazh*. Moscow: Sovetskii Khudozhnik, 1989.

Klokov, Sergei. "The Commercialization of Soviet Art." *Apollo* (January 1990): 22–25.

Kornetchuk, Elena. "The Politics of Soviet Art." *Bulletin of the Atomic Scientists* 33 (October 1977): 32–37.

————. "The Politics of Soviet Art." Ph.D. dissertation, Georgetown University, Washington, D.C., 1982. Ann Arbor: University Microfilms International, 1983.

Kunstmuseum Bern. *Ich Lebe-Ich Sehe: Künstler der Achtziger Jahre in Moskau*. Exhibition catalogue. Bern, Switzerland: Kunstmuseum Bern, 1988.

Milner, John. *Vladimir Tatlin and the Russian Avant-Garde*. New Haven and London: Yale University Press, 1983.

Misiano, Viktor. "Back in the U.S.S.R." *Contemporanea* (June 1988): 97–107.

Mitta, Yevgeny. "... the Young Guard." *Apollo* (January 1990): 20–21.

Modern Art Museum of Fort Worth, USSR Ministry of Culture, and Inter Cultura. *10 + 10: Contemporary Soviet and American Painters*. Exhibition catalogue. Modern Art Museum of Fort Worth, 1989–1990.

Morozov, A. I. *Pokoleniya molodykh: Zhivopis' sovetskikh Khudozhnikov 1960–kh–1980–kh godov*. Moscow: Sovetskii Khudozhnik, 1989.

Nuding, G. Prescott. "The Art Market: Here Come the Russians (But Are They Going to Stay?)." *Apollo* (January 1990): 26–35, 69–70.

"Out from under the Hammer?" *Apollo* (January 1990): 3.

Peschler, Eric A. *Künstler in Moskau: Die Neue Avantgarde*. Schaffhausen: Edition Stemmle Verlag Photographie AG, 1988.

Phillips. *Russian 20th Century & Avant-Garde Art.* Auction catalogue. London: November 27, 1989.

Pohribny, Arsen, Peter Spielman, and Helmut Lumbro, eds. *Progressive Strömungen in Moskow, 1957–1976.* Bochum: Heinrich-Druckerei GmbH., 1974.

Reid, Susan. "Glasnost and the Avant-Garde." *New Art Examiner* (January 1990): 25–30.

Rudenstine, Angelica Zander. *The George Costakis Collection: Russian Avant-Garde Art.* New York: Harry N. Abrams, 1981.

Russian Museum, Leningrad. *Soviet Art 1920s–1930s.* New York: Harry N. Abrams, 1988.

Schaire, Jeffrey. "Secret Fires: The Private World of Soviet Artists." *Art and Antiques* (September 1988): 83–93.

Sjeklocha, Paul, and Igor Mead. *Unofficial Art in the Soviet Union.* Berkeley and Los Angeles: University of California Press, 1967.

Smithsonian Institution Traveling Exhibition Service. *Moscow: Treasures and Traditions.* Seattle: University of Washington Press, 1990.

Sokolov, Mikhail. "Russian Art: The Crucial Century." *Apollo* (January 1990): 4–11.

Sopotsinsky, Oleg, ed. *Art in the Soviet Union: Painting, Sculpture, Graphic Arts.* Leningrad: Aurora Art Publishers, 1978.

Sotheby's. *Russian Avant-Garde and Soviet Contemporary Art.* Auction catalogue. Moscow: July 7, 1988.

———. *Post War and Contemporary Art.* Auction catalogue. London: October 26, 1989.

Tacoma Art Museum (Washington) and the Institute of Contemporary Art (Boston). *Between Spring and Summer: Soviet Conceptual Art in the Era of Late Communism.* Boston: Institution of Contemporary Art, 1990.

Tamruchi, N. O., comp. *Prostranstvo Kartiny: Sbornik statei.* Moscow: Sovetskii Khudozhnik, 1989.

Taylor, Brandon. "Russians on the Road: Vienna (Part 1)." *Art in America* (October 1988): 33–47.

Thomas Levy Galerie et al. *Russische Malerei Heute: Bilder, Gouachen, Grafik.* Hamburg: 1982.

Tupitsyn, Margarita. *Margins of Soviet Art: Socialist Realism to the Present.* Milan: Giancarlo Politi Editore, 1989.

Turine, Roger-Pierre. *Soviet Art from Lenin to Gorbachev: Catalogue and Facts.* Brussels: Vie Ouviere, 1988.

Walker, Richard W. "The Making of a Market." *ARTnews* (March 1989): 138–143.

Wallach, Amie. "Import/Export: Marketing Perestroika." *Art in America* (April 1989): 53–67.

Weiss, Evelyn, ed. *Sowjetkunst Heute.* Cologne: Museum Ludwig, 1988.

Zamkov, Vladimir. "The Old Guard and…." *Apollo* (January 1990): 18–19.

INDEX

Names in capital letters are of artists whose works appear in this exhibition. Page numbers and plate numbers in boldface signify color illustrations.